LAND, PROTO-INDUSTRY AND POPULATION IN CATALONIA, c. 1680–1829

Land, Proto-Industry and Population in Catalonia, c. 1680–1829

An Alternative Transition to Capitalism?

JULIE MARFANY

University of Oxford, UK

Routledge
Taylor & Francis Group

LONDON AND NEW YORK

First published 2012 by Ashgate Publishing

2 Park Square, Milton Park, Abingdon, Oxon OX14 4RN

711 Third Avenue, New York, NY 10017, USA

Routledge is an imprint of the Taylor & Francis Group, an informa business

First issued in paperback 2016

British Library Cataloguing in Publication Data
Marfany, Julie.
  Land, proto-industry and population in Catalonia, c.1680-1829 : an alternative transition to capitalism?. – (Modern economic and social history)
  1. Capitalism – Spain – Catalonia – History – 18th century. 2. Industrialization – Social aspects – Spain – Catalonia – History – 18th century. 3. Agriculture – Economic aspects – Spain – Catalonia – History – 18th century. 4. Social structure – Spain – Catalonia – History – 18th century.
  5. Catalonia (Spain) – Population – History – 18th century. 6. Catalonia (Spain) – Rural conditions.
  7. Igualada (Spain) – Social conditions – 18th century. 8. Igualada (Spain) – Economic conditions – 18th century.
  I. Title II. Series
  306.3'09467'09033-dc23

Library of Congress Cataloging-in-Publication Data
Marfany, Julie.
  Land, proto-industry and population in Catalonia, c. 1680-1829 : an alternative transition to capitalism? / Julie Marfany.
     p. cm. – (Modern economic and social history)
  Includes bibliographical references and index.
  ISBN 978-1-4094-4465-7 (hbk) 1. Catalonia (Spain) – Economic conditions – 18th century.
  2. Catalonia (Spain) – Economic conditions – 19th century. 3. Catalonia (Spain) – Social conditions – 18th century. 4. Catalonia (Spain) – Social conditions – 19th century. 5. Agriculture – Economic aspects – Spain – Catalonia – History – 18th century. 6. Agriculture – Economic aspects – Spain – Catalonia – History – 19th century. 7. Industrialization – Spain – Catalonia – History – 18th century. 8. Industrialization – Spain – Catalonia – History – 19th century. 9. Capitalism – Spain – Catalonia – History – 18th century. 10. Capitalism – Spain – Catalonia – History – 19th century. I. Title.

  HC387.C25M34 2012
  330.946'705 – dc23

                                                                              2012005584

ISBN 978-1-4094-4465-7 (hbk)
ISBN 978-1-138-26695-7 (pbk)

Contents

To James, Isabel and Dominic with love

List of Figures

List of Tables

List of Abbreviations

ACA   Arxiu de la Corona d'Aragó, Barcelona
AHCB   Arxiu Històric de la Ciutat de Barcelona
AMI   Arxiu Municipal d'Igualada
ANI   Arxiu Notarial d'Igualada (references follow Marta Vives Sabaté, *L'arxiu de protocols del districte d'Igualada* (Barcelona, 1997))
API   Arxiu Parroquial d'Igualada
AT   Arxiu Torelló (Institut d'Història Jaume Vicens Vives, Universitat Pompeu Fabra)
BC   Biblioteca de Catalunya
FEG   Fons Erasme de Gònima
FC   Fons Comercial
FJC   Fons Junta de Comerç
NI   Notariales, Igualada

Notes

The Catalan money of account was the *lliura*: 1 *lliura* = 20 *sous*, 1 *sou* = 12 *diners*.
Some payments were made in *rals d'ardit* (1 *ral* = 2 *sous*).
A *jornal* = 0.4986 hectares.
A *quartera* of wheat = 0.694 hectolitres
A *càrrega* of wine = 1.21 hectolitres
The Junta de Comerç was the equivalent of a Chamber of Commerce.

To save space, references to archival sources have been kept to the minimum, often just the catalogue number. I have also eliminated second surnames both for modern authors and for historical individuals, except where two individuals share the same first surname. Then, as now, Catalans combined the father's and the mother's surname. Women took their husband's surname in addition to their own, but I have usually just referred to them under their maiden names. Place names are in Catalan except where there is an established English form e.g. Majorca. All translations are my own unless otherwise stated.

Acknowledgements

Thanks are due first to Richard Smith, who supervised the PhD with which this project began and who has offered patient, enthusiastic and sound advice throughout, as only he can. Jaume Torras was a huge help in the initial stages. My debt to his work will be evident. James Thomson, Tony Wrigley, Ramon Garrabou and Sheilagh Ogilvie have read and commented on drafts and outlines. I was immensely privileged to do my PhD at the Cambridge Group for the History of Population, a uniquely supportive and stimulating environment. Many of the results in this work are due to the technical wizardry of Jim Oeppen, Ros Davies and Peter Kitson. The friendship of Tracy Dennison, Alysa Levene and Rhiannon Thompson has been absolutely crucial. Further research was made possible by a fellowship at Homerton College, Cambridge, with thanks to my colleagues there for their friendship. The final stages benefited from financial support from the Spanish Ministry of Science and Technology, grant HAR2008-02960/HIST. Thanks to the late Assumpta Fabré for the generous loan of microfilms of the Igualada parish registers and the University of Cambridge for funding to scan the remainder. Francesc Valls generously provided me with some of his data. Dr Christy MacHale produced the maps at very short notice. Thanks to all the archivists of the archives consulted, especially Marta Vives and Mariluz Cristóbal in Igualada. Rosa Congost, Biel Jover, Natàlia Mora-Sitjà, Bélen Moreno, Enric Saguer, Leigh Shaw-Taylor and James Simpson have offered insights along the way. Finally, my parents, Val and Joan-Lluís, have helped out in numerous ways, including hours of childcare. My father has taken as much interest in my research as in his own. My children, Isabel and Dominic, have slowed progress down, but given me a sense of perspective. Last, thanks and love are due to my husband, James, who has done more than anyone to keep this on track.

General Editor's Preface

Economic and social history has been a flourishing subject of scholarly study during recent decades. Not only has the volume of literature increased enormously but the range of interest in time, space and subject matter has broadened considerably so that today there are many sub-branches of the subject which have developed considerable status in their own right.

One of the aims of this series is to encourage the publication of scholarly monographs on any aspect of modern economic and social history. The geographical coverage is world-wide and contributions on the non-British themes will be especially welcome. While emphasis will be placed on works embodying original research, it is also intended that the series should provide the opportunity to publish studies of a more general thematic nature which offer a reappraisal or critical analysis of major issues of debate.

Derek H. Aldcroft
University of Leicester

PART I
Transitions to Capitalism?

Chapter 1
Rethinking the Transition to Capitalism

Introduction

On 2 August 1709 a notary in the small Catalan town of Igualada drew up an
inventory recording the possessions of a clothier, Lluís Francolí.[1] Francolí's
inventory shows him to have been a fairly typical example of a well-to-do artisan
for that time and place. From other sources, he is known to have been one of the
town's most successful clothiers.[2] He had a substantial amount of equipment for
carding and spinning in his workshop, as well as a dyeing vat. Like other clothiers,
he was involved in the preparatory stages of woollen-cloth production, putting out
wool to other carders and spinners and then to weavers, and marketing the finished
product. His income was not solely derived from wool, however; like many other
artisans, he owned 5 hectares of land, planted with vines and grain and a small
vegetable plot, as well as a mule and a plough. He also owned two houses. The one
in which he lived was as well furnished as those of most of his contemporaries. He
had equipment for baking and for at least the preliminary stages of wine-making.
There were no books and few ornaments, but there were nine pictures on the
walls, a substantial stock of linen and a set of silverware, including six spoons.
The inventory records a list of 12 debtors, who owed regular sums to be paid on
censals, loans disguised as investments, but all were relatively small amounts.

Francolí was one of the better-off clothiers in Igualada and appears to have
owned more capital equipment, but the differences at this stage between him and
his contemporaries are relatively slight. Just over 100 years later, inventories tell
a different story. On 16 June 1817 another notary began to draw up the inventory
of Josep Anton Fàbregas, a calico manufacturer.[3] Fàbregas's calico-printing
workshop was in a separate building from the main house, which was not unusual,
given that printing required space, including a bleaching meadow. Fàbregas was
presumably buying his cotton cloths ready-woven from other producers, since
there are no references to spinning or weaving cotton, only to the printing stages.
He still owned land, however, including a separate farmhouse in the nearby village
of Rubió, with sheep, goats, two mules and a donkey. This farm was probably
cultivated by tenants, though the inventory lists furniture there belonging to
Fàbregas. Of the 17 remaining hectares, mostly planted with vines, at least three

[1] ACA NI 791, fos 170r–177r.

[2] These sources are discussed in Chapter 3. For context, see Jaume Torras, *Fabricants
sense fàbrica: Els Torelló, d'Igualada (1691–1794)* (Vic, 2006), pp. 27–36.

[3] ANI 663, fos 49r–58r.

plots were cultivated by sharecroppers. He owned six houses and the mortgage on another. His main residence, in Igualada, testifies to the continued domestic production of many goods, especially foodstuffs. He owned a wine-press and equipment for baking bread and for curing meat. The family kept six hens and a cockerel. There is also evidence of a lifestyle marked by a greater degree of comfort than that of Lluís Francolí's household. The rooms suggest an increasing specialisation of function: there were separate storerooms, a cellar and a room just for baking, as well as a kitchen, a dining room and a sitting room with 18 chairs round a large table, suggesting entertainment on a certain scale. This room was decorated with five maps, while most of the other rooms had pictures. Three of the bedrooms had mirrors, calico bedspreads and bed curtains. There were still no books, but there were two writing-desks, a clock and a guitar. Clothing was not itemised, but there were 65 sheets listed among the substantial linen stocks, which did not include those owned by Fàbregas's widow and daughter-in-law. Three chocolate-pots were listed, as well as 17 sets of silver cutlery and 6 wooden spoons and forks, either for everyday use or for the servants. There was at least one maidservant living in the house. Fàbregas had credit of 3,090 *lliures*, in the form not of small loans to neighbours (though these may also have existed), but of payments owed for calicoes by merchants in Barcelona, Valencia, Saragossa and elsewhere.

Five years later, on 3 July 1822, a very different inventory was drawn up for another cotton producer, this time a weaver named Jaume Vallès.[4] Vallès and his wife Teresa lived in just two rented rooms, a bedroom and a kitchen. Vallès owned nothing relating to his occupation as a weaver: he presumably either rented his loom or, more likely, worked in someone else's workshop. He had no land. The sole furniture was a table and a bench in the kitchen, with a bed, four chairs, two chests and a cradle in the bedroom. Otherwise, Vallès owned a few pots and pans, a set of six dishes and plates, six wooden spoons and forks, a lamp, a broom, some bedding, two changes of clothes, a cape and a hat. He had 30 *lliures* in cash, and the only other income mentioned is 18 *lliures* interest on a loan.

The differences between the inventories, between Francolí's and the two later ones but also between those of Fàbregas and Vallès, illustrate a series of profound transformations taking place in Igualada, in Catalonia and in Europe as a whole, transformations which form the subject of this work. The first shift is from the production of wool to cotton. For centuries, Igualada and other Catalan towns had specialised in the production of woollens. Over the eighteenth century, wool was replaced by cotton, 'the fibre that changed the world', to cite a recent publication.[5] It certainly changed lives in Igualada, drawing many, like Fàbregas, into wider commercial networks outside of Catalonia and ultimately across the globe. The Barcelona and Valencia merchants with whom Fàbregas was trading

---

    [4]   ANI 695, fo. 48.
    [5]   D. Farnie and D. Jeremy (eds), *The Fibre that Changed the World: The Cotton Industry in International Perspective, 1600–1990s* (Oxford, 2004).

were undoubtedly selling calicoes on to the colonies. Fàbregas was one of the lucky ones. He was able to exploit the opportunities the new fibre offered to invest in calico-printing and improve his lifestyle. At the same time, he did not abandon other sources of income; rather, he diversified, investing in land, particularly commercial viticulture. Like many other Catalan landowners, he took advantage of the demand for wine and spirits by increasing grape production and exploiting the labour of sharecroppers. His lifestyle testifies to increased wealth but also to changes in material culture and consumption over the century or so separating him from Francolí. New colonial products such as chocolate were being consumed, and the picture is one of increased comfort, if not luxury.

Not all the changes were so positive. Vallès's inventory shows a different kind of transformation: one from an artisan-style of production, as represented by Francolí, with ownership of the means of production and a certain degree of independence, to one of semi if not total proletarianisation. Vallès did not even own a loom: he was entirely dependent upon waged labour provided by manufacturers such as Fàbregas or, more likely, those who specialised in spinning and weaving cotton cloths before they were printed. How high his wages were is unknown, but his lifestyle was extremely modest and precarious, with no obvious source of income other than the interest on a loan to see him through any of the many downturns in the cotton industry. The only evidence of any change in his lifestyle relative to that of a century before is the set of wooden spoons and forks, which began to appear in Igualada inventories during the eighteenth century.

These three men and their families were among many Catalan and European households to be caught up in the profound transformations which can together be described as constituting the rise of capitalism. Ever since Marx, an impressive array of scholarship has attempted to explain how Europe moved from being a feudal to a capitalist society over the course of the early modern period. Unease about the Marxist overtones of much of the debate has not been sufficient to prevent its continued importance for economic historians. For a time some eschewed such ideologically laden terms as 'a transition to capitalism' in favour of 'economic growth'. More recently, however, the older debate has undergone a reappraisal.[6] As Maarten Prak points out, the concept of a 'transition to capitalism' is more useful than simply describing 'economic growth': 'transition' conveys the complex and incomplete nature of the process.

It is a major contention of this work that an investigation into this transition is best carried out at the level of the household. It is in studying the interactions of households with other households and with markets, as producers and consumers, that the specific relations of production that defined nascent capitalism can be identified and studied. Moreover, a focus on the household enables us to see the interactions between different sectors of the economy more clearly. It is also often

---

[6] Maarten Prak, 'Early Modern Capitalism: An Introduction', in id. (ed.), *Early Modern Capitalism* (London, 2001), pp. 1–21.

at the micro-level that tensions between capitalist and older relations of production become most evident.

To investigate households and markets is hardly novel, but it has not been exhausted as an approach. More importantly, it is an approach that has tended to be confined to limited geographical areas. The dominant scholarship, or at least the scholarship in English, has focused on areas of north-western Europe: England and the Netherlands above all.[7] The strongest challenge so far has come from historians of East Asia.[8] Differences within Europe have received far less attention. If an understanding of regional dynamics is what is needed, then a study such as this, with a southern European focus, can make a major contribution.

The agrarian roots of European capitalism

In the debates surrounding the transition to capitalism, the changes that took place on the land have perhaps been some of the most disputed. Debate has been conditioned for years by Robert Brenner's seminal article on the subject.[9] Brenner argued that economic growth required the emergence of capitalist relations on the land, in other words, replacing small peasant properties with large farms cultivated using hired labour. Brenner based his arguments on what he saw as the differences between England and France. England's increase in agricultural productivity and thus her ability to industrialise was due to the early emergence of a tripartite structure of landlords, tenants and hired labourers respectively owning, renting and cultivating large farms that had come into existence through a process of enclosure and engrossment in which peasants had been squeezed off the land. In France, by contrast, peasant properties had survived, thus discouraging investment in land and participation in markets. Brenner attributed the dispossession of English peasants on the one hand and the survival of French peasants on the other to differences in the balance of power

[7] This is despite the relevance of many earlier works, such as those by historians of the *Annales* school, for example, and important studies such as that of Bartolomé Yun, *Sobre la transición al capitalismo en Castilla; Economia y sociedad en Tierra de Campos (1500–1830)* (Valladolid, 1987).

[8] This question is discussed in more detail below; see also K. Pomeranz, *The Great Divergence: China, Europe and the Making of the World Economy* (Princeton, 2000); K. Sugihara, 'The East Asian Path of Economic Development: A Long-Term Perspective', in G. Arrighi, T. Hamashita and A. Selden (eds), *The Resurgence of East Asia: 500, 150 and 50 Year Perspectives* (London, 2003), pp. 78–123.

[9] Robert Brenner, 'Agrarian Class Structure and Economic Development in Pre-Industrial Europe', in T.H. Aston and C.H.E. Philpin (eds), *The Brenner Debate: Agarian Class Structure and Economic Development in Pre-Industrial Europe* (Cambridge, 1985), pp. 10–63.

between landlords and peasants in the two countries over the later Middle Ages, rather than to demographic pressures or the growth of markets. In Brenner's view, the capacity of the agrarian economy to respond to these latter forces depended on the prevailing class structure.

Brenner's argument came under attack almost immediately.[10] Perhaps the most important counterargument that has been presented is evidence that small peasant properties were in fact compatible with growth in many areas of Europe, including France and the Low Countries.[11] Indeed, a large body of literature now stresses the survival of peasant production on a global scale up to the present day, with development economists now often arguing for the merits of small-scale over large-scale farming.[12] The English experience increasingly appears to be the exception to be explained, rather than the model against which all other transitions to agrarian capitalism are to be judged.

Explanations for the survival of peasant production and its compatibility with economic growth are not hard to find. From a Marxist perspective, Bernstein has argued that capitalist primitive accumulation does not require agrarian capitalism.[13] Intensified exploitation of the peasantry, in the form of state taxation, rent squeezes and debt, coupled with colonial plunder, may be as effective as dispossession. More generally, capitalist farming does not necessarily require capitalist farms: where capital tends to be more concentrated and more obviously 'corporate' within the agrarian sector is in areas 'upstream' (farm machinery, chemicals) or 'downstream' (food processing) from farming itself. There are well-known explanations for why capital may not be attracted to agriculture, namely, the risks posed by uncertain natural conditions, the disparity between labour time and production time (the delay between planting and harvest) and the greater expense of supervising labour in a field compared with in a factory.[14]

The recognition that peasant production survives within capitalist systems, while vital, has tended to muddy the conceptual waters. It is no longer clear

---

[10]   Many of the responses to Brenner are brought together in Aston and Philpin, *Brenner Debate*. For two valuable reappraisals of Brenner which inform many of the ideas presented here, see P. Hoppenbrouwers and J.L. van Zanden (eds), *Peasants into Farmers? The Transformation of the Rural Economy and Society in the Low Countries (Middle Ages–19th Century) in Light of the Brenner Debate* (Turnhout, 2001); Jane Whittle, *The Development of Agrarian Capitalism: Land and Labour in Norfolk 1440–1580* (Oxford, 2000), esp. ch. 1.

[11]   Philip T. Hoffman, *Growth in a Traditional Society: The French Countryside 1450–1815* (Princeton, 1996); Hoppenbrouwers and van Zanden (eds), *Peasants into Farmers?*.

[12]   H. Bernstein, 'Agrarian Classes in Capitalist Development', in L. Sklair (ed.), *Capitalism and Development* (London, 1994), pp. 40–71; F. Ellis, *Peasant Economics: Farm Households and Agrarian Development* (2nd edn, Cambridge, 1993), ch. 10.

[13]   Bernstein, 'Agrarian Classes', pp. 43–4.

[14]   S.A. Mann and J.A. Dickinson, 'Obstacles to the Development of a Capitalist Agriculture', *Journal of Peasant Studies*, 5 (1978), pp. 466–81.

what the differences between 'peasant' and 'capitalist' are, nor if historians should even be looking for the disappearance of the former and emergence of the latter.[15] Definitions based on farm size have been shown to be particularly inadequate, especially when confused with the idea of family farms as opposed to those using hired labour.[16] For some, including Brenner, it is the social relations of property, that is, the conditions of ownership and tenure of land, that distinguish peasant agriculture from capitalist agriculture; particularly, in Brenner's view, if these property relations determine the capacity of different groups for surplus extraction.[17] As has already been pointed out, however, the extraction of more and more surplus does not necessarily require the dispossession of the peasantry. The survival of family-based ownership or tenure has led some to distinguish between 'peasant farms' and 'commercial family farms', bringing us to the final criterion used by economists and historians attempting to identify a transition to capitalism, namely, commercial orientation. In the crudest version of this, that of Le Roy Ladurie, peasant society is a *societé immobile*, characterised by a lack of a spirit of innovation.[18] At the other extreme, however, Jan de Vries sees 'risk aversion' as a myth and peasants, at least in Holland, as independent agents of economic growth, responding freely to market demand.[19] Most historians and economists can probably be situated somewhere between these two extremes: few would regard risk and uncertainty as a myth, but where agreement is lacking is on the degree of commercial orientation required for peasants to be regarded as capitalists. Thus Ellis's definition of 'peasant' centres on the idea that peasants are 'only partially integrated into incomplete markets'.[20]

Greater clarity on the issue of commercialisation is provided by Hoppenbrouwers and van Zanden, in particular their recognition of Brenner's subtle distinction

[15] See Whittle, *Development of Agrarian Capitalism*, pp. 10–16.

[16] Ellis, *Peasant Economics*, pp. 219–20. In part, the issue is one of ascertaining accurate thresholds for small and large farms, but, with issues such as monitoring of labour, it becomes unclear whether what matters is simply size or the differences in motivation that can be attributed to family and hired labour.

[17] As has been pointed out, Brenner tends to conflate property relations with surplus-extraction relationships, even though there were other ways in which landlords could extract a surplus than through land rent (see P. Hoppenbrouwers and J.L. van Zanden, 'Restyling the Transition from Feudalism to Capitalism: Some Critical Reflections on the Brenner Thesis', in eid. (eds), *Peasants into Farmers?*, pp. 19–40 (pp. 31–5).

[18] E. Le Roy Ladurie, *Les payans de Languedoc* (2nd edn, 2 vols, Paris, 1985), vol. 1, pp. 634, 639–44.

[19] Jan de Vries, 'The Transition to Capitalism in a Land without Feudalism', in Hoppenbrouwers and van Zanden (eds), *Peasants into Farmers?*, pp. 67–84.

[20] This is also part of Whittle's definition (see *Development of Agrarian Capitalism*, p. 11).

between involvement with markets and dependence upon them.[21] For Brenner, crucially, as long as non-market access to the means of subsistence remained an option for both peasants and landlords, neither group was compelled to compete in factor or output markets. As Hoppenbrouwers and van Zanden point out, the important thing then becomes to identify the historical circumstances under which peasants were induced or forced out of subsistence production and into specialised market-dependent production.[22] The question of market incentives is also central to the arguments of Epstein, who sees no reason in principle 'why peasants should avoid markets, although the degree of involvement will be tempered by market inefficiencies, susceptibility to exogenous shocks like warfare, access to credit, information costs and the like'.[23] For Epstein, a major flaw in the works of both neo-Malthusians, such as Le Roy Ladurie, and Brenner is the excessive focus on staples such as grain at the expense of pastoral and rural manufacturing activities, which offered sections of the rural population opportunities to participate in markets.[24]

Proto-industrialisation

The importance of rural manufacturing activities is at the heart of another of the debates on the transition to capitalism, namely, the importance or otherwise of 'proto-industrialisation'.[25] As is well known, the term was coined by Franklin Mendels and given shape in the work of Peter Kriedte, Hans Medick and Jürgen Schlumbohm.[26] Proto-industrialisation can be understood as the expansion of a new form of industrial production for non-local markets, production that usually

---

[21] Hoppenbrouwers and van Zanden, 'Restyling the Transition from Feudalism to Capitalism', pp. 26–8. Brenner makes this distinction in 'The Agrarian Roots of European Capitalism', in Aston and Philpin, *Brenner Debate*, pp. 213–327 (pp. 300–2), in contrast to the more simplistic views expressed in his earlier article. See also M. Aymard, 'Autoconsommation et marchés: Chayanov, Labrousse ou Le Roy Ladurie?', *Annales ESC*, 38 (1983), pp. 1392–1410.

[22] Hoppenbrouwers and van Zanden, 'Restyling the Transition from Feudalism to Capitalism', p. 26.

[23] S.R. Epstein, *Freedom and Growth: The Rise of States and Markets in Europe, 1300–1750* (London, 2000), pp. 38–49 (p. 48).

[24] Though in some cases, such as the growth of urban markets, grain production could also offer rural populations opportunities for market involvement, as in early modern Castille (see Yun, *Sobre la transición al capitalismo*).

[25] This section draws on ideas already discussed in J. Marfany, 'Is it Still Helpful to Talk about Proto-Industrialisation? Some Suggestions from a Catalan Case Study', *Economic History Review*, 63 (2010), pp. 942–73.

[26] Franklin Mendels, 'Proto-Industrialization: The First Stage of the Industrialization Process', *Journal of Economic History*, 32 (1972), pp. 241–61; Peter Kriedte, Hans Medick and Jürgen Schlumbohm, *Industrialization before Industrialization* (Cambridge, 1981).

remained rural and domestic in nature and was practised alongside agriculture, yet required greater input of capital and changes in the organisation of production than traditional artisanal activities, precisely because of production for non-local markets.[27] It was thus a hybrid form of industrial production, neither traditional crafts nor modern factory industry. The original proposal saw proto-industry as potentially, though not always, providing the basis on which subsequent factory industry could be built through the accumulation of skilled labour and capital.

The validity, however, of proto-industrialisation as a framework for explaining the origins and subsequent development of factory-based industrialisation has been much debated and frequently rejected. Many empirical studies have now demonstrated the lack of a connection between the spread of dispersed rural manufacturing in Europe and the later development of factory industry.[28] The variety of contexts in which proto-industry developed, the variation in structures and forms of organisation within these industries and the marked differences in the impact of proto-industry on economic, social and demographic behaviour have belied the explanatory and predictive powers of the original theory.[29]

Proto-industrialisation has therefore had a bad press over the 40 or so years it has been part of the vocabulary of economic history, yet it proves to be durable as a concept. To reject proto-industrialisation because not all areas that developed proto-industry subsequently industrialised is to take too narrow a view of the original framework outlined by Kriedte, Medick and Schlumbohm, which was intended as 'a point of departure', not as a checklist of rigid criteria.[30] It is also to ignore the many areas for which clear links can be demonstrated between proto-industry and subsequent industrialisation, of which Catalonia is one. If, as with the transition to agrarian capitalism, we look beyond England, proto-industrialisation continues to be of relevance, as is evident in the work of many French and Dutch historians.[31]

---

[27] This definition follows that given by Sheilagh Ogilvie and Markus Cerman, 'The Theories of Proto-Industrialization', in id. (ed.), *European Proto-Industrialization* (Cambridge, 1996), pp. 1–11 (p. 1); see Marfany, 'Is it Still Helpful to Talk about Proto-Industrialisation?', pp. 943–4.

[28] See e.g. S.C. Ogilvie, *State Corporatism and Proto-Industry: The Württemberg Black Forest, 1580–1797* (Cambridge, 1997); D.C. Coleman, 'Proto-Industrialization: A Concept too Many', *Economic History Review*, 36 (1983), pp. 435–48; F.M.M. Hendrickx, *In Order not to Fall into Poverty: Production and Reproduction in the Transition from Proto-Industry to Factory Industry in Borne and Wierden (The Netherlands), 1800–1900* (Amsterdam, 1997).

[29] For an overview of many of the criticisms of Mendels, Kriedte, Medick and Schlumbohm, see Ogilvie and Cerman, 'Theories of Proto-Industrialization'.

[30] See M. Werner, 'Présentation: Proto-industrialisation et *Alltagsgeschichte*', *Annales HSS*, 4 (1995), pp. 719–23.

[31] P. Deyon, 'Proto-Industrialization in France', in Ogilvie and Cerman, *European Proto-Industrialization*, pp. 38–48; G. Lewis, 'Proto-Industrialization in France', *Economic History Review*, 47 (1994), pp. 150–64; B.J.P. van Bavel, 'Early Proto-Industrialization? The Importance and Nature of Market-Oriented Non-Agricultural Activities in the Countryside

Proto-industrialisation forces us to focus on combinations of structures and forms of behaviour that are both capitalist and non-capitalist and enables us to 'rethink historical alternatives to mass production'.[32] As will be shown, it was the flexibility of many proto-industrial producers in adapting to changing circumstances that gave proto-industry advantages over other forms of production.

Population growth: escaping the Malthusian trap

While historians may differ on the causes and patterns of economic growth, what is incontrovertible is that Europe was able, at some point during the eighteenth and nineteenth centuries, to break free of the Malthusian trap in a way that other areas of the globe were unable to manage. In other words, economic growth became for the first time both rapid and sustained, and higher output from both agriculture and non-agricultural sectors could be achieved alongside sustained population growth and without declining living standards. Historians disagree as to whether Asia and Europe had already diverged in terms of population growth and living standards before 1800, but none appear to argue against subsequent divergence.[33] Europe's population rose rapidly over the eighteenth and nineteenth century to levels never previously attained. By comparison, in much of Asia, maintaining a stable population was as much as the economy could manage. Labour-intensive techniques were able to avoid the trap of diminishing returns from land, and even to raise per capita output over the eighteenth century, but left the economy caught in what both Elvin and Sugihara term a 'high-level equilibrium trap': welfare could not be raised and further population growth could not occur without radically new changes, which were eventually introduced from outside in the form of new technology.

For some of those on the side of early divergence, what distinguished Europe or north-western Europe from the rest of the world was not landholding structures or proto-industrialisation, but long-standing and more fundamental

---

in Flanders and Holland, c.1250–1570', *Revue Belge de philologie et d'histoire*, 81 (2003), pp. 1109–65; J.L. van Zanden, 'A Third Road to Capitalism? Proto-Industrialization and the Moderate Nature of the Late Medieval Crisis in Flanders and Holland, 1350–1550', in Hoppenbrouwers and van Zanden (eds), *Peasants into Farmers?*, pp. 85–101.

[32]   Charles F. Sabel and Jonathan Zeitlin, 'Historical Alternatives to Mass Production: Politics, Markets and Technology in Nineteenth-Century Industrialization', *Past and Present*, 108 (1985), pp. 133–76; eid., 'Stories, Strategies, Structures: Rethinking Historical Alternatives to Mass Production', in eid. (eds), *World of Possibilities: Flexibility and Mass Production in Western Industrialization* (Cambridge, 1997), pp. 1–33.

[33]   Pomeranz, *The Great Divergence*; Sugihara, 'The East Asian Path of Economic Development'; Mark Elvin, *The Pattern of the Chinese Past* (Stanford, 1973), ch. 17; James Z. Lee and Wang Feng, *One Quarter of Humanity: Malthusian Mythology and Chinese Realities, 1700–2000* (Cambridge, MA, 1999).

features of society, namely, demographic structures and behaviour. As Eric Jones puts it, it was Europe's ability to hold population growth at levels a little below the theoretical maximum that allowed for forms of capital investment such as livestock farming that would lay the basis of future growth.[34] In particular, it was the propensity of Europeans to practise Malthus's preventative check that is seen as giving them an advantage over other parts of the globe. Perhaps the most famous expression of this view is John Hajnal's seminal description of a 'north-west European marriage pattern', whereby marriage was late and substantial proportions of men and women never married, thus contributing to lower levels of fertility than the theoretical maximum and enabling population growth to adjust itself to real wage levels.[35] Elsewhere, population was held in check by high mortality, manifested in pre-industrial economies by the tendency of harvest failure and subsistence crises to become mortality crises. Moreover, these marriage patterns were the result of a cultural preference for setting up independent households upon marriage, rather than retaining adult, especially married, children within the household of birth.[36] As well as the restraining influence of these marriage patterns upon population growth, they are also viewed as promoting independence, particularly for women: children of both sexes not only left the parental home when they married, they often left before in order to go into service and save for their future households.[37] The 'north-west European marriage pattern' probably owes its origin in part, and certainly its survival, to the presence of well-developed labour markets for both men and women. In David Reher's formulation, family ties in northern Europe have traditionally been 'weak', whereas those in southern Europe have been 'strong', with loyalty to the family unit in the latter area taking priority over loyalty to the community or to the state.[38]

The reality of the north-west European pattern of marriage and household formation is not in question, even if one concedes that Hajnal's overview glosses

---

[34] E. Jones, *The European Miracle: Environments, Economies and Geopolitics in the History of Europe and Asia* (3rd edn, Cambridge, 2003).

[35] John Hajnal, 'European Marriage Patterns in Perspective', in D.V. Glass and D.E.C. Eversley (eds), *Population in History: Essays in Historical Demography* (London, 1965), pp. 101–47. Hajnal descibes this simply as a 'European marriage pattern', covering the area west of a line from Leningrad to Trieste, but less dominant in southern Europe.

[36] John Hajnal, 'Two Kinds of Pre-Industrial Household Formation System', *Population and Development Review*, 8 (1982), pp. 449–94; Peter Laslett, 'Characteristics of the Western Family Considered Over Time', in id., *Family Life and Illicit Love in Earlier Generations* (Cambridge, 1977), pp. 12–49.

[37] Tine de Moor and Jan Luiten van Zanden, 'Girl Power: The European Marriage Pattern and Labour Markets in the North Sea Region in the Late Medieval and Early Modern Period', *Economic History Review*, 63 (2010), pp. 1–33.

[38] D.S. Reher, 'Family Ties in Western Europe: Persistent Contrasts', *Population and Development Review*, 24 (1998), pp. 203–34.

over much variation in family forms across Europe and fails to recognise that families everywhere were never static. This explanation of European divergence, however, remains a hypothesis. The precise ways in which family forms contributed to different types of growth require careful definition and much closer study than they have received before now. It is not self-evident that 'weak' families were necessarily better placed to respond to market opportunities and economic change than 'strong' families. The former may perhaps have been more dynamic and have allowed a greater degree of independence to family members, though this is hard to prove, but they were less able to withstand hardship than the latter and therefore more reliant on support from the 'collectivity', to use Peter Laslett's term.[39] Indeed, it may have been the availability of support from the collectivity, in the form of poor relief, rather than the form of the family itself, that explains at least England's early escape from the Malthusian trap and subsequent sustained economic growth.[40]

Not only does the focus on nuclear or 'weak' families carry the danger of ignoring contextual features such as labour markets and the poor law that may have sustained such household forms, even if they did not create them; but the focus on marriage as the hinge on which population turned also ignores or downplays other aspects of the demographic regime, chiefly mortality. While the importance of nuptiality and fertility is well established in the English case at least, it is rarely recognised that the preventative check may have been strong here precisely because the positive check was weak by European standards. Had life expectancy been as low as in southern Europe, for example, less restraint on marriage might have been needed in order to keep population growth within bounds. This is not to argue that the preventative check was absent in southern Europe, quite the contrary, as will become evident, but simply to suggest that the north-west European marriage pattern may have evolved from a background of relatively benign demographic conditions.

The industrious revolution

The 'weak' nuclear family of north-western Europe is the protagonist of one particular explanation for the transition to capitalism: Jan de Vries's 'industrious

---

[39] Peter Laslett, 'Family, Kinship and Collectivity as Systems of Support in Pre-Industrial Europe: A Consideration of the 'Nuclear-Hardship' Hypothesis', *Continuity and Change*, 3 (1988), pp. 153–73.

[40] P.M. Solar, 'Poor Relief and English Economic Development Before the Industrial Revolution', *Economic History Review*, 48 (1995), pp. 1–22; R.M. Smith, 'Social Security as a Developmental Institution? Extending the Solar Case for the Relative Efficacy of Poor Relief Provisions Under the English Old Poor Law', available at <www.bwpi.manchester. ac.uk/resources/WorkingPapers/bwpi-wp-5608>. See also Lee and Feng, *One Quarter of Humanity*, p. 136: 'what distinguishes China from Europe, however, is not the nature of demographic checks, but rather the social context of demographic behaviour'.

revolution'.[41] De Vries originally developed his concept in order to explain an apparent conundrum: that real wages appear to have been falling across Europe for most of the early modern period, yet the evidence available from inventories points to increased consumption and an ever greater and more varied world of goods. De Vries argued that, over the early modern period, a broad range of households across much of Europe and North America shifted the allocation of their productive resources, thereby altering the supply of goods and labour and also the demand for marketed goods. Put more precisely, households both reduced their leisure time and specialised more in production for the market rather than home consumption. Driving this shift, de Vries claims, was the desire to consume more and better goods. Areas of agricultural specialisation and proto-industry were at the forefront of this shift, given the favourable market conditions for the allocation of labour, particularly female labour, in these areas.

There is much that is appealing about de Vries's theory. It forces us to consider production and consumption in close relation to each other, whereas other studies often tend to focus exclusively on supply or demand. It also forces us to examine how large-scale changes in supply and demand were worked out at the micro-level of the household. It also recognises that, as many other historians have stressed, pre-industrial societies were not operating at a ceiling as regards productive capacity.[42] Even in the absence of technology, considerable increases in output could be achieved through intensification of labour inputs. In many ways, however, the industrious revolution is a problematic concept.

First is the question of how necessary the concept in fact is. It may solve the apparent conundrum of how falling real wages can be matched to an increased world of goods, but does the conundrum actually exist? All the historians who have used inventories are forced to concede their social bias: those with little or no property and therefore those most likely to be wholly or partly dependent upon wages are less likely to have left inventories than those of more substantial means. De Vries, following work by Anne McCants and Peter King, is optimistic that new consumer demand encompassed a broad swathe of the social spectrum, rather than being confined to a wealthy minority.[43] Overton et al., however, have

[41] De Vries originally set out his ideas in two articles: 'Between Purchasing Power and the World of Goods: Understanding the Household Economy in Early Modern Europe', in J. Brewer and R. Porter (eds), *Consumption and the World of Goods* (London: 1993), pp. 85–132; 'The Industrial Revolution and the Industrious Revolution', *Journal of Economic History*, 54 (1994), pp. 249–70. Since then he has refined his hypotheses and synthesised a large volume of empirical evidence from the secondary literature in *The Industrious Revolution: Consumer Behaviour and the Household Economy, 1650 to the Present* (Cambridge, 2008).

[42] Yun, *Sobre la transición al capitalismo*, pp. 510–12; Jones, *European Miracle*; Aymard, 'Autoconsommation et marchés', p. 1393.

[43] De Vries, *Industrious Revolution*, pp. 149–54; Anne McCants, 'Poor Consumers as Global Consumers: The Diffusion of Tea and Coffee Drinking in the Eighteenth Century',

warned that the English inventories, according to their calculations, exclude around the lowest 40 per cent of the social hierarchy.[44] The problem of social bias within inventory samples will figure largely in later chapters. For now, it is worth bearing in the mind the possibility that greater material wealth and new forms of consumer behaviour among the elite and maybe the middling sorts were still compatible with declining living standards among the poor.

More controversial still is de Vries's placing of consumer desire at the centre of the industrious revolution. He is emphatic that ultimately, the industrious revolution was driven not by 'external constraints' but by the 'willingness' of consumers to shift their tastes and hence reallocate their labour.[45] Such a reallocation of labour was voluntary: time-discipline did not have to be imposed upon a reluctant workforce as suggested so forcefully by E.P. Thompson.[46] Active consumer choice is what differentiates de Vries's 'industrious revolution' from the original use of the term by Japanese historians.[47] These have used the term to denote a 'labour-intensive' path towards industrialisation, an alternative to the capital-intensive path followed by north-western Europe. In this model, East Asian economies responded to population pressure by applying still more labour to the land, mainly through rice cultivation and other intensive farming methods. Such additional labour inputs were achieved not just through longer working days and greater self-exploitation but through greater discipline and organisation within peasant households, attributes which were later transferred to and facilitated the emergence of, the industrial sector. Purchasing power remained low, however; industrious behaviour was not driven in East Asia by the desire to consume new goods. This type of 'industrious revolution' in fact chimes with the description of many areas of Europe, where smallholders could meet their needs only through the intensification of labour in various forms.[48]

The emphasis on consumer desire as motivating household behaviour relates to the final and perhaps most controversial point, namely, de Vries's insistence on pinning the industrious revolution down to a specific type of household in a fairly restricted geographical area. In his more recent work, de Vries goes a step

---

Economic History Review, 61, special issue (2008), pp. 172–200; Peter King, 'Pauper Inventories and the Material Lives of the Poor in the Eighteenth and Early Nineteenth Centuries', in T. Hitchcock, P. King and P. Sharpe (eds), *Chronicling Poverty: The Voices and Strategies of the English Poor, 1640–1840* (Basingstoke, 1997), pp. 155–91.

[44]   M. Overton et al., *Production and Consumption in English Households, 1600–1750* (London, 2004), p. 26.

[45]   De Vries, *Industrious Revolution*, pp. 113–21.

[46]   E.P. Thompson, 'Time, Work-Discipline and Industrial Capitalism', in id., *Customs in Common*, 2nd edn (Harmondsworth, 1993), pp. 352–403.

[47]   The term was first coined by Akira Hayami in a Japanese-language publication in 1967 (see de Vries, *Industrious Revolution*, pp. 78–82; Sugihara, 'The East Asian Path of Economic Development', pp. 78–9).

[48]   Aymard, 'Autoconsommation et marchés'.

further than in his earlier articles to make the explicit claim that the industrious revolution could only be a north-west European phenomenon.[49] According to de Vries, only in north-western Europe could the requisite combination of nuclear families, urban networks and open markets be found. While the absence of corporal and institutional constraints on consumer behaviour was important, de Vries places more weight on the tendency towards nuclear-family formation and late age described above as the defining demographic features of north-western Europe. De Vries views nuclear families as permitting a greater degree of autonomy and flexibility than extended families. This autonomy and flexibility could be translated into innovative and independent consumer behaviour in ways not possible within 'the claustrophobic bonds of extended kinship'.[50] In particular, it was the relative freedom for women to consume and to supply their labour to the market that allowed the industrious revolution to take off in north-western Europe.

It does appear to be the case that the desire to consume in north-western Europe was unhindered by the kind of institutional or cultural constraints, such as sumptuary legislation, identified for other areas.[51] In the main, however, there are difficulties with de Vries's claims. First, consumption patterns in southern Europe over the seventeenth and eighteenth centuries are largely unknown. De Vries rather takes it for granted that there was a lack of significant change in consumer behaviour in this region.[52] In comparison with north-western Europe, he may be right, but much more research is needed. Second, as will be discussed in subsequent chapters, not all historians of north-western Europe would endorse his claims for the greater agency of households and women in this region. Perhaps most controversial as far as this work is concerned, however, is that the restrictive nature of the extended family is also asserted rather than proved. More will be said on this question in later chapters, but it is not clear that extended families should a priori be incapable of adapting their consumer behaviour and working practices. Indeed, the East Asian example discussed above would rather seem to negate this claim.

---

[49] De Vries, *Industrious Revolution*, pp. 9–19. In his earlier work ('The Industrial Revolution', pp. 261–2), de Vries appears to view greater individualism within families and the augmentation in the decision-making power of women within the household as effects of the industrious revolution. In this most recent work, they are seen as causal mechanisms.

[50] De Vries, *Industrious Revolution*, p. 18.

[51] H. Medick, 'Une culture de la consideration: Les vêtements et leurs couleurs à Laichingen entre 1750 et 1820', *Annales HSS*, 4 (1995), pp. 753–74 (pp. 755–63); S.C. Ogilvie, *A Bitter Living: Women, Markets and Social Capital in Early Modern Germany* (Oxford, 2003), pp. 136–8.

[52] There is only one reference to Iberia in the entire work, in relation to the consumption of colonial groceries. Here, de Vries admits that 'little can be said with confidence' (*Industrious Revolution*, p. 162).

Households and markets

The question therefore becomes one of establishing: first, to what extent were households becoming more industrious in their behaviour and, second, to what extent was this behaviour an autonomous response to changing commodity markets? The idea that peasant households were capable of adapting to changing markets is hardly new. Indeed, it forms the background of decades of criticisms of Chayanov's model of the peasant family farm as an isolated unit of production and consumption and is inherent in the very notion of a proto-industrial family economy. Some precision is needed, however, in how historians think about both households and markets.

First, to which markets are households supposed to adapt? Historians need to differentiate between factor and commodity markets.[53] The former are usually viewed as subject to more institutional constraints than the latter so, for example, land markets may be restricted by prevailing inheritance laws, or labour markets by guild regulations that place outsiders at a disadvantage. The ability of households to adapt to markets and the means by which they do so will thus vary depending on the type of market in question.

Second, markets may be formal or informal. Not only are the latter harder for historians to assess, but they are frequently more important to rural households. Credit may be more readily available informally; similarly, in the absence of a formal labour market, labour may be supplied by families or systems of mutual help within communities.[54]

Moreover, markets are rarely independent of each other. This mutual interdependence can take two forms. The first is what is known as 'interlocking markets', whereby smallholders such as tenants or sharecroppers are often dependent upon landowners for access to equipment such as ploughs, to draught animals and to credit. Interlocking markets are discussed in more detail in Chapter 2. The second form of interdependence is less specific. Quite simply, it is the fairly obvious point that changes in one market sector may have an impact upon another. For example, a rise in the demand for foodstuffs may lead to greater activity in land markets and possibly also to a greater demand for labour. At the same time, rising food prices may affect demand for other commodities and thus the demand for labour in those areas. These interrelationships are precisely what de Vries is trying to capture, although his industrious revolution is formulated more narrowly in terms of the interrelationship between labour and commodity markets.

Finally, market growth itself is not straightforward. As Epstein points out, it can take two forms, 'deepening' and 'widening'.[55] The former refers to an increase in the volume, number and quality of commodities exchanged, the latter to an increase

---

[53]   R. Domínguez, *El campesino adaptativo: Campesinos y mercado en el norte de España, 1750–1850* (Santander, 1996), pp. 16–23.

[54]   Ibid., pp. 181–90.

[55]   Epstein, *Freedom and Growth*, p. 57.

in the geographical range of exchanges. Deepening has three forms: an increase in per capita consumption of already commercialised goods, an increase in the traded proportion of total output and an increase in the range of traded goods. As is obvious, these ideas are formulated with commodity markets in mind, although arguably factor markets can also be subject to widening and to some forms of deepening, such as increases in the total and per capita volume of credit, for instance.

The precise ways in which markets grow will have different impacts upon producers and consumers. Increases in the traded proportion of total output, for example, may result in less self-sufficiency among households. An increase in the range of goods produced may be possible simply through intensification of labour, but an increase in quality may require the acquisition of new skills. Both may require a greater subordination of labour to control and supervision. Similarly, widening and deepening will often be interrelated. As will be seen in Chapter 3, attempts by Catalan clothiers to capture extra-regional markets such as Madrid required a higher quality of output, which in turn necessitated greater flexibility of and control over production.

Just as sophistication is required in terms of thinking about markets, so it is with households. Current thinking has evolved considerably from the original idea of a straightforward shift from a peasant family economy to a proto-industrial family economy to a family wage economy.[56] Now historians recognise that most households depended upon a changing mixture of incomes from different sources, including land, proto-industrial production and wage labour. The notion of an 'economy of makeshifts' or an 'adaptive family economy' is felt to capture better the complex reality of how households operated in the past.[57] Members of households shifted the allocation of their labour across a range of activities depending upon the life-cycle of the family, the time of year, changes in labour and commodity markets and so on. Alongside this is the recognition that households did not have to be egalitarian or harmonious, often the opposite. Hierarchies of gender and age frequently dominated. For historians of the household economy, women's work remains one of the most crucial, if elusive aspects. In adapting to changing markets, Domínguez suggests households combined diversification of productive activities with an intensification of family labour, especially that of women and children. As discussed above, de Vries sees changes in the allocation of female time within the household economy as crucial to the industrious revolution.

Crucially, both households and markets need to be situated in their demographic context. The interaction between households and markets was both influenced by

---

[56] For a critical overview of the literature, see Ad Knotter, 'Problems of the "Family Economy": Peasant Economy, Domestic Production and Labour Markets in Pre-Industrial Europe', in Prak (ed.), *Early Modern Capitalism*, pp. 135–60.

[57] The first term was coined by Olwen Hufton in *The Poor of Eighteenth-Century France, 1750–1789* (Oxford, 1974), pp. 15–6; the second by Richard Wall, 'Work, Welfare and the Family: An Illustration of the Adaptive Family Economy', in L. Bonfield et al., *The World We have Gained: Essays Presented to Peter Laslett* (Oxford, 1986), pp. 261–94.

and influenced the prevailing demographic situation. Population growth or decline determined the size of markets. Similarly, the formation of new households and their survival were conditioned by demographic factors. At the same time, demographic behaviour could adapt to economic conditions. Nuptiality, most obviously, could and did change in response to economic changes, such as rising real wages. One of the most contested claims made for proto-industry has been that it lowered the age at marriage and raised fertility. Even mortality could be influenced by household choices, such as the time allocated by women to breastfeeding and childcare or the expenditure on food consumption and housing.

An important consideration here is the extent to which population growth meant increased social differentiation among households. For many historians, social differentiation between peasant households is an essential feature of the transition to capitalism. As already discussed, increased consumption often appears to have relied upon the emergence of elite and middling sorts, while the growth of agrarian capitalism on the one hand and the emergence of proto-industry were often dependent upon the labour of proletarian or semi-proletarian households.

Why Catalonia?

Having described the various avenues that current research has thrown up as fruitful directions in which to pursue an investigation of the transition to capitalism, it remains to justify the choice of Catalonia as a region for study. In the first place, it is essential to escape the current focus on north-western Europe. All too often, the dominant literature, whether on the transition to agrarian capitalism, on proto-industrialisation or on the industrious revolution refers to a European experience that, on closer inspection, turns out to be that of England and the Netherlands. Yet, as already mentioned in the context of agrarian capitalism, the English experience may well have been exceptional. Similarly, proto-industry may have had less impact in England than elsewhere in Europe. The demographic experience of both England and the Netherlands in the early modern period was certainly unique in terms of the high levels of urbanisation of both countries and the precocity of the English economy in escaping from the Malthusian trap. Studies of other areas, which were both less wealthy and, in terms of environment, less healthy than England and the Netherlands, are urgently needed in order to confirm or modify the current picture of development.

Catalonia's interest as a subject of study lies in its distinctive status as one of the few areas on the 'periphery' of Europe, as Sidney Pollard noted, that experienced a degree and type of industrialisation in the eighteenth and nineteenth centuries comparable with that of the 'core'.[58] Both the region's

---

[58]   S. Pollard, *Peaceful Conquest: The Industrialization of Europe 1760–1970* (Oxford, 1981), p. 206.

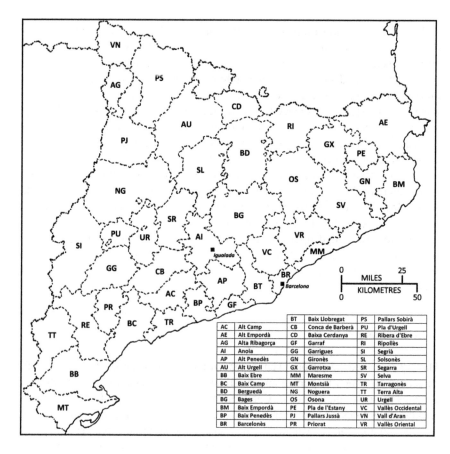

AC	Alt Camp	CB	Conca de Barberà	PU	Pla d'Urgell
AE	Alt Empordà	CD	Baixa Cerdanya	RE	Ribera d'Ebre
AG	Alta Ribagorça	GF	Garraf	RI	Ripollès
AI	Anoia	GG	Garrigues	SI	Segrià
AP	Alt Penedès	GN	Gironès	SL	Solsonès
AU	Alt Urgell	GX	Garrotxa	SR	Segarra
BB	Baix Ebre	MM	Maresme	SV	Selva
BC	Baix Camp	MT	Montsià	TR	Tarragonès
BD	Berguedà	NG	Noguera	TT	Terra Alta
BG	Bages	OS	Osona	UR	Urgell
BM	Baix Empordà	PE	Pla de l'Estany	VC	Vallès Occidental
BP	Baix Penedès	PJ	Pallars Jussà	VN	Vall d'Aran
BR	Barcelonès	PR	Priorat	VR	Vallès Oriental
BT	Baix Llobregat	PS	Pallars Sobirà		

Figure 1.1   Catalonia, showing division into *comarques*

exceptionalism in the Iberian context and its comparability with northern Europe have long been recognised by historians and were already evident to contemporaries. One eighteenth-century Castilian writer described the Catalans as 'the Dutch of Spain'.[59] To another, Catalonia was 'a little England', while a Catalan author proudly claimed that 'it cannot be denied that this province is the most populated, industrious, commercial and active of all Spain'.[60]

In referring to Catalonia as a region, I mean the area represented in Figure 1.1, governed by the autonomous parliament of Catalonia, with its division into

---

[59]   José de Cadalso, *Cartas marruecas*, ed. E. Martínez and N. Glendinning (Barcelona, 2000), pp. 77–8.

[60]   Cited in Pierre Vilar, 'La Catalunya industrial: Reflexions sobre una arrencada i sobre un destí', *Recerques*, 3 (1974), pp. 7–22 (p. 9); Junta de Comerç de Barcelona, *Discurso sobre la agricultura, comercio e industria del Principado de Cataluña (1780)*, ed. E. Lluch (Barcelona, 1997), p. 114.

comarques or districts.[61] It does not encompass all areas where Catalan is currently and has been spoken, including the French Pyrenees, Valencia and the Balearic Islands. The modern administrative region does, however, correspond to a distinct geographical area, delineated by various natural frontiers such as the Pyrenees to the north and the Ebro delta to the south and a zone of extremely low population density along the western frontier with Aragon. Moreover, this region in the past had various institutional features, such as its own system of customary laws, including property rights and inheritance customs, that differed from elsewhere in Spain and were, as will be shown, of crucial importance for historical developments.

Above all, Catalonia's distinctiveness lay in the rapid economic and social transformations of the eighteenth century, which paved the way for an industrial revolution in the nineteenth century, accompanied by a growing nationalism. Pierre Vilar's seminal work, *La Catalogne dans l'Espagne moderne*, provided an account of these transformations which was breathtaking both in the sophistication of its analysis and the wealth of the research on which this analysis was based. As will be seen in later chapters, Vilar described a transition to capitalism on the land based on peasant production, accompanied by rapid demographic growth and increasing commercialisation, with a regional economy that rapidly became more interconnected with wider, particularly Atlantic, markets. Although Vilar devoted some attention to proto-industry, he did not manage to write the fourth volume of his work, which was to have been dedicated to industrialisation. This gap has since been filled to some extent by others. As will be discussed in detail in Chapter 3, Catalonia witnessed a significant degree of proto-industrialisation, which took the form first of an expansion and reorientation of the traditional woollen industry, followed by the introduction of cotton and the displacement of the former by the latter. The cotton industry remained for a long time a largely rural and domestic industry, with mechanisation only slowly necessitating the concentration and restructuring that would lead to the factories of the 1830s and onwards.

Many scholars have followed Vilar's lead in trying to ascertain why Catalonia followed such a different trajectory from the rest of the Iberian peninsula. In doing so, they have revealed numerous ways in which the region's experience can be compared with that of other areas of Europe and also ways in which it differed. In short, Catalonia shared many of the features of the transition to capitalism in northern Europe: agricultural specialisation, proto-industrialisation, the expansion of market networks and, as contemporaries recognised, signs of a growing industriousness. In particular, it resembles inland Flanders in combining small peasant holdings with proto-industry, though arguably in a more dynamic fashion.[62] Such changes

---

[61] This definition follows Pierre Vilar, *La Catalogne dans l'Espagne moderne: Recherches sur les fondements économiques des structures nationales* (3 vols, Paris, 1962), vol. 1, pp. 171–97.

[62] E. Thoen, 'A "Commercial Survival Economy" in Evolution: The Flemish Countryside and the Transition to Capitalism', in Hoppenbrouwers and van Zanden (eds), *Peasants into Farmers?*, pp. 102–57.

were happening, however, in the context of very different patterns of demographic behaviour and landholding. The 'claustrophic bonds of extended kinship' deplored by de Vries have been extolled by contemporaries and some historians alike as being one of the causes of Catalonia's economic strength relative to other areas of Spain. The Catalan system of impartible inheritance and the formation of extended families, along with use rights to land that were in practice quasi-property rights, are credited with providing the security and stability required for economic growth. As will become clear, I am sceptical about whether all participants in the process enjoyed the same degree of security, but I am in agreement with other historians that family structure contributed in important ways to ensuring an effective supply of labour. In this regard, however, it may be more appropriate to describe Catalonia as a 'little Japan' rather than a 'little England'. Similarly, in terms of population dynamics, Catalonia did not entirely avoid the Malthusian trap, or at least it came closer to the precipice than did north-western Europe and paid a heavier price for its economic development.

Hitherto, however, studies of Catalonia have tended to focus on one particular aspect of the transition to capitalism, be it changes on the land, proto-industry or, more recently, consumer behaviour. It is the aim of this work to draw together these different strands, through an in-depth focus on the household economy. A focus on household economy by definition requires micro-level history. In this case, such history takes the form of a community study, in which the experiences of households during the transition to capitalism have been reconstructed as far as the sources permit. The community in question is the town of Igualada, situated in central Catalonia, some 60 km west of Barcelona (see Figure 1.1). Over the course of the eighteenth century, it became the most important centre in the region for the production of woollen cloths and later an important centre of the new cotton industry, second only to Barcelona for spinning.[63] Cotton continued to dominate until the 1860s, when the increasing need for steam or hydraulic power made it difficult for Igualada to compete with other localities that were better-placed in this regard. Other important activities were leather and hat manufacturing. At the same time, it participated in the expansion of commercial viticulture that characterised the transition to agrarian capitalism in Catalonia. Alongside these economic changes came rapid population growth: from around 1,630 inhabitants in the census of 1717 to 4,925 in 1787 to around 7,730 by 1830.[64]

Igualada thus represents in microcosm many of the significant transformations taking place in eighteenth-century Catalonia. Moreover, the surviving sources are exceptionally rich. Unusually for Spain, Igualada's parish registers survive virtually intact from the early sixteenth century to the present, allowing for

---

[63]   For an overview of Igualada's economic development during the eighteenth and nineteenth centuries, see J.M. Torras Ribé, 'Trajectòria d'un procés d'industrializació frustrat', *Miscellanea aqualatensia*, 2 (1974), pp. 151–97.

[64]   Population figures taken from J. Iglésies, *Evolució demogràfica de la comarca d'Igualada* (Igualada, 1972), pp. 12–14.

a reconstitution of some 8,700 families for the period 1680–1819. A wealth of other sources such as marriage contracts, inventories, tax listings and manorial surveys permit the demographic information derived from the reconstitution to be supplemented with information on landholding, material goods and inheritance practices.

Chapter 2 will investigate the transition to agrarian capitalism, which in Catalonia mainly took the form of an expansion of commercial viticulture. The distinctive system of property rights that prevailed in Catalonia meant that this expansion was facilitated through a proliferation of smallholdings, many through a type of sharecropping contract. The changes in the structure of landholding in Igualada will be compared with those for other localities, and the implications of such changes for smallholders examined, particularly in terms of market involvement. The small size of most holdings meant that households were forced to engage in activities other than viticulture in order to survive. Proto-industry was the main activity complementing viticulture, which will be investigated in Chapter 3. The main focus of this chapter is the reasons for the success of Igualada's woollen industry compared with that of other localities, reasons which are to be found in the industry's ability to adapt to rapidly changing markets. Important continuities between the woollen and cotton industries explain the shift from one fibre to the other towards the end of the eighteenth century. Again, the household remained the main unit of production throughout these changes. The advantages of small-scale domestic production were slow to disappear.

Chapter 4 will put the changes described in the previous chapters into their demographic context, exploring the factors underlying Igualada's rapid population growth and contributing to a better understanding of Catalan population growth in general. The changing economic basis for household formation provided by easier access to land and proto-industry had important implications for marriage and fertility, in part by undermining the rigid inheritance customs that had hitherto determined marriage behaviour, in part as a result of the greater demands upon the time of married women. Despite the ability of Catalan households to be relatively dynamic and flexible, however, Malthusian constraints could not be entirely avoided. Population growth was sustained without a decline in real wages, yet growth in an unhealthy Mediterranean context created other problems in terms of pressure on resources and higher mortality.

Part II focuses on the issue of an industrious revolution. It brings together aspects of the previous chapters in a closer examination of the household economy, based mainly on the findings of probate inventories. These are used in Chapter 5 to reveal how households adapted to changing markets by shifting their productive activities between land, proto-industry and other activities and between production for use and production for exchange. The chapter also considers what evidence there is of an intensification of work, particularly by women. While there is certainly evidence that households were working harder and shifting their productive activities, it remains less clear that the desire to consume was driving these changes, as opposed to processes of forced commercialisation. Chapter 6 will describe some new forms of consumer behaviour, including the appearance of new goods in inventories, but will also question how far down the social scale such changes penetrated. Instead, new forms of consumption reflected and contributed to a process of increasing social differentiation.

Overall, the aim of this work is to show that the Catalan experience can be used to modify our picture of the transition to capitalism in Europe by testing and querying many of the arguments described above. Some aspects of the Catalan transition will appear familiar, but others are sufficiently different to suggest that there were clear alternatives, inside as well as outside Europe, to the transition to capitalism described by so many scholars for England.

Chapter 2
A Transition to Agrarian Capitalism?

Introduction

The previous chapter outlined ways in which recent scholarship enables us to escape the hitherto dominant picture of transition to agrarian capitalism along English lines. Catalonia provides a valuable comparison with northern Europe in this regard. Brenner had already singled the region out as an exceptional case, believing that it had achieved 'significant and continuing agricultural advance' during the early modern period despite the consolidation of a strong peasantry after the fifteenth-century peasant wars.[1] Brenner compared Catalonia to England as an 'equally capitalist system based on large-scale owner-cultivators also generally using wage labour' on 'typically a very large but compact farm'. In fact, Brenner was misled by the then current Catalan scholarship as to the triumph of the Catalan peasantry and wrong in his characterisation of Catalan agrarian society.[2] Catalonia actually stands alongside parts of France and the Low Countries, as well as areas outside Europe, as an example of agricultural transformation achieved in parallel with the persistence of family farming, small units of production and, to an extent, of property and the absence, by and large, of a rural proletariat. Catalan historians have been able to show that even big estates in terms of ownership tended to be territorially dispersed and that productivity was higher when these estates were left to sharecropping or other forms of family-based tenure than when they were farmed directly using hired labour.[3]

Catalonia is also important, however, in terms of its differences from the areas of northern Europe discussed above. First, it had a particular system of emphyteutic property rights, to which contemporaries ascribed much of the economic advances of the eighteenth century. Second, sharecropping played an important role in the transformation of the agrarian economy during the eighteenth century. Work on Catalonia thus contributes to the important reassessment among development economists and historians whereby sharecropping is no longer seen as typical of and responsible for agricultural 'backwardness'. Finally, the persistence of feudal forms in early modern Catalonia, in contrast to areas such as Holland, allows for

---

[1]   Brenner, 'Agrarian Class Structure', pp. 35, 40, 49 n. 81.

[2]   See Jaume Torras, 'Class Struggle in Catalonia: A Note on Brenner', *Review*, 4 (1980), pp. 235–65.

[3]   R. Garrabou, J. Planas and E. Saguer, *Un capitalisme impossible? La gestió de la gran propietat agrària a la Catalunya contemporània* (Vic, 2000).

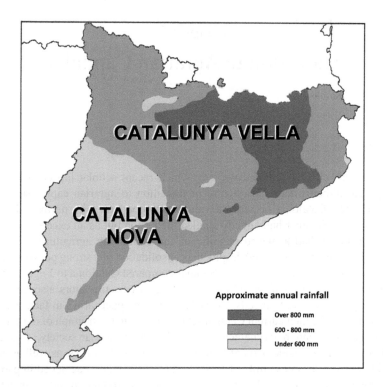

Figure 2.1   Old and new Catalonia

a re-introduction of class conflict in rural society, alongside the role of markets in the investigation of the transition to agrarian capitalism in Europe.

The Catalan rural economy in the eighteenth century

The evolution of Catalan property rights

As shown in Figure 2.1, Catalonia can be divided into two distinct zones: a relatively humid north-eastern zone and a dryer south-western one. The distinction is more than simply climatic, however; there are also historical differences that can be traced back to the earliest stages of the Christian Reconquest. North-eastern Catalonia, traditionally known as *Catalunya vella* (old Catalonia) is an area of dispersed settlement, particularly family farms known as *masos* (singular: *mas*), wrongly characterised by Brenner as 'very large but compact'.[4] The south-west, *Catalunya*

---

[4]   The size of the average *mas* varied considerably, from 90–120 hectares in the Bages district (see Figure 1.1), to 50–65 hectares in the late eighteenth-century Penedès, and 20–50 hectares in the Girona district during the mid-nineteenth century. Not all the

nova (new Catalonia), is characterised by more nucleated settlements and smaller holdings. Both areas, however, shared the same distinctive property rights, a legacy of the Middle Ages.

Central to these property rights was a division between *domini directe* (seigneurial rights) and *domini útil* (use rights).[5] The *domini directe* has to be distinguished from three other categories of seigneurial rights: judicial rights, territorial rights and participation in ecclesiastical rents (tithes).[6] The holder of the *domini directe* received rent payments known as *censos*, and could claim other payments, discussed in the final section below. The holder of the *domini útil*, ceded to him or his predecessors at some point in the past, was obliged to pay *censos* and any other payments or services stipulated, but was free to determine how the land should be cultivated, subject only to the requirement in the original cession or *establiment* to improve the land. For every plot of land, therefore, there was a feudal lord (*senyor directe*) and an owner of the use rights, usually described as the owner (*propietari*) of the land. The two sets of rights could be sold or transferred independently of each other. Both sets of rights were perpetual. The difference, however, was that the same person might and often did, exercise *domini directe* over a wide area, whereas the *domini útil* tended to be much more fragmented as small plots had gradually been ceded over time. The emphyteutic nature of use rights meant these could be ceded, sold, leased or otherwise transferred, in exchange for payments in cash or kind or on a sharecropping basis, so long as the rights of the *senyor directe* were recognised. The importance attached to emphyteusis by contemporary observers will be discussed below in the context of the agrarian expansion of the eighteenth century.

Over the early modern period, the *censos* and other payments due to the *senyor directe* declined in value, strengthening the position of the holders of use rights, who paid relatively little and were able to control production in order to extract the maximum of surplus. During the sixteenth and seventeenth centuries, a process of social differentiation took place, whereby some peasant families were able to accumulate emphyteutic tenures through purchase, marriage or inheritance at

---

area would necessarily be cultivated, however, so size cannot be taken as an indicator of labour use. See Llorenç Ferrer, *Pagesos, rabassaires i industrials a la Catalunya central* (Barcelona, 1987), pp. 648–51; Belén Moreno, *Consum i condicions de vida a la Catalunya moderna: El Penedès, 1670–1790* (Vilafranca del Penedès, 2007), p. 62; Rosa Congost, *Els propietaris i els altres: La regió de Girona 1768–1862* (Vic, 1990), pp. 79–81.

[5] For this section, see Vilar, *La Catalogne*, vol. 2, pp. 491–501; Congost, *Els propietaris i els altres*, pp. 33–52.

[6] On these sets of rights, often hard to distinguish in practice, see Gaspar Feliu, *El funcionament del règim senyorial a l'edat moderna: L'exemple del Pla d'Urgell* (Lleida, 1990), ch. 2. Judicial rights implied civil and criminal jurisdiction over a certain area. Territorial rights included vassalage, labour services and taxes on mills, markets, roads and the like. Tithes belonged to the parish in *Catalunya vella*, but in *Catalunya nova* had been ceded to secular lords early on in the Christian Reconquest in a bid to encourage resettlement of the land.

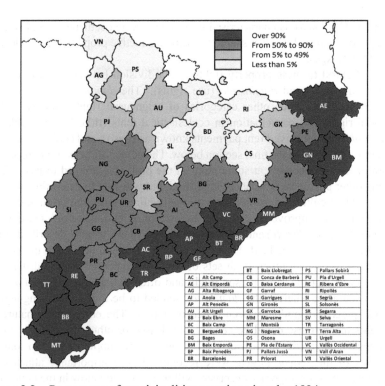

Figure 2.2   Percentage of municipalities growing vines by 1824

the expense of others. As the former accumulated land beyond their capacity to cultivate it, often because holdings were not adjacent, they ceded some or all of it to others. By the eighteenth century most holders of *domini útil*, particularly of *masos*, were no longer the cultivators of the land they owned.

The transformations of the eighteenth century

The agricultural transformation of Catalonia was a three-way process of extension, intensification and specialisation of cultivation.[7] The initial stimulus to this process came from the rising foreign demand, from the late seventeenth century onwards, for wine and spirits. The hostility aroused in England and Holland by Colbert's protectionist measures allowed the Iberian peninsula to gain the predominance in the English and Dutch markets formerly enjoyed by French wines and spirits.[8] This demand stimulated viticulture across the region, illustrated in Figure 2.2, which shows the districts according to how many municipalities were growing

---

[7]   Vilar, *La Catalogne*, vol. 2, pp. 189–327.

[8]   Francesc Valls, *La Catalunya atlàntica: Aiguardent i teixits a l'arrencada industrial catalana* (Vic, 2003), pp. 50–63.

vines by 1824. Viticulture dominated in the southern and coastal areas, where the soil was unsuited to large-scale grain production and there was easy access to ports.[9] Cereal production tended to be more important in western Catalonia, where soils were better, while, as will be described in Chapter 3, rural industry became concentrated in the central, mountainous area of Catalonia, where soils were also poor, but the climate often too cold for vines.

The extension of cultivation took the form first of replanting land that had long lain fallow after the economic crisis of the seventeenth century and second of breaking previously uncultivated land (areas of poor soil and woodland) in order to plant it, usually with vines.[10] In the Lleida district, for example, the area under cultivation almost doubled between 1716 and 1785, from 6,355 to 11,020 *jornals*.[11]

The intensification of cultivation took various forms. As will be discussed in more detail below, most historians agree that it was primarily through an intensification of labour that output was increased. There were some technical innovations, however, such as an increase in irrigation, usually small-scale and localised because of the cost, an improvement in the quality of ploughs used and changes to crop rotations that either shortened the fallow period or substituted nitrogen-fixing crops instead.[12] There are fewer figures for increase in output per hectare available than for expansion of cultivation, but one estimate for the Penedès district gives a rise from 3 *cargues* of wine to 8 per hectare between the mid-eighteenth and early nineteenth centuries and from 2.8 to 4 *quarteres* of grain.[13]

Throughout Catalonia, these three strands of extension, intensification and specialisation of cultivation were largely achieved through the medium of long-term emphyteutic contracts, different variants of the *establiment* or cession of plots of land described above. Properly speaking, these were *subestabliments*, since the original cession of the *domini útil* had already taken place long before, and it was now the holder of the *domini útil*, not the feudal lord, who was ceding the land for cultivation. While fixed-length and non-emphyteutic contracts did exist, known as *arrendaments*, they were rare except in well-irrigated areas where yields were higher than average, where proximity to an urban centre meant high demand for both land and output or, most importantly, where *masos* required tenant farmers for the short-term.[14]

---

[9] For a summary, see Ramon Arnabat, *Vins, aiguardents, draps i papers* (Vilafranca del Penedès, 1996), pp. 46–53.

[10] Vilar, *La Catalogne*, vol. 2, pp. 191–241.

[11] Enric Vicedo, *Les terres de Lleida i el desenvolupament català del set-cents: Producció, propietat i renda* (Barcelona, 1991), p. 65.

[12] Vilar, *La Catalogne*, vol. 2, pp. 242–303; Vicedo, *Les terres de Lleida*, pp. 101–12.

[13] My calculation from figures provided by Arnabat, *Vins, aiguardents, draps i papers*, p. 60.

[14] Vilar, *La Catalogne*, vol. 2, pp. 515–9; Vicedo, *Les terres de Lleida*, pp. 268–72; Congost, *Els propietaris i els altres*, pp. 67–8; Ferrer, *Pagesos, rabassaires i industrials*, pp. 479–83.

The emphyteutic contract, the *establiment* or *subestabliment*, was thus the norm. The owner ceded the *domini útil* in perpetuity, in exchange for an annual payment (*cens*) which could be in cash or kind, fixed or a share of the crops and an entry payment (*entrada*), which could be a sum of money, poultry or a more symbolic payment such as a glass of water. Particularly important was the variant of this contract known as the *rabassa morta* which ceded the use rights to a small plot of land for the life of the vines in return for the clearing, planting and cultivating of the land and a share of the crop.[15] The ability to extend the life of the vines by grafting meant that the contract was in practice indefinite, although not perpetual.

The *establiment*, especially the *rabassa morta*, has been hailed as the basis of Catalonia's economic prosperity in this period.[16] Contemporaries, native and foreign alike, stressed the importance of emphyteusis in providing the landlord with the freedom to be flexible, compared with other areas of Spain where the transfer of land was often heavily restricted, and providing the producer with the stability of quasi-property rights:

> To the power retained by [landlords] of making emfiteutic contracts, has with reason been attributed the cultivation of such waste lands as are most susceptible of tillage, and the constant increase of population. Industry has been promoted, new families have been called into existence and many, rescued from poverty and wretchedness, are now maintained in comfortable affluence.[17]

As Congost points out, however, the fiction of property rights embodied in emphyteusis masks very real differences in the implications of the contract for the different parties. She contrasts the nominal payment of, for example, a hen by the owner of the *domini útil* to the *senyor directe*, with the third of the produce the former could claim from the smallholder to whom he had ceded the use of a small parcel of his land.[18] For the cultivator, the advantages of the *rabassa morta* as a sharecropping contract lay in the low entry costs and relatively small share of the harvest to be handed over. For the holder of the *domini útil*, in a context of abundant labour and scarce capital and in view of the risks associated

---

[15] For an overview in English, see Juan Carmona and James Simpson, 'The "Rabassa Morta" in Catalan Viticulture: The Rise and Decline of a Long-Term Sharecropping Contract, 1670s–1920s', *Journal of Economic History*, 59 (1999), pp. 290–315. The most detailed study is Belén Moreno, *La contractació agrària a l'Alt Penedès durant el segle XVIII: El contracte de rabassa morta i l'expansió de la vinya* (Barcelona, 1995); see also Ferrer, *Pagesos, rabassaires i industrials*, pp. 439–65; F. Valls, *La dinàmica del canvi agrari a la Catalunya interior: L'Anoia, 1720–1860* (Igualada, 1996), ch. 5.

[16] See Vilar, *La Catalogne*, vol. 2, pp. 495–501.

[17] Joseph Townsend, *A Journey Through Spain in the Years 1786 and 1791* (3 vols, London, 1792), vol. 3, pp. 328–33 (here p.332).

[18] Congost, *Els propietaris i els altres*, pp. 64–7.

with viticulture, they lay in reduced monitoring costs and the maximum income resulting from the self-exploitation of the cultivator's household, particularly if other dues could be transferred to the cultivator. As will be discussed below, sharecropping is often viewed as lowering monitoring costs. Emphyteusis is seen to have lowered them still further. For Carmona and Simpson, ownership of the vines and the indefinite length of the contract provided 'the best incentive' for careful cultivation.[19] In fact, in the eighteenth century, the *rabassaire* owned not just the vines, but also the land.[20]

Despite these advantages, there were attempts to change the nature of the *rabassa morta*. The main conflict was over the indefinite length of the contract, in particular, the legality of the process whereby dead or dying vines could be replaced by forms of grafting. Attempts by the courts to fix the length of contracts at 50 years were largely ignored. Other conflicts were more specific, usually concerning attempts by landlords to make contracts more restrictive. The significance of these changes can only be addressed by looking at how land was held and transferred in practice, what its importance was at the level of the household economy and what transfers meant for those ceding and those taking on the land.

Landholding in Igualada

Changes in cultivation during the eighteenth century

Igualada's location in central Catalonia places it more or less on the border between *Catalunya nova* and *Catalunya vella*. The parish was small in the eighteenth century, extending not much further than the town itself. Apart from small irrigated plots for vegetables (*horts*), most residents who held land did so outside the parish and municipal boundaries, in the neighbouring municipalities of Òdena, Vilanova del Camí and Santa Margarida de Montbui (see Figure 2.3). There do not appear to have been any *masos* within the municipality of Igualada itself, but ownership of *masos* in the area during the eighteenth century can be identified in several cases from inventories, particularly to the north, in Òdena, Jorba and Rubió. In general, however, small-scale property seems to have been the norm, as will be shown.

---

[19] Carmona and Simpson, '"Rabassa Morta"', p. 293.
[20] Although Carmona and Simpson claim that the *rabassaire* owned just the vines ('"Rabassa Morta"', p. 293 n. 9), it seems that this was only true by the late nineteenth century. Previously, the wording of the *rabassa morta* contract specified the transfer of the *domini útil* and thus the 'ownership' of the land (see Moreno, *La contractació agrària*, p. 40 n. 12; Emili Giralt, 'El conflicto *rabassaire* y la cuestión agraria en Cataluña hasta 1936', in id., *Empresaris, nobles i vinyaters* (Valencia, 2002), pp. 115–39 (p. 120)).

Figure 2.3   The Anoia district

Igualada, as the centre of the Anoia district, was also on the border between different zones of production.[21] It is situated in a valley known as the Conca d'Òdena (see Figure 2.3). To the west and north-west, the high plateau of the Segarra district was dominated by cereal production, though soils were poor. To the south, Igualada bordered on the Penedès, a district of commercial viticulture, oriented towards the coastal ports of the south-east. To the north-east and east, the Bages and Llobregat districts were also developing viticulture, though at a slower rate than the south and not producing as high quality wine and spirits. As will be discussed in Chapter 3, they, like Igualada, were also proto-industrial zones, characterised by relatively poor soils, as noted by the mayor of Igualada in 1784:

> It is a wonderful sight to see how the people of this region, too numerous for the land available, work this land, bringing more of it under cultivation. Though it would seem that extracting the fruits of these plots would be hopeless, they turn over the soil and fertilise it to such an extent that finally they manage to reap

[21]   On the geography of the Anoia, see Valls, *La dinàmica del canvi agrari*, pp. 19–24; J.M. Torras Ribé, *La comarca de l'Anoia a finals del segle XVIII: Els 'questionaris' de Francisco de Zamora i altres descripcions (1770–1797)* (Barcelona, 1993), pp. 87–100.

some produce, the reward for their constant efforts in cultivating the soil, efforts which defy the hopelessness of the task.[22]

The same process of expansion, intensification and specialisation of cultivation described above can be shown for the Anoia. Around 1720 only about 31 per cent of the land was under cultivation, with the remainder wooded or wasteland.[23] Between 1720 and 1860 approximately 9,700 hectares of land were brought under new cultivation in a sample of eleven villages, tripling the total cultivated area.[24] Valls has calculated that 93 per cent of this new land was planted with vines.[25] Around 1720 the proportion of land under vines was 24.8 per cent, rising to 66.6 per cent in 1860.

Landholding in Igualada

The source that historians have normally used to analyse landownership in eighteenth-century Catalonia is the *cadastre*, a new tax introduced by the Bourbon administration in 1716.[26] It included payments on all forms of fixed property, of which land was the most important. In the case of Igualada, however, the *cadastre* rolls (commonly referred to as *cadastres* too) are of little use as a guide to landholding, since they only record payments on property owned within the parish. As mentioned above, most Igualada residents held land in the neighbouring parishes, for which the *cadastres* have not been found.

In order to link landholdings to households, I have therefore used two alternative sources to reconstruct the structure of landowning in Igualada during the eighteenth century. The first source is the *capbreu*, the document by which the *domini directe* over areas of land was asserted.[27] The *capbreu* took the form of a declaration by each holder of the *domini útil* to a plot of land that he (occasionally she) recognised the *senyor directe* of the land in question and stated the title by which he had come to hold the land since the original concession of use rights, whether through inheritance, purchase or mortgage. These changes in title were traced back over generations, often over two centuries, in the case of Igualada usually ending with reference to previous *capbreus* in the seventeenth and sixteenth centuries. The *capbreus* rarely record cases where land had been ceded through *subestabliments*, *rabassa morta* contracts or similar arrangements, even

22   Torras Ribé, *La comarca de l'Anoia*, pp. 283–4.
23   Valls, *La dinàmica del canvi agrari*, pp. 32–7.
24   Ibid., pp. 76–9.
25   Ibid., pp. 85–91.
26   For a discussion of the *cadastre* in general including that of Igualada, see J. Marfany, 'Proto-Industrialisation and Demographic Change in Catalonia, c.1680–1829' (PhD, University of Cambridge, 2003), pp. 61–8.
27   On the *capbreu*, see Feliu, *El funcionament del règim senyorial*, pp. 19–20.

though these theoretically involved the transfer of use rights and thus supposedly of ownership.

Numerous *capbreus* survive for the Igualada region. I have collated two sets, one for the 1720s, and one for the 1760s, covering the surrounding municipalities of Òdena, Vilanova del Camí and Montbui. While some Igualada residents did own land further afield, as evidenced by inventories, such cases were rare. The 1720s and 1760s were chosen as being decades for which *cadastres* survive for Igualada, thus allowing the landholding population recorded in the *capbreus* to be compared with the population as a whole. There is a difference in that the *cadastres* refer to single years, namely, 1724 and 1765, whereas the *capbreus* were compiled gradually over a series of months and years in some cases. I have tried to restrict the years covered and to control for changes in ownership within these.[28] The declaration of ownership was almost always made by the head of household, usually male, although widows headed households and could thus also declare title. In the case of married women, who continued to own property under Catalan law, the title is recognised as theirs, their husbands declaring only the usufruct. Where both a husband and a wife owned property in their own right, I have counted these properties together as those of one household.

The second source is inventories *post mortem*. This source is discussed in more detail in subsequent chapters. For the period 1680–1829, 522 inventories have been located for Igualada. The advantage of inventories over the *capbreus* is that all land held by households in any parish are recorded, as is land held by forms of *establiment*, including *rabassa morta* contracts. There are also inventories for households who did not own land, whereas the *capbreus* by definition were only concerned with those who did. Inventories have two disadvantages as regards landholding, however. The first is their selective nature: only certain households chose to inventory their property, usually the better-off. The second is that the dimensions of plots are not always given. In the case of Igualada, 257 (21 per cent) of all plots recorded in inventories did not have dimensions, including almost all *masos*. Rather than excluding households for which the extent of some landholdings were missing, particularly since this would involve the biggest landowners, I preferred to estimate total landholdings by adding in estimates for missing figures. In the case of *masos*, the dimensions of two owned by the Padró family, minor nobles, are known: Mas Roxel.la, in Òdena, was 40 *jornals*, Can Rafecas, in Montbui, was 36 *jornals*.[29] These were on the small side for *masos* elsewhere in Catalonia, though within the range for those in recorded in a *capbreu*

---

[28]   The *capbreus* are in ACA, NI. For the 1720s, the references are 797 (Vilanova del Camí); 815(7), 800(1), 800(11) (Òdena); 818 (Montbui). For the 1760s: 836 (Vilanova del Camí); 839, 864 (Òdena); 843 (Montbui). I am grateful to Francesc Valls for allowing me to use some of his data for the 1720s.

[29]   See J.M. Torras Ribé, *Evolució social i econòmica d'una família catalana de l'antic règim: Els Padró d'Igualada (1642–1862)* (Barcelona, 1976), p. 99.

Table 2.1a   Land ownership in Igualada according to *capbreus*

Jornals	1720s			1760s	
	Households	Percentage		Households	Percentage
<2	23	16.3		38	26.4
2–4.9	68	48.2		73	50.7
5–9.9	33	23.4		24	16.7
>10	17	12.1		9	6.3
Total	141			144	

Table 2.1b   Land ownership in Igualada according to inventories

Jornals	1680–1754			1755–1829		
	N	Percentage of house-holds with land	Percentage of all households	N	Percentage of house-holds with land	Percentage of all households
No land	38		22.2	107		27.8
<2	11	8.3	6.4	18	7.4	5.6
2–4.9	43	32.3	25.1	103	42.2	28.0
5–9.9	33	24.8	19.3	63	25.8	18.4
10–49.9	39	29.3	22.8	47	19.3	16.5
50–99.9	4	3.0	2.3	8	3.3	2.3
>100	3	2.3	1.8	5	2.0	1.5
Total with land	133			244		
Total	171			351		

for Orpí, near Igualada.[30] The 30 *masos* in Igualada inventories were thus all estimated at 40 *jornals*, a conservative but not unreasonable estimate. For other holdings, I used the modal values for those plots for which size was recorded. For vegetable plots, the mode was 1 *jornal*, for all other types of crop, it was 2 *jornals*, so these values were assigned to missing dimensions accordingly. Adjusting sizes of landholdings for households in this manner had more of an effect for bigger landowners. Before adding in missing figures, the number of households inventoried with 10 or more *jornals* was 88, after inflation the figure was 106. By contrast, the number of households with under 2 *jornals* only fell from 33 to 29 after adjustment.

Table 2.1a shows the patterns of land ownership revealed by the two sets of *capbreus*; Table 2.1b those revealed by the sample of inventories. The first comment

[30]   For the Orpí *masos*, see ibid., pp. 225–32. On the size of *masos* in general, see n. 4 above.

to be made is the relative absence of substantial landowners. Even though the inventories confirm that the *capbreus* underestimate total holdings for the biggest landowners, the numbers of households with over 50 *jornals* recorded by the two sources are low, with next to no change over time. Instead, both sources testify that most landholdings in Igualada were small-scale. Very few households had even as much as 10 *jornals* (just under 5 hectares), and most, even after adjustment for missing plot sizes, were still in the smallest categories of holdings.

Second, there is a clear shift over time towards a greater presence of smaller landholders in Igualada, according to the *capbreus*. The proportion of the population with 2 *jornals* or fewer increased, while the percentage of households with more than 5 and particularly with more than 10 *jornals* decreased. These patterns are less marked in the inventory sample, but neither source captures the substratum of households who had some rights over land in the form of *rabassa morta* contracts or *establiments*. Only 34 inventories record land held on a *rabassa morta* contract, and only 4 held *establiments*. By contrast, there were 446 *establiments* of land for cultivation found in the notarial records, of which 321 were *rabassa morta* contracts. The *capbreus*, as mentioned, do not record *subestabliments* at all. In the 1724 *cadastre*, however, there were 311 households recorded in Igualada. In 1765 there were 630. There is thus a marked decline in the proportion of Igualada households recording land tenure in the *capbreus* from 45 per cent in the 1720s, to 22.9 per cent in the 1760s. The missing households were either landless or owned land only through forms of *subestabliment*.

The majority of Igualada households, therefore, if they held land at all, had only small holdings. In this regard, they were not atypical in the Catalan context.[31] In the Penedès district, two-thirds of all plots ceded on *rabassa morta* contracts were under 2 hectares.[32] Most households thus had insufficient land to meet their needs, since the consensus is that 5 or 6 hectares was the minimum requirement for self-sufficiency.[33] For most, therefore, participation in other activities alongside the cultivation of vines would be essential for survival. The assumption has been that these other activities would have taken the form of waged labour on other farms. In the Girona district in particular, the *rabassa morta* contract has been viewed as a means of fixing a labour force on the *mas*. In the Igualada district, however, there were few landowners with sufficient land to require extra labour on a regular basis. Proto-industry was therefore the more likely alternative, as will be discussed in Chapter 5.

A further point to make here concerns the existence not just of a semi-proletariat, with insufficient land, but of a total proletariat, with no land. This rural proletariat cannot be quantified with any precision, as explained above. Nonetheless, if

---

[31]   Ferrer, *Pagesos, rabassaires i industrials*, pp. 226–9, 265–7; Vicedo, *Les terres de Lleida*, pp. 220–32.

[32]   Arnabat, *Vins, aiguardents, draps i papers*, pp. 56–7.

[33]   Congost, *Els propietaris i els altres*, p. 79; Ferrer, *Pagesos, rabassaires i industrials*, p. 210; Aymard 'Autoconsommation et marchés', p. 1394 (summarising a range of studies).

around 25 per cent of inventories record no land, and the social bias of inventories is such that the landless are likely to be under-represented, the rural proletariat in Igualada must have been of a considerable size by the late eighteenth century.

The existence of a rural proletariat is important since Catalan historians have claimed that Catalonia's particular version of agrarian capitalism was achieved without the creation of such a class.[34] Garrabou, Planas and Saguer argue that, even as late as the second half of the nineteenth and beginning of the twentieth century, no significant process of proletarianisation can be observed. Although waged labour existed, these authors see it as supplementing inadequate landholdings or as work undertaken only at certain times of the life-cycle. In part, they attribute the lack of a proletariat to the insecurities of waged labour and low levels of wages over the course of the nineteenth century. The Igualada evidence, however, suggests that a not insignificant proportion of households may have been dependent upon wage labour at a much earlier date. How atypical Igualada may have been in this regard is hard to judge. Contemporary comments suggest landlessness was rare for the most part. Vicedo believes, however, that an increasing, if unquantifiable proportion of the population of Lleida became landless agricultural labourers during the eighteenth century.[35] In Igualada, the emergence of a rural proletariat may have been facilitated by proto-industrialisation, another theme which will be addressed in Chapter 5.

Other forms of landholding

Returning to the substratum of landholders not captured by the *capbreus*, the most commonly used mechanisms for the transfer of land, other than actual sales, in the Igualada district were the *subestabliment* and its variant, the *rabassa morta* contract. I have located 446 *subestabliments*, of which 321 were *rabassa morta* contracts, used to cede plots of land for cultivation over the period in question. As described above, the *rabassa morta* differed from the more general form of *subestabliment* in two ways. *Rabassa morta* contracts stipulated the plantation of vines and were usually for uncultivated or neglected land, while the *subestabliments* only stipulated what crops were to be grown in 33 cases (26.4 per cent). The *subestabliment* was more often for a fixed rent in cash or kind and involved a higher entry payment than the *rabassa morta*. Nonetheless, these differences were blurred in practice. In Igualada, there were 52 cases of *rabassa morta* contracts with a fixed cash rent and 53 with a rent in kind. Similarly, while cash entry payments were both more frequent and for larger amounts with *subestabliments* proper than with *rabassa morta* contracts, both types of contract could come with entry payments in kind, usually poultry, or symbolic payments, occasionally a glass of water but more usually token cash payments of a few *sous*. The first contract in the dataset is from 1739, but it is clear that many earlier contracts were not signed before notaries. Instead, they were either

---

[34] Garrabou, Planas and Saguer, *Un capitalisme impossible?*, pp. 188–95.
[35] Vicedo, *Les terres de Lleida*, pp. 279–85.

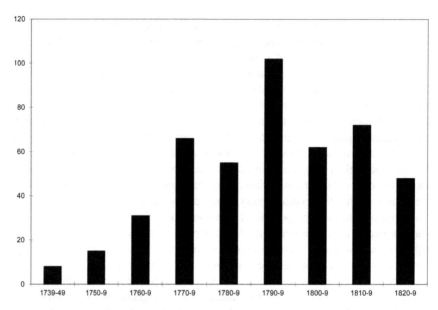

Figure 2.4   Emphyteutic land transfers in Igualada

private or oral contracts.[36] Establishing a precise chronology is thus difficult, made more so by the tendency of landowners to formalise several transfers on the same day. Figure 2.4 shows the breakdown of all types of contract according to the decade in which they appear in the notarial records. The figures for the 1760s and 1770s are inflated by numerous contracts signed in these decades, but with references to agreements in place since an earlier date. The rise in the number of transfers over time was thus less dramatic than appears. There was no tendency for one type of transfer to be more common in certain decades than in others. A similar chronology can be found for other areas, such as the Penedès.[37]

More importantly, there was little difference in terms of the size of plot ceded under either type of contract. As Table 2.2 shows, the tendency was overwhelmingly towards ceding very small plots of land, regardless of the purpose or terms of the transfer. The mean area of land ceded by *subestabliment* was 3.4 *jornals* (around 1.66 hectares), compared with a mean by *rabassa morta* of 2.6 *jornals* (around 1.3 hectares). In both cases, however, the mode was 2 *jornals*.

Neither type of transfer allowed for gradual accumulation of land by particular households. A close examination of those who took on land reveals that most households rarely appear more than once in the dataset. The figures are shown in Table 2.3a. Allowing for some errors in identification, 363 households took on land

---

[36]   For examples that refer to previous oral or private contracts, see ANI 551, fos 133–4; ANI 355, fo. 389.

[37]   Arnabat, *Vins, aiguardents, draps i papers*, pp. 56, 62–7.

Table 2.2   Size of plots transferred by *rabassa morta* and other *subestabliments*

Jornals	Rabasses mortes		Subestabliments	
	Plots	Percentage	Plots	Percentage
Not stated	5	1.6	4	3.2
<1	17	5.3	28	22.4
1–1.9	98	30.5	31	24.8
2–4.9	179	55.8	47	37.6
5–9.9	18	5.6	8	6.4
>10	4	1.2	7	5.6
	321		125	

over the period.[38] Of these, 301 (82.9 per cent) appear only once, accounting for just over two-thirds of all transfers. Among the rare instances of several transfers being made to the same household or individual, the greatest number, six, were made to Macari Planas, a smallholder from Montbui. Five of these contracts were signed on the same day, when Pere Borràs and Pere Borràs Bas, father and son, transferred five small parcels totalling 7.5 *jornals* to Planas on *rabassa morta* contracts.[39] The transfers seem to be of oddly sized parcels, perhaps not worth ceding and cultivating on their own. Eight years later, Planas took on a further plot of 3.2 *jornals*, this time from Josep Castells, a tanner of Igualada.[40] He thus represents a rare case of someone able to build up a reasonably sized holding over a relatively short time. Similarly, Anton and Miquel Soteras, father and son (and probably also a grandson), smallholders from Orpí, signed five contracts, but this time over three decades.[41] While it was clearly possible, therefore, to take on a parcel of land, break it, plant it with vines or another crop, cultivate it for a while, then take on another plot until fairly substantial holdings had been acquired, few households did so.

Rather than accumulating land, many households were acquiring it for the first time. In particular, Francesc Valls and Belén Moreno have suggested that the *rabassa morta* contract provided a basis for family formation, especially for younger sons whose access to land had previously been limited by impartible inheritance customs.

In Igualada, no kin relationships were detected between those ceding land and those taking it on, although it is likely that where *concedents* preferred their kin as cultivators, the transfers may not have been formalised before a notary. What can be shown is that *rabassaires* and those with *subestabliments* were often younger

---

[38]   Contracts signed by different members of the same household were grouped together, as far as these could be identified.

[39]   ANI 602, fos 59–61.

[40]   ANI 696, fos 134–5.

[41]   The three contracts signed by Miquel Soteras are far enough apart to make it likely that we have two different generations of the same name (see ANI 503, unfol.; 505, unfol.; 586, fos 153–4; 605, fo. 267v.

Table 2.3a   Households taking on land

Contracts per household	Households	Contracts	Percentage of all households	Percentage of all contracts
6	1	6	0.3	1.3
5	1	5	0.3	1.1
4	3	12	0.8	2.7
3	8	24	2.2	5.4
2	49	98	13.5	22.0
1	301	301	82.9	67.5
	363	446		

sons. From a combination of marriage contracts and baptismal information, 45 cultivators could be identified definitely as being younger sons. Another 47 were born outside the parish, and thus likely to be mostly younger sons, given that younger sons were more likely to leave their place of birth to set up home elsewhere. One or two marriage contracts do confirm the use of *rabassa morta* contracts to set up households for younger sons. Gayetano Barral received land in Òdena held by his family on a *rabassa morta* contract as part of his marriage portion.[42] In fact, the *rabassa morta* contract had been signed 5 years earlier, when Gayetano and his brother Josep signed contracts for two presumably adjacent plots owned by Pere Joan Pelfort.[43] In another example, land held on an oral *rabassa morta* contract became the dowry for Maria Vila on her marriage to a younger son, Maurici Balil.[44] The couple appeared as joint signatories when the contract was eventually formalised more than 20 years later.[45]

If we turn to those households that ceded land, as shown in Table 2.3b, what stands out instantly is the extreme concentration of such cessions in the hands of a few households, with just four responsible for nearly a third of all plots ceded. One household in particular, the Padró family, accounted for 97 *subestabliments* and *rabassa morta* contracts, just under 22 per cent of the total, ceded over three generations by Liberata Vilossa, widow of Ramon Ignasi Padró, her son Anton Mariano Padró and her grandson, Josep Anton Padró. A long way behind them, the Massaguer family, merchants, ceded 18 plots of land over two generations, followed by Serafina Llucià, widow of a peasant, and her son Valentí Biosca, with ten contracts. A handful of households, and the Padró family in particular thus controlled much of the extension of cultivation taking place in the Igualada region. As can be seen from Table 2.3b, however, this control was not absolute. At the other end of the scale, just under 30 per cent of all land transfers were made by 132 households (nearly 70 per cent), each responsible for just one transfer in the dataset.

---

[42]   ANI 586, unfol.

[43]   ANI 563, fos 173–5, fos 184–5.

[44]   ANI 381, fos 94r–97r.

[45]   ANI 306, fos 196–9.

Table 2.3b   Households ceding land

Contracts per household	Households	Contracts	Percentage of all households	Percentage of all contracts
97	1	97	0.5	21.9
18	1	18	0.5	4.1
10	1	10	0.5	2.3
9	1	9	0.5	2.0
7	4	28	2.1	6.3
6	2	12	1.0	2.7
5	4	20	2.1	4.5
4	9	36	4.7	8.1
3	9	27	4.7	6.1
2	27	54	14.1	12.2
1	132	132	69.1	29.8
	191	443		

Note: Excludes eight contracts of land ceded by a monastic house, the hospital and the silk-weavers' guild.

This pattern, whereby numerous households ceded small parcels of land on a one-off basis, is intriguing, since it does not fit the image usually presented of the *subestabliment* and *rabassa morta* contract, which is closer to that of the Padró family. It may have represented an adjustment of land–labour ratios, either at certain times in the life-cycle or because of a preference for engaging in other activities. It is likely that it was cheaper to do so than to cultivate the land directly, especially where this was a case of breaking new land for vines. It is noticeable that 43 households (22.5 per cent) that ceded land were headed by women, mostly widows, as opposed to only 6 of the households taking on land. For women with young children, the time constraints of cultivating their land may have meant that it made most sense for them to transfer the land to someone else, while still receiving an income in the form of cash or a share of the harvest. Marianna Querol and Coloma Sabater ceded 6 *jornals* of land to Anton Centellas in return for shares of the harvest to feed their families and a cash payment of 150 *lliures* to pay a legacy and a dowry to two children.[46] Similarly, Josepa Viladès i Batlle ceded a holding of 40 *jornals* to Josep Carner in return for 10 *càrregues* of wine, 8 *quarteres* of grain and 4 *cortans* of olive oil a year and the promise of 1,000 *lliures* in cash should Carner end the arrangement at any point.[47] Josepa made the arrangement 'to feed her numerous family' in 1812, when prices were exceptionally high.

[46]   ANI 467, fos 200r–205r. Marianna and Coloma were either sisters-in-law or mother and daughter-in-law.

[47]   ANI 652, fos 349–50.

Why sharecropping?

Transfers of land by *subestabliments* could therefore mean very different things depending on the circumstances of the households involved. Some of the theoretical implications of sharecropping and emphyteusis have been described above, and can now be examined in further detail. There is an abundant literature on sharecropping in different areas of Europe that stresses the capacity of this form of tenure to be as efficient and productive as any other.[48] Historians and economists tend to explain preferences for sharecropping according to three different arguments, which are not mutually exclusive. The first is that sharecropping allowed landlords to attract risk-averse tenants. The second is that it minimised monitoring costs or avoided problems of moral hazard. The third is that sharecropping made sense where access to capital was limited. Catalan historians, as described above, have also tended to emphasise the quasi-property rights conferred by the *subestabliment* when explaining the ability of the *rabassa morta* to contribute to the transformation of the Catalan economy.

Of the three general arguments, the third is the most straightforward to assess where Catalan contracts were concerned. The *subestabliment*, particularly the *rabassa morta*, kept start-up costs low in theory, by keeping entry payments to landowners to a minimum, and in practice, by being associated with viticulture, which could be labour-intensive rather than capital-intensive and thus suited to small plots. Arthur Young praised the vine's potential for smallholders as its cultivation depended 'almost entirely on manual labour … demanding no other capital than the possession of the land and a pair of arms; no carts, no ploughs, no cattle'.[49] Planting involved some capital costs, but the main costs were still labour.[50] In Catalonia, one of the principal purposes of the *rabassa morta* was the clearing of, and planting on, rocky soil. It was precisely because of the high labour

---

[48]   See J.S. Cohen and F.L. Galassi, 'Sharecropping and Productivity: "Feudal Residues" in Italian Agriculture, 1911', *Economic History Review*, 43 (1990), pp. 646–56; Philip T. Hoffman, 'The Economic Theory of Sharecropping in Early Modern France', *Journal of Economic History*, 44 (1984), pp. 309–19; D.A. Ackerberg and M. Botticini, 'The Choice of Agrarian Contracts in Early Renaissance Tuscany: Risk Sharing, Moral Hazard or Capital Market Imperfections?', *Explorations in Economic History*, 37 (2000), pp. 241–57.

[49]   Cited in Juan Carmona and James Simpson, 'Why Sharecropping? Explaining its Presence and Absence in Europe's Vineyards, 1750–1950', Universidad Carlos III, Departamento de Historia Económica e Instituciones Working Papers in Economic History, 11 (2007), available at <www.uc3m.es/dpto/HISEC/working_papers/working_papers_general.html> , p. 8.

[50]   Badosa calculates that 83 per cent of the cost of planting a hectare with vines consisted of labour, with only 27 per cent for tools, manure and vines, which might or might not have been provided by the landowner (E. Badosa, *Explotació agrícola i contractes de conreu, 1670–1840: Les finques del clergat de Barcelona* (Barcelona, 1985), pp. 172–6, 200–11).

costs involved that most landowners preferred to cede plots rather than break the ground and plant the vines themselves with hired labour. Ferrer estimates on the basis of eighteenth-century accounts that a single man could clear and plant just under half a *jornal* in a year, given that the season for such work lasted only three months (December to February).[51] Planting 2 *jornals* would thus take 4 years, perhaps half that if family labour can be factored in. Most contracts stipulate that planting should be completed after 2–4 years. Capital costs are hard to estimate. Rather than purchasing new vines, the usual practice in Catalan viticulture seems to have been to graft from other vines, which was cheaper but involved a longer delay before the vines were productive. We have no idea if this involved payment or if vines were grafted from those of a family member or friend. Similarly, few cultivators owned ploughs and work animals, as will be seen below, so when these were required, they would need to be borrowed or hired.

Capital requirements were thus fairly low, but cultivators faced at least 2 years of intensive labour before any returns would be forthcoming. Moreover, despite the theory, entry payments were not always symbolic. Cash payments were stipulated in 68 contracts, a smaller proportion than in other *subestabliments*, but significant nonetheless. While these cash payments tended to be for smaller amounts than in *subestabliments*, with a mean value of 36.9 *lliures* and a maximum of 240 *lliures* for the former compared with values of 108.8 *lliures* and 650 *lliures* for the latter, they were hardly symbolic. Moreno suggests that the highest entry payments were for land that had already been all or partially planted and where the landowner was thus recuperating costs.[52] Whether this was the case or not, it still represented a start-up cost for the cultivator which could not be met except by raising cash.

As has already been seen, monitoring costs receive considerable attention in the literature. In general, sharecropping is viewed as an optimal arrangement with valuable assets such as vines or animals, where both negligence and over-production carried greater costs than with cereals. Specific studies have also shown that sharecropping was more likely if landlords resided at a distance, were female, lacked adult children, or were in occupations other than agriculture.[53] In Igualada, we have noted a marked presence of women among those ceding land in this way. More recently, Carmona and Simpson have argued with reference to France that monitoring costs included not just the supervision of labour but also the costs of dividing the harvest.[54]

Catalan historians have tended to stress emphyteusis as the ultimate solution to monitoring costs. It was not simply the stake the cultivator had in the harvest that guaranteed maximum care and effort, but the quasi-property rights he had over the land. There is little evidence that the cost of dividing the harvest was an

---

[51] Ferrer, *Pagesos, rabassaires i industrials*, pp. 128–35.

[52] Moreno, *La contractació agrària*, p. 84.

[53] On distant landlords, see Hoffman, 'The Economic Theory of Sharecropping'; on other characteristics, see Ackerberg and Botticini, 'The Choice of Agrarian Contracts'.

[54] Carmona and Simpson, 'Why Sharecropping?', p. 10.

issue in Igualada. In three cases, the Padró family set a fixed rent rather than shares 'to avoid arguments and concealment and to encourage the said sharecropper … to cultivate the land, which today from the indigence of other cultivators is excessively decayed'.[55] Whereas some contracts in the Penedès district specified that the landlord would choose whether to divide the harvest by rows of vines or by weight of grapes, the most that Igualada contracts ever stipulate is that the *rabassaire* had to give plenty of notice before the harvest, so that someone could be sent to make the division and that it was the *rabassaire*'s responsibility to transport the landowner's share.[56] In fact, the *rabassa morta* contract may have worked in Catalonia for the same reasons that Carmona and Simpson offer for France: namely, because wine was produced in the landlord's own cellar. Contracts do not specify where wine was to be produced but, as will be seen shortly, very few cultivators possessed the means to do so themselves. Moreover, as Carmona and Simpson admit elsewhere, monitoring costs of the kind they describe were less likely in small communities where reputation for honesty mattered.[57]

As regards the final reason, the significance of risk aversion has been seen as minimal in the more recent literature.[58] To say that both parties to the contract were risk neutral, however, seems a step too far, given fluctuations in wine prices and the delay before new plantings would yield any profit. Moreover, the literature tends only to consider risk in a limited form; that is, the assumption tends to be that landlords needed to attract tenants who would otherwise consider taking on the land too risky.[59] There were other types of risk involved, in the Catalan case at least. The greatest was precisely that of specialisation in viticulture at a time when grain prices were rising almost continuously. The more land was given over to growing vines, the more those who owned it, both cultivators and those merely receiving rent, were dependent on the market for grain. There were two responses to this risk. The first was the opportunity or obligation to plant other crops alongside the vines, primarily grain. The second was to change the terms of the contract to reflect price movements. As regards the first, *rabassa morta* contracts usually stipulated shares not just in wine, but also in grain, olives and fruit. In most cases, these are hypothetical shares, to be claimed only if the cultivator chose to plant such crops. What is hard to ascertain is how often cultivators did so. There is anecdotal evidence that grain was grown in between rows of vines. No contracts forbade

---

[55]   ANI 587, fos 180v–182v, 193r–195r, 201–2. The same phrasing occurs in all three contracts.

[56]   Moreno, *La contractació agrària*, p. 76.

[57]   Carmona and Simpson, '"Rabassa Morta"', p. 294.

[58]   Carmona and Simpson assume that both parties were risk neutral ('Why Sharecropping?'). For an empirical case where risk aversion does not seem to have been a factor, see Ackerberg and Botticini, 'The Choice of Agrarian Contracts'.

[59]   This is the assumption made by both Hoffman, 'Economic Theory of Sharecropping' and Ackerberg and Botticini, 'The Choice of Agrarian Contracts'. If the landlord is subject to risk, it is associated with monitoring costs and problems of moral hazard.

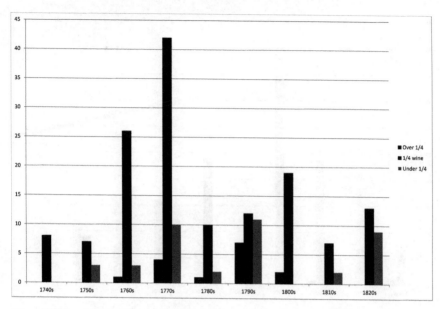

Figure 2.5a   Shares of wine in contracts

the practice, although two set limits to how much grain could be planted and only seven contracts carried the obligation to do so. This is in contrast to the Penedès district, where some contracts did forbid planting other crops.[60] The failure of the Igualada contracts to be explicit on this point does not mean, however, that diversification was necessarily a matter of choice for the cultivator. The second response to rising grain prices was to set the terms of the contracts accordingly. Either the *concedent* could demand larger shares of the crop, or he or she could set a fixed rent in cash or kind instead. In Igualada, both options were pursued. The norm was for the *concedent* to take one-quarter of the wine, one-sixth of the cereals and up to half of the olives, fruit or vegetables. Over time, important shifts took place in these shares. Figures 2.5a and 2.5b compare variations over time in the numbers of contracts specifying different shares of grapes and cereals. To simplify matters, the range of options has been reduced to the norm (one-quarter wine, one-sixth cereals) and either less or more than the norm. Olives, fruit and vegetables have not been included, since it is harder to establish a norm with such crops, and price trends are impossible to reconstruct.

The figures show an interesting contrast in that, in decades where wine prices were high, such as the 1770s and 1790s, more contracts deviated away from the norm of a quarter share of wine, but in both directions and much more towards taking less than a quarter. *Concedents* were not trying to benefit from high prices by claiming a greater share of the grape harvest. What they did instead was to claim a greater share of cereals, particularly in the 1790s, when prices experienced

---

[60]   Moreno, *La contractació agrària*, p. 79.

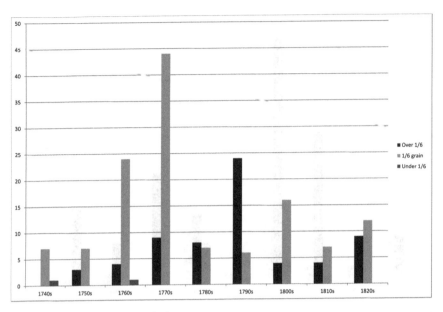

Figure 2.5b   Shares of grain in contracts

a particularly sudden jump. Moreno has found similar trends for the Penedès.[61] Moreover, what these figures do not show is the switch in many contracts after the 1780s to fixed rents instead of shares and, even more importantly, the variation from fixed rents in kind to in cash. If in kind, they were never in wine and almost always in wheat or barley, sometimes alongside poultry or olive oil. From the 1780s, both types of contract alternated between a predominance of fixed rents in cereals, 1780–4; cash, 1785–94; cereals, 1795–1802; cash, 1803–10; a slightly mixed picture during the war years, 1810–14; then cash dominating until 1817. After that, interestingly, the contracts part company, with the *rabassa morta* returning to being almost exclusively a sharecropping contract again, while other *subestabliments* continued to alternate between cereals for 1819–21, then cash again from 1821–9. Essentially, the trend follows relative movements in prices, with cereals preferred when grain prices were particularly high, but with a shift to cash when wine prices were on an upwards trend. These fixed rents had the double effect of protecting the *concedent* from the market while making the cultivator more dependent upon it, both for his own subsistence and to meet the terms of his contract. The degree of dependence would be determined by the amount, if any, of grain the *rabassaire* could plant alongside vines. The situation in Igualada may not have been as harsh as in the Penedès, where a fixed rent in wheat or barley was often demanded even in contracts where the *rabassaire* was explicitly banned from growing cereals, and where fixed rents were often

---

[61]   Moreno, *La contractació agrària*, pp. 79–80.

in addition to, not replacement of shares.[62] Nonetheless, the risk of poor grain harvests was disproportionately borne by the cultivator.

Finally, the *concedent* had the ultimate protection from risk in that the *rabassa morta* contract could be terminated, an issue that has tended to be overlooked in the literature, where it is the shift to non-emphyteutic contracts that tends to be emphasised with regard to this point. Despite all that has been said on the subject of quasi-property rights and the supposed security these afforded both parties, in fact, it was the *concedent* who benefited most. Essentially, he or she could not lose. If the *rabassaire* did invest the maximum in his 'property', then the *concedent* would be the beneficiary of this labour input. If, however, he failed to meet the agreed terms, then the *concedent* was free to find someone else to take over the land, while the *rabassaire* lost the investment of labour and any capital that had been put into cultivation.

In practice, in Igualada at least, the termination of contracts was relatively frequent: 43 cases can be identified, 13.4 per cent of the sample. Some of these were sales by one *rabassaire* of his rights to another, but more often, land was taken back by the original *concedent* to be ceded anew because the original *rabassaire* had failed to meet the terms of the contract. There were numerous examples of these. On 16 December 1800, Anton Mariano Padró took back land ceded 5 years previously to Josep Grau, and signed a new *rabassa morta* contract with Josep Bou. Grau had failed to plant the land and missed two payments.[63] In a particularly poignant case, Jaume Santasusanna took on land from Serafina Llucià and her son Valentí Biosca on 31 August 1806. Santasusanna died on 3 November, and his widow Rosa was forced to give up the land, which was transferred two weeks later to Josep Mestre. On 29 January 1812 the Mestre family gave the land back to Serafina and Valentí, because 'the expenses outweighed the income'.[64] These examples serve to highlight once more the fictitious nature of these property rights, which conferred less security on their possessors than the champions of emphyteusis would have had contemporaries and historians believe.

Market involvement or market dependence?

The different forms of *subestabliment* thus placed the *concedent* and the cultivator in different relationships to the market in terms of risk. There remains, however, the important question of how far households were dependent upon markets, rather than simply involved with them as they chose. As discussed in the previous chapter, historians disagree over how to measure market involvement: whether

---

[62]   Ibid., pp. 86–8. Moreno suggests fixed rents in addition to shares may have been in order to satisfy tithe payments.

[63]   ANI 637, fo. 183.

[64]   ANI 635, fos 183–5, 274–6; ANI 658, fos 34–5.

Table 2.4   Ownership of livestock in inventories

	Number inventories	Percentage of inventories	Percentage of livestock owners
Mules	76	14.6	52.8
Donkeys	37	7.1	25.7
Horses	8	1.5	5.6
Oxen	2	0.4	1.4
Cows	3	0.6	2.1
Sheep	8	1.5	5.6
Goats	3	0.6	2.1
Pigs	11	2.1	7.6
Poultry/rabbits	35	6.7	24.3
Bees/silkworms	3	0.6	2.1
Unspecified	2	0.4	1.4

Note: Unspecified refers to the generic description *bestiar* which could be sheep, cows or oxen.

it is specialisation or diversification that best captures greater involvement. Specialisation and diversification over the whole range of economic activity of households will be examined in Chapter 5. If we limit our analysis to land cultivation, the most obvious point to make is that households were specialising in at least one way, namely, choosing to plant vines rather than other crops. Since Catalan viticultural expansion in this period was primarily commercial, households were in this sense responding to market stimuli, although in terms of the conditions upon which land was available to them, not entirely as free agents. Moreover, as the previous section has made clear, specialisation in this instance could be risky for the cultivator. Whether or not cultivators specialised entirely in vines or grew some other crops, the terms of their contracts were such as to insulate from the market the *concedents* to whom they owed rent or shares, while they themselves were forced into market dependence.

There was also little diversification in ownership of livestock. Table 2.4 shows the different types of livestock found in the 522 inventories. Only 144 (28 per cent) recorded any livestock, and the presence of animals rarely involved diversification on a significant scale, as will be shown in Chapter 5. In most cases, as Table 2.4 indicates, households owned either a mule, used in areas of viticulture for ploughing but also for transport, or a donkey, which performed similar functions, though less efficiently. Otherwise, only poultry and rabbits had a significant presence.

The ownership of agricultural tools is another good indicator of the economic status of households. On a generous definition, whereby tools such as axes are included, 254 households owned tools of some kind. Overwhelmingly, however, these were tools for manual labour: hoes, spades, rakes and the like. Ownership of ploughs was much rarer. Only 69 inventories recorded complete ploughs, as opposed to just parts, such as yokes. Similarly, very few households owned the means to turn grapes into wine or spirits for market. While 144 households did have a *cup*, a form of tub or sometimes a tiled pit for the first stage of crushing grapes, only 14 had a wine press for the more elaborate stages of processing, and only 11 had equipment for distilling spirits.

While for most smallholders keeping mules or oxen, like ploughs or wine-making equipment, did not make sense financially, it meant they were caught in a trap frequently associated with sharecropping: that of interlocking markets.[65] In other words, access to land may come with the obligation to perform labour services, and the cultivator may be dependent on the landowner for credit and working capital. While direct evidence of this for Catalonia is lacking, Garrabou, Planas and Saguer have found some examples for the Segarra district whereby ploughing was done in return for labour services, with a strict account kept in cash.[66] No account books have been found for Igualada, but it is not unreasonable to suppose that cultivators were dependent on a handful of wealthier landowners for ploughs, animals and the means to make wine, whether this was paid for in cash, labour or kind. Nor is it unreasonable to suppose that these wealthier landowners made use of interlocking markets to reinforce paternalistic relationships between themselves and the class of cultivators.

Class conflict

The issue of relationships between landowners and cultivators brings us back to the question of class conflict. The recent reappraisal of Brenner by historians of north-western Europe has tended to place less emphasis on class conflict than on other factors, partly because of the particular conditions prevailing in England and especially Holland, where the feudal class structure is argued to have 'disintegrated' at an early date.[67] In contrast, historians continue to emphasise class conflict in the transition to capitalism in Catalonia in various ways. It is now generally accepted that the early modern period, as mentioned above, saw the strengthening of those peasants who were owners of the *domini útil*, as the dues they owed were minimised by inflation.

Several historians have argued for a gradual loss of seigneurial rights and income over this period, as the effect of inflation was exacerbated by resistance to

---

[65]   See esp. Pranab K. Bardhan, *Land, Labor and Rural Poverty: Essays in Development Economics* (Delhi, 1984).

[66]   Garrabou, Planas and Saguer, *Un capitalisme impossible?*, pp. 188–9.

[67]   Peter Hoppenbrouwers, 'Mapping an Unexplored Field: The Brenner Debate and the Case of Holland', in Hoppenbrouwers and van Zanden (eds), *Peasants into Farmers?*, pp. 41–66. This is not to say that these historians ignore class conflict, merely that they do not see it as fundamental to the transition to capitalism after a certain date.

the payment of dues.[68] Such resistance took the more passive form of fraud as well as active forms, often in the form of legal challenges to what were, or were perceived as, new charges. As sales and transfers of titles increased during the eighteenth century, so did attempts to impose new exactions or revive ones that had fallen into disuse, with corresponding resistance on the part of the peasantry. From the point of view of the owners of *domini directe*, the most important forms of income were those that were not fixed and thus not rendered insignificant by inflation, namely, tithe (claimed by secular as well as ecclesiastical lords in Catalonia) and *lluïsme*. The *lluïsme* was a fine payable every time land changed hands except as an inheritance. In theory, it could be a third of the value of the sale or transfer price and, although in practice the amount varied, it was usually substantial. The ability of landlords to maximise their income from *lluïsmes* at a time when such transfers were ever more frequent depended on the degree to which they could be kept informed of changes in land ownership. Rosa Congost has argued that landlords were increasingly kept in the dark through what she terms 'asymmetric information strategies', whereby the notaries recording sales deliberately failed to record the identity of the *senyor directe*.[69] Similarly, Belén Moreno has found that only 44 per cent of *rabassa morta* contracts in the Penedès district stated who held *domini directe*.[70] Even the *capbreu*, supposedly the instrument par excellence for safeguarding feudal rights during this period, was increasingly in the hands of local notaries by the eighteenth century. While titles could not be denied in the *capbreus*, which were instigated by the lords themselves, there was considerable scope for omitting information.

For Igualada, the evidence is ambiguous. There is little sign of asymmetric information strategies being practised in the way described by Congost and Moreno. Only in nine land transfers was the title not recorded at all, in a further nine the phrase *incert senyor* (disputed title) was used, three claimed not to know who held the title, four claimed there was no overlord and one used the formula frequently found in Congost's sales: 'the lord who shall prove his title' (*lo senyor qui se demostrará*). In total, therefore, only 6 per cent of *subestabliments* failed to record title. That Igualada should be different in this regard probably reflects the prominence of the Padró family among those ceding land, since these represent a rare case of land being ceded by those who held *domini directe* as well as *domini útil* and who could thus exercise a much greater degree of control than more distant landowners.

---

[68] Feliu, *El funcionament del règim senyorial*, pp. 147–55; Albert Cots, 'Aproximació a l'estudi dels conflictes senyorials a Catalunya (1751–1808)', *Estudis d'història agrària*, 6 (1986), pp. 241–68; Ramon Arnabat, 'Notes sobre la conflictivitat senyorial al Penedès (1759–1800)', *Estudis d'història agrària*, 8 (1990), pp. 101–22; Arnabat, *Vins, aiguardents, draps i papers*, pp. 18–20, 28–33.

[69] Rosa Congost, 'Derechos señoriales, análisis histórico y estrategias de información: El ejemplo catalán', in idem., *Tierra, leyes, historia* (Barcelona, 2007), pp. 159–90.

[70] Moreno, *La contractació agrària*, pp. 104–11.

Nonetheless, this is not to say that resistance was non-existent. It is significant that the Cardona-Medinaceli family in particular repeated their *capbreus* for the Anoia district twice as often in the eighteenth century as in the seventeenth and how prolonged the process of declaration became, suggesting that owners of *domini útil* dragged their heels more and more when summoned to declare their holdings. A decline in income has been documented for this family, the biggest feudal lords in Catalonia, but whose possessions were extremely fragmented.[71] It is precisely this fragmentation that may have made them vulnerable to loss of income and authority. Moreover, in the Anoia district, their rights were increasingly challenged or at least the subject of confusion in the records, since in many places they shared jurisdiction with others.[72]

A conflict for which a detailed study exists is that which took place between the Cardona-Medinaceli family and the Padró family of Igualada over the right to claim dues in the municipality of Orpí.[73] The Padró family had purchased the title of lordship in 1677, but the Cardona-Medinaceli family claimed to be overlords and challenged the right of the Padró family to carry out *capbreus*. The resulting legal suit dragged on until 1707. Interestingly, the Cardona-Medinaceli family had the support of the more substantial peasantry of Orpí, who, as Torras Ribé points out, preferred to maintain the status quo of a distant lord than to pay dues to a new and exacting one and indeed resisted paying dues throughout the eighteenth century.

This particular conflict highlights a problem for historians in studying class conflict in Catalonia during this period: the use of legal sources reveals only those episodes which reached some stage in the judicial process and thus involved either better-off individuals or communal resistance.[74] This is not to say that smallholders did not also resist seigneurial power, but merely to point out that such resistance is far less visible in the sources. Moreover, while the owners of *domini útil* might be protesting against seigneurial power, they were able in turn to intensify pressure on the direct cultivators of the land. Particularly relevant here is the phenomenon described as the 'denaturalisation' of the *rabassa morta* contract.[75] As mentioned above, there were legal disputes as early as 1765 over the length of the contract. Though attempts were made to fix the length at 50 years or to ban techniques such as grafting, neither was successful. To ban grafting was in no one's interests, since landlords did not want to take back an exhausted vineyard. Despite legal

---

[71]   M. Caminal et al., 'Moviment de l'ingrés senyorial a Catalunya (1770–1835)', *Recerques*, 8 (1978), pp. 51–72.

[72]   Torras Ribé, *La comarca de l'Anoia*, pp. 119–50.

[73]   Torras Ribé, *Evolució social i econòmica d'una família catalana*, pp. 85–92.

[74]   On this point, see Cots, 'Aproximació a l'estudi dels conflictes senyorials', pp. 242–3; Arnabat, 'Notes sobre la conflictivitat senyorial al Penedès', pp. 102–3, who differ in the sources they use.

[75]   See Giralt, 'El conflicto *rabassaire* y la cuestión agraria', pp. 119–25; Moreno, *La contractació agrària*, pp. 67–97

prescriptions, therefore, very few contracts were restricted to 50 years before 1830.[76] By this date, however, the contract in many areas was less likely to be described as an emphyteutic contract. Either the formula *estableixo y en emfiteusim concedeixo* was replaced by the more ambiguous *concedeixo a parts*, or the phrase *rabassa morta* disappeared, to be replaced by the term *parceria* (sharecropping). This shift away from emphyteusis made the contract, even when still indefinite in length, less a permanent transfer of property rights and more a lease arrangement. Some historians view these changes as part of a more general shift to short-term leasing arrangements such as the *arrendament*. Even when emphyteusis remained, many contracts increasingly became more rigid in the definition of tasks and payments imposed upon the cultivator.

Some aspects of this process have already been described for Igualada, such as the shift at certain times to fixed-rent agreements in cash or kind. It was, however, uncommon in Igualada for contracts not to be emphyteutic. Only two contracts are described as *parceria* contracts, and in both cases they are for *masos* rather than small plots.[77] The *arrendament* was also rare in Igualada. Of ten instances in the dataset, four were for the collection of shares of harvests or tithes, rather than land proper, and a fifth was for a *mas*. All ten were after 1800, and the Padró family was responsible for half of them.

Some tightening-up of the contract can, however, be observed in Igualada in terms of the particular sub-clauses governing both the methods of cultivation and the dues to be paid by the cultivator. With regard to the first, the earliest contracts, as elsewhere in Catalonia, tended not to be prescriptive, usually summarising all directions under the standard requirement that the land should be cultivated 'according to the customs and practices of a good farmer' (*a ús i costum de bon pagès*). Over time, however, the contracts include more and more directions, such as the distance between rows of vines, how the soil was to be fertilised, how often different tasks were to be carried out and so on. At the same time, the burden of costs was increased for the cultivator. There was a shift over time from merely specifying that the cultivator was to give the *concedent* notice of the harvest so that someone could be sent to collect the latter's share to making the cultivator pay the wages of the labourer concerned. Similarly, more dues were passed on to the cultivator. The obligation to pay the *cadastre* was a standard feature of most contracts from the start, but it also became increasingly common from the 1770s to see the obligation to pay the *cens* and the *lluïsme* to the holder of *domini directe* as well. The increased exploitation of the cultivator is starkly and cynically revealed in one of the rare *arrendaments*, when Josep Anton Padró, leasing his shares of crops from different *rabassa morta* contracts to Celdoni Ribas, stipulated that the *cadastre* payments for the respective plots of land would be Ribas's responsibility, but that he could then recoup the amounts from the *rabassaires*.[78]

---

[76] No contracts were fixed-term in Igualada.
[77] ANI 485, unfol.; ANI 615, fos 240–2.
[78] ANI 512, fos 267r–268r.

It is interesting to compare the situation in Igualada with elsewhere in Catalonia. It is clear that few landowners in the eighteenth century were able to go so far as abandoning the *subestabliment* altogether. Only for the Barcelona district has a significant shift been documented from the *rabassa morta* contract to the *arrendament*.[79] This shift was in a context where land was in high demand and the labour supply plentiful, because of high population density. Elsewhere in Catalonia, those ceding land were unable to dictate the terms of access entirely. The *rabassa morta* contract would be the most cost-effective means of cultivating land for a long time. The power of *concedents* to vary the terms of the contract and to exploit the cultivators, however, varied from place to place. The tightening-up of the *rabassa morta* contract was less severe in Igualada than in the Penedès district, despite the unusual degree of control over land exercised by the Padró family. It seems plausible that the availability of alternative employment in proto-industry in Igualada gave cultivators some room for bargaining or at least made the demand for land less urgent than elsewhere. It is to the emergence of proto-industry that the argument will now turn.

---

[79] Badosa, *Explotació agricola*, pp. 271–5, 304–32. Even here, contracts were long-term.

Chapter 3
Proto-Industry and the Origins of the Industrial Revolution

Introduction

As described in Chapter 1, perhaps the most striking aspect of Catalonia's economic transformation over the eighteenth century for contemporaries and historians alike is the early industrialisation and commercialisation of the region, which was well ahead of the rest of Spain. Arthur Young commented that Barcelona displayed 'great and active industry; you move no where without hearing the creak of stocking-engines'.[1] More importantly, Young saw enough of the interior and coastal regions during his brief visit to see that industry was not limited to Barcelona: numerous locations were described as 'animated' with manufacturing or 'exceedingly industrious'.[2]

Young's comments reflect an important feature of Catalan industrialisation, that it was not confined to Barcelona but largely rural in origin. Historians increasingly now follow the original suggestions of Pierre Vilar in seeing continuities between what can be thought of as a first proto-industrial phase in the expansion of cotton, from the 1790s to the 1830s, and the second phase of factory-based industrialisation, from the 1830s onwards. Still longer continuities, however, can be seen between the woollen industry of the eighteenth century and this first phase of the cotton industry in terms of market orientation and reorganisation of production. Historians have begun to acknowledge these continuities between wool and cotton, particularly in the nature of the labour force involved, but a systematic study is lacking. As already stated, the only way to make sense of this transformation is in terms of proto-industrialisation: examining the ways in which capital inserted itself into the production process, and how relations of production became increasingly market-oriented as a result, yet with the household remaining the unit of production. The way in which these two proto-industrial phases emerged and developed shaped subsequent industrialisation. It is these continuities from proto-industry to the factory that make Catalonia such a valuable area for study in a European context. Within Catalonia, Igualada is an obvious choice, given that it was the largest woollen-cloth manufacturing centre by the 1760s and the second for spinning and fourth for weaving cotton by 1820. At the same time, comparing

---

[1] Arthur Young, 'Tour in Catalonia', *Annals of Agriculture*, 8 (1787), pp. 193–275 (pp. 235–41).

[2] Ibid., pp. 231–2, 247–9.

Igualada with other localities reinforces the argument of Kriedte, Medick and Schlumbohm that proto-industry could develop in various ways. Relations of production in Igualada appear to have differed from those that predominated in other areas of Catalonia and Europe more widely. Understanding the different ways in which capital could insert itself into the production process and trying to understand why such differences might have arisen not only adds a valuable contribution to the debate on proto-industrialisation but also sheds considerable light on one of the major themes identified for this work: how households reoriented themselves towards the market.

The nature of the proto-industrial household economy will be discussed in Chapter 5. This chapter sets out the development of the woollen and cotton industries in Igualada and Catalonia, comparing the specific ways in which relations of production developed in Igualada with elsewhere and highlighting the continuities in scale of production, labour and market involvement through the transition from one fibre to the other. The woollen industry and the reasons for its particular success in Igualada have been extensively studied by Jaume Torras. I build upon Torras's work by showing how this success prepared the ground for the introduction and establishment of cotton in the 1790s. In particular, this chapter picks up on an important theme in Torras's work: namely, the shift from traditional, artisan ways of production to a more capitalist mentality.[3] It is the changes inherent in such a shift that were to have a significant impact on household formation and the nature of the household economy described in subsequent chapters.

The woollen industry

The Catalan woollen industry was in many ways a classic example of a proto-industry as described in earlier studies.[4] First in terms of its location, as shown in Figure 3.1, based on the numbers of looms reported in a survey of 1760. It was concentrated in areas of relatively poor soils for cereal crops in the central mountainous part of the region, where the problem of low yields was exacerbated by the small size of landholdings. Studies of other proto-industrial areas have played down the importance of poor soils and subsistence-based agriculture in determining the location of proto-industry. Gay Gullickson's study of the Pays de Caux, a region of commercial agriculture and proto-industry combined, is a

---

[3]   Torras, *Fabricants sense fàbrica*.

[4]   Kriedte, Medick and Schlumbohm, *Industrialization before Industrialization*, pp. 13–21, 26–8. For other case studies, see R. Braun, *Industrialization and Everyday Life* (Cambridge, 1990); Joan Thirsk, 'Industries in the Countryside', in F.J. Fisher (ed.), *Essays in the Economic and Social History of Tudor and Stuart England* (Cambridge, 1961), pp. 70–88; D. Levine, *Family Formation in an Age of Nascent Capitalism* (New York, 1977).

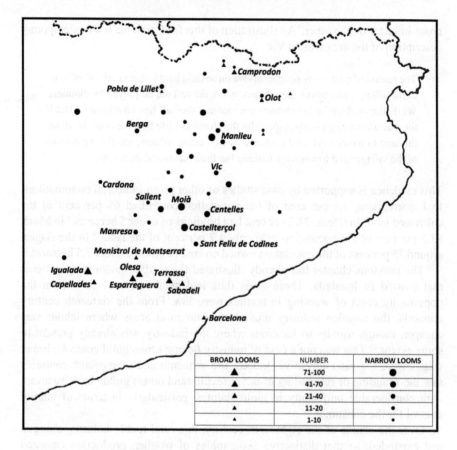

BROAD LOOMS	NUMBER	NARROW LOOMS
▲	71-100	●
▲	41-70	●
▲	21-40	●
▲	11-20	•
▲	1-10	•

Figure 3.1   Distribution of looms in the Catalan woollen industry, 1760

case in point.[5] Nonetheless, it remains the case that proto-industry seems always to have developed in areas where the opportunity costs of working outside the agricultural sector were low, whether because of the quality of the soil, the small size of landholdings or seasonal unemployment, as in inland Flanders and the Pays de Caux.[6] Even when proto-industry arose in regions of commercial agriculture and fertile soils, as in the Cambrésis, there was still a correlation at the village level between access to land and poverty on the one hand and the strength of

[5]   G. Gullickson, *Spinners and Weavers of Auffay: Rural Industry and the Sexual Division of Labour in a French Village, 1750–1850* (Cambridge, 1986).

[6]   On this relationship, see the comments by Kriedte, Medick and Schlumbohm in response to some of their critics ('Proto-Industrialization Revisited: Demography, Social Structure and Modern Domestic Industry', *Continuity and Change*, 8 (1993), pp. 217–52 (pp. 226–32)).

proto-industry on the other.[7] An illustration of this for Catalonia is a contemporary description of the area around Vic:

> The reason why so many people survive on so little land is that nearly all of those in the villages and towns are artisans, while the rest are employed by clothiers. While the clothiers' manufactures are running, they all live comfortably. But if the manufactures go badly, especially the clothiers', life becomes very hard, for the land to which I referred is owned by rich estate owners, and the inhabitants of the villages and towns have nothing but their hands and their wits.[8]

This evidence is supported by case studies of other proto-industrial communities. In Esparreguera, 3.1 per cent of the population controlled 65 per cent of the cultivated land. In Olesa, 74.2 per cent had holdings of under 5 hectares.[9] In Moià, 83.5 per cent of the population held only 4.7 per cent of the land.[10] In the Bages, around 75 per cent of the population owned no land or plots of under 2.5 hectares.[11]

The previous chapter has already illustrated the similar landholding patterns that existed in Igualada. These areas thus had a labour force for whom the opportunity costs of working in textiles were low. From the sixteenth century onwards, the woollen industry moved out into rural areas where labour was cheaper, though usually to locations where the industry was already present to some extent.[12] This was not a case of industry fleeing urban guild controls: lower wages were a greater incentive. Indeed, the sixteenth and seventeenth centuries saw the founding or refounding of many textile (and other) guilds in these areas, with considerable uniformity in guild statutes, particularly in terms of quality control for the consumer.

Over the course of the eighteenth century, this rural textile industry changed and expanded, so that distinctive geographies of woollen production emerged within Catalonia.[13] In the mountainous area around Berga and Pobla de Lillet, by the 1780s, the woollen industry tended to be focused on spinning. In central Catalonia, around small centres such as Moià, Centelles and Sant Feliu de Codines

---

[7]   D. Terrier, *Les deux âges de la proto-industrie: Les tisserands du Cambrésis et du Saint-Quentinois, 1730–1880* (Paris, 1996), pp. 78–99.

[8]   F. de Zamora, *Diario de los viajes hechos por Cataluña*, ed. R. Boixareu (Barcelona, 1973), pp. 62–3.

[9]   Assumpta Muset, 'Protoindustria e industria dispersa en la Cataluña del siglo XVIII: La pañería de Esparreguera y Olesa de Montserrat', *Revista de historia económica*, 7 (1989), pp. 45–67.

[10]   L. Ferrer, 'El Moianès en els segles XVIII i XIX: De l'especialització llanera a la decadència per manca d'aigua', *Modilianum*, 22 (2000), pp. 64–92 (pp. 73–80).

[11]   Ferrer, *Pagesos, rabassaires i industrials*, pp. 226–44, 265–74.

[12]   Torras, *Fabricants sense fàbrica*, pp. 49–52.

[13]   J. Torras, 'Especialización agrícola e industria rural en Cataluña en el siglo XVIII', *Revista de história económica*, 2 (1984), pp. 113–27.

and larger towns such as Vic the industry grew considerably during the eighteenth century, initially producing cheaper cloths for mass consumption but with some expansion into medium and higher quality cloths of 1,800 to 2,400 threads to the warp, which were marketed locally and across the peninsula. Finally, around Terrassa, the mountain centres of Olesa and Esparreguera, and Igualada, the woollen industry was more specialised, producing higher quality cloths, of 2,600 to 3,200 threads to the warp, which were mainly marketed outside the region. This specialisation is reflected in Figure 3.1 in the concentration in these localities of broad looms, suited to weaving finer cloths. By choosing to manufacture this type of what were relatively light-weight woollen broadcloths, often known elsewhere as Dutch or Spanish-style cloths, the cloth manufacturers of these localities were capturing an important niche in the market.[14] They could not compete with foreign manufacturers of super-fine woollens and worsteds, where English and Dutch techniques were superior, but they could command the market for this particular range of cloths, which came to be recognised as a distinctive product. It is noticeable that other areas of Spain, such as Béjar, near Segovia, in which the woollen industry was to enjoy long-term prosperity and eventual mechanisation, were also those places where manufacturers decided to specialise in fine woollens.[15] This type of cloth was also behind the success of the woollen industry in Clermont-de-Lodève.[16]

Proto-industrialisation could only develop successfully in places where the industry already enjoyed a certain presence, guaranteeing a sufficient concentration of capital, knowledge and commercial links.[17] The availability of labour was a necessary, but not sufficient condition. The failure of linen production in the Segarra district (see Figure 1.1) to become more than simply a local industry can be attributed to the local concentration of the raw materials, the production and the demand, leaving no space into which mercantile power might insert itself.[18] Locations such as these, where the textile industry failed to capture markets of its own tended to find themselves drawn into the putting-out networks of other centres of production. The Segarra, along with the Conca de Barberà to the south-west, became part of the putting-out network for the Igualada textile industry.

It was thus the ability to capture distant markets that distinguished areas of traditional rural industry from proto-industrial ones. This distinction can be applied more widely to Catalonia than to other Spanish regions. Catalan merchants and

---

[14] Ángel García Sanz, 'Competitivos en lanas pero no en paños: Lana para la exportación y lana para los telares nacionales en la España del Antiguo Régimen', *Revista de história económica*, 12 (1994), pp. 397–434.

[15] Rosa Ros, *La industria textil lanera de Béjar (1680–1850)* (Valladolid, 1999).

[16] J.K.J. Thomson, *Clermont-de-Lodève 1633–1789: Fluctuations in the Prosperity of a Languedocian Cloth-Making Town* (Cambridge, 1982), pp. 94–5.

[17] Torras, 'Especialización agrícola e industria rural'. Similar arguments are made for late medieval Italy by Epstein (*Freedom and Growth*, pp. 107–9, 117–19).

[18] E. Tello, *Cervera i la Segarra al segle XVIII* (Lleida, 1990), pp. 431–66.

manufacturers were more successful than any others in taking advantage of the abolition of customs barriers within Spain after the War of the Spanish Succession, establishing networks across the kingdom. A shared language, on occasion family links and the use of Catalan muleteers, especially from the villages of Calaf and Copons (see Figure 2.3), facilitated the functioning of these networks.[19]

These patterns of commercialisation, particularly in terms of a shift towards extra-regional markets, can be illustrated clearly for Igualada. Although in the 1690s, only one in every twenty cloths manufactured in Igualada was sold in the town itself, most sales were to Barcelona (almost a quarter), and to markets in the Catalan interior (almost half).[20] Fifty years later, some clothiers had managed to penetrate much more distant markets. Jaume Torras has used the accounts and correspondence of the Torelló family, one of the most successful in Igualada, to show this participation in market networks. Accounts drawn up in 1745 for the company founded by Josep Torelló Mas and his son Josep Torelló Galofré reveal interesting patterns.[21] The 29 debtors from Igualada, out of a total of 49 (if institutions are counted as single debtors), accounted for only 5 per cent of the total value of the debt owed, while just one merchant in Madrid, Josep Boter, owed 2,109 *lliures* (38 per cent). Madrid was the most distant market, but also important were markets en route, with six merchants in Lleida and Balaguer in western Catalonia (36 per cent) and two in Aragon (11 per cent). The Torelló family had thus widened their markets to include Aragon and Madrid.

Most importantly, these connections were with other Catalans, in keeping with the description of mercantile networks above. Josep Boter, with whom the Torelló family maintained a commercial relationship through the 1750s, was Catalan. From 1762 onwards the family used another Catalan merchant, Ramon Nadal, as their Madrid agent. One of the shops in Aragon was owned by Bartomeu Borrull, a brother-in-law of Josep Torelló Galofré. From the 1750s to the 1780s the family continued to extend their marketing networks across Castille, through Catalan contacts.

For other Igualada clothiers, the information is patchier, but occasional evidence of similar contacts can be found. The inventory of Josep Anton Lladó, to be discussed later, lists among his debtors merchants in Madrid, Aragon and Castile.[22] Again, one Madrid contact dominates: a Manuel de la Dehesa, who was responsible for 68 per cent of the total debt owed. In fact, Lladó's commercial

---

[19]   On the muleteers and merchants of Calaf and Copons, see A. Muset, *Catalunya i el mercat espanyol al segle XVIII. Els traginers i els negociants de Calaf i Copons* (Barcelona, 1997).

[20]   Torras, *Fabricants sense fàbrica*, pp. 61–2.

[21]   ANI 347, fos 313–19. For a discussion, see Torras, *Fabricants sense fàbrica*, pp. 102–6. My figures, derived from the original source, differ slightly from Torras's in that I count 29 debtors for Igualada, owing a total of 255 *lliures* in round numbers, while he has 30 owing 225 *lliures*. In percentage terms, the difference is minimal.

[22]   ANI 394, fos 205–18.

contacts seem to have been even more focused on Castile than those of the Torelló family. Only two debtors are listed outside Igualada who were Catalan, one of whom may have been Lladó's son-in-law. Studies of other Catalan localities where proto-industry flourished, such as Terrassa and Sabadell, show a similar presence in Madrid and other Castilian markets, compared with the more modest performance of places such as Esparreguera and Olesa de Montserrat, where producers were less involved in the commercialisation of their products.[23]

The ability to trade with other Catalans explains how these networks could function so efficiently once in place, yet cannot explain the initial success in capturing Castilian markets. There were other areas of Spain with a strong tradition of local cloth manufacturing and much greater proximity not only to Madrid, but also to raw materials.[24] Wool from Aragon and Castile was needed for cloths of medium quality and above, Catalan wool was inadequate. The removal of customs barriers within Spain after 1714 did not give Catalans any particular advantage compared with any other group: theoretically, Castilians could have penetrated Catalan markets just as easily as Catalans did Castilian ones. Moreover, selling in Madrid was not straightforward: there were still internal tariffs to pay of 8 per cent and the retail guilds held a strong monopoly over wholesale goods, hence the need for intermediaries such as Boter and Nadal.[25] Nevertheless, by the last third of the eighteenth century, an eighth of all cloths sold by wholesale merchants within the retail guild and a quarter of those sold that were manufactured in Spain were Catalan, mainly from Igualada, Sabadell, Terrassa and Barcelona.[26] The proportions sold by *roperos* (those who sold ready-made clothing), by smaller, specialised shops and by pedlars are likely to have been much higher.

Explaining Catalan success is therefore not easy. In particular, why some clothiers took the initial decision to specialise in this particular range of cloths is unknown. Rosa Ros has been able to point to some factors likely to have played a part in influencing the Béjar manufacturers, such as an influx at the end of the seventeenth century of Flemish immigrants with particular skills and a deliberate policy of promoting industry on the part of the local ducal family.[27] These factors

[23]   J.M. Benaul, 'La comercialització dels teixits de llana en la cruïlla dels segles XVIII i XIX: L'exemple de la fàbrica de Terrassa "Anton y Joaquim Sagrera"', *Arraona*, 2 (1988), pp. 35–47; J.M. Cobos, *Pagesos, paraires i teixidors al Llobregat montserratí* (Barcelona, 2006), pp. 276–92.

[24]   On Molina de Aragón, where most Catalan purchases of wool were made, but where local industry failed to thrive, see Torras, *Fabricants sense fàbrica*, pp. 163–5.

[25]   Ibid., pp. 106–11, 122–5; García Sanz, 'Competitivos en lanas pero no en paños', pp. 410–11.

[26]   J. Cruz and J.C. Sola Corbacho, 'El mercado madrileño y la industrialización en España durante los siglos XVIII y XIX', in J. Torras and B. Yun (eds), *Consumo, condiciones de vida y comercialización. Cataluña y Castilla, siglos XVII–XIX* (Valladolid, 1999), pp. 335–54.

[27]   Ros, *La industria textil lanera de Béjar*, pp. 39–66.

were not present in Catalonia. In the case of the Torelló family, a large part seems to have been flexibility in adapting to demand. Even then, flexibility was aided precisely by having contacts with first-hand knowledge of markets. The Torelló sons thus spent much time travelling around in order to maintain these contacts and to gain such knowledge themselves.[28] In particular, colour was one area where demand changed frequently and needed to be met with exactitude. In this regard, it helped that the Torelló family were one of the first in Igualada to own their own dye-house, as will be seen. In a letter dated 8 April 1752, for example, Boter wrote expressing the hope that Torelló would 'do all that was possible to achieve the exact colours required'.[29] Later, on 14 November 1764, Josep Torelló Borrull (known as Po) wrote to his father from one of his many trips to the fair at Valdemoro that dark and black cloths had not done well, but 'other colours had sold well'. Three days later, he wrote to recommend sending more cloths in yellow shades and of lead colour to Ramon Nadal in Madrid, since these had sold well at Valdemoro. In 1771 Nadal wrote that cloths in a pearl colour were popular, but green ones 'no longer have the success they used to'.[30]

Displacing English fabrics was another way in which the Igualada clothiers, particularly Torelló, could adapt to changing demand. In the 1780s a greater part of production was given over to simpler, yet softer woollens, known as *baietes*, and in particular a form of these described as *ratinades* or *arratinades* (ratines or rateens).[31] English forms of these had enjoyed great success in Madrid until war cut off trade in 1779. In 1782–3 Torelló and another clothier, Josep Jover, wrote to the Junta de Comerç claiming to have successfully imitated English *baietes* and asking for official recognition.[32] Even when peace was restored, clothiers such as Torelló still benefited from the higher tariffs to which English merchants found themselves subject after 1783. By 1788, according to a contemporary, Catalan manufacturing had 'managed to displace English *ratinados* thanks to the great consumption of those from Igualada, which are of the best quality'.[33]

---

[28]   First-hand knowledge of markets and ability to adapt to demand are also highlighted as reasons for success elsewhere (C. Poni, 'Fashion as Flexible Production: The Strategies of the Lyons Silk Merchants in the Eighteenth Century', in Sabel and Zeitlin (eds), *World of Possibilities*, pp. 37–74; C. Petillon, 'S'adapter a la mode et tenir la qualité: La Fabrique rurale de Roubaix au XVIIIe siècle', in G.L. Fontana and G. Gayot (eds), *Wool: Products and Markets (13th–20th Century)* (Padua, 2004), pp. 1103–13).

[29]   The letters cited here are in AT, *lligall* 1567. They are discussed by Torras, *Fabricants sense fàbrica*, pp. 141–5, 160–70, 180–1; id., 'The Old and the New: Marketing Networks and Textile Growth in Eighteenth Century Spain', in M. Berg (ed.), *Markets and Manufactures in Early Modern Europe* (London, 1991), pp. 93–113.

[30]   Ramon Nadal, letter (12 Oct. 1771).

[31]   Torras, *Fabricants sense fàbrica*, pp. 208–12.

[32]   AHCB, FJC, vol. 57, fos 81r–83r, 109r–125v.

[33]   E. Larruga, *Memorias políticas y económicas* (15 vols, Saragossa, 1995–6), vol.1, pp. 313–14.

The question still remains, however, as to how some clothiers were able to be more flexible than others. To a large extent, the answer comes down to the organisation of production and especially the freedom that clothiers had to dictate this. To begin with, there were structural features associated with their peculiar role that meant clothiers were better placed than weavers to assume control over the manufacturing process. In Catalonia, the functions of the clothier (*paraire*) matched those of occupations labelled elsewhere as *marchand-drapeur* or *marchand-drapier*.[34] He took care of the initial preparatory stages such as washing the wool and often did the carding as well. If not, he was certainly in charge of distributing it for carding and spinning, then collecting it back and redistributing it to weavers. The finishing stages of fulling, dyeing and shearing could be carried out by specialists, but often fell to clothiers as well. If so, specialised technical knowledge such as of mixing dyes could also give the clothier an advantage over other producers.[35] Finally, it was the clothier who sold the finished product, either directly to the consumer or to a merchant. Particularly important was the control over raw materials which clothiers had. Often clothiers' guilds were empowered to buy wool in bulk, which was then sold to members at a fixed price. This was the case in Igualada until some point in the late seventeenth century, although Torras believes only smaller clothiers relied on guild stocks for supply.[36] Clothiers with sufficient credit could purchase their own wool. It was this control over raw materials above all, as M.J. Deyá has pointed out, that gave them the advantage over other textile producers.[37] As mentioned above, those Catalan clothiers who produced the higher quality cloths that were more competitive in distant markets were those with access to wool from Aragon and Castile.

Clothiers therefore often enjoyed a strategic advantage over other producers with regard to access to markets and organisation of production. Given the various stages involved in the process of production and commercialisation, there was also often scope for differentiation among clothiers. An initially modest degree

---

[34] Similar organisational functions are described for Languedocian *marchands-drapeurs* by Thomson, *Clermont-de-Lodève*, pp. 31–5 (but with a distinction between Upper and Lower Languedoc in terms of involvement in the production process); C.H. Johnson, 'Capitalism and the State: Capital Accumulation and Proletarianization in the Languedocian Woollens Industry, 1700–1789', in T.M. Safley and L.N. Rosenband (eds), *The Workplace Before the Factory: Artisans and Proletarians, 1500–1800* (Ithaca, 1993), pp. 37–62 (pp. 42, 45–6). Despite the etymological similarities, *paraire* corresponds to a broader range of tasks than the French *pareur*.

[35] The surviving Torelló papers include a book of recipes for mixing dyes (Torras, *Fabricants sense fàbrica*, pp. 31–2). Dyeing techniques and the ability to sidestep the ducal monopoly on the local dye-house were also key features behind commercial success in Béjar (Ros, *La industria textil lanera de Béjar*, pp. 53–4, 56–9).

[36] Torras, *Fabricants sense fàbrica*, pp. 58–9.

[37] M.J. Deyá, 'La industria rural textil en la Mallorca moderna: producción y formas de comercialización interior', *Estudis d'Història Econòmica*, 2 (1988), pp.15–41 (p. 32).

of differentiation could enable some clothiers to gain the upper hand when it came to the production of higher quality goods. It is here that the question of organisation of production becomes key. Organisation of production could take varied forms along the spectrum between the ideal types of *Kaufsystem* (artisan production subject to merchant capital) and *Verlagssystem* (putting-out system involving divisions of labour) described by Kriedte, Medick and Schlumbohm. Where historians have placed particular examples along this spectrum depends on which aspects of these ideal types are stressed. James Thomson, for example, emphasises both the role of merchant capital in the *Kaufsystem* and the differences in scale of production as the key features distinguishing one from the other in his comparison of Carcassone and Clermont-de-Lodève.[38] Robert Duplessis and Pat Hudson, by contrast, stress the relative independence of producers as the most important difference.[39] In Hudson's comparison of the woollen and worsted industries of the West Riding of Yorkshire, the former remained more of a *Kaufsystem* in that clothiers retained their independence for longer, whereas the worsted industry developed along more putting-out lines.[40] Certainly, merchant capital could also dominate a putting-out system without the merchants being directly involved in production, though often it was certain producers who emerged as merchant–manufacturers, supplying raw materials, selling finished products but also co-ordinating production.[41] The range of tasks within cloth production and the inevitable resulting division of labour made a putting-out system more likely in the textile industry and made it more likely that it would be the clothier who emerged as merchant–manufacturer. Deyá also points out that a *Verlagssystem* with the clothier as merchant–manufacturer was more likely to develop in locations where both spinners and weavers were available.[42]

Not only were putting-out systems more likely in the textile industry compared with others, but, more importantly, the extent to which they developed in different localities could determine the success of industry in these places. While there were disadvantages to the *Verlagssystem* in terms of the greater difficulties in supervising

---

[38]   J.K.J. Thomson, 'Variations in the Industrial Structure of Pre-Industrial Languedoc', in M. Berg, P. Hudson and M. Sonenscher (eds), *Manufacture in Town and Country Before the Factory* (Cambridge, 1983), pp. 61–91.

[39]   P. Hudson, *The Genesis of Industrial Capital: A Study of the West Riding Wool Textile Industry c.1750–1850* (Cambridge, 1986), pp. 59–60; R. Duplessis, *Transitions to Capitalism in Early Modern Europe* (Cambridge, 1997), pp. 38–42, 124–8, 267.

[40]   Ibid., pp. 30–41.

[41]   The former situation is described for Upper Languedoc by Thomson (*Clermont-de-Lodève*, pp. 31–2), in contrast to Lower Languedoc, where the figure of the *marchand-fabricant* was more common. In Béjar, some manufacturers were of non-textile, usually commercial origins, but many also emerged from the ranks of the traditional woollen industry (Ros, *La industria textil lanera de Béjar*, pp. 69–77).

[42]   Deyá, 'La industria rural textil', p. 33.

production, these disadvantages seem to have been outweighed in most instances by its greater advantages.[43] As Thomson notes, putting-out systems were better suited to capturing particular markets, especially distant markets, where success depended upon developing higher quality cloths but also on flexibility in adapting to changes in demand.[44] Johnson attributes the success of the Lodève woollen industry to the emergence of a hierarchical putting-out system that had created 'a factory system without machines' by the eve of the French revolution.[45] He argues that it was precisely the ability to organise and command labour that determined success in the woollen industry, given the lack of effective mechanisation in this sector on the continent prior to 1800.

In Catalonia, organisation of production varied as much as elsewhere. On the whole, merchant capital seems to have been relatively unimportant in the Catalan woollen industry. Only in Esparreguera and Olesa was it important in funding the purchase of raw materials.[46] In Majorca, clothiers owned the raw materials and maintained control of production but did not market the finished products themselves.[47] In the other places for which information is available, it seems to have been local producers who came to fund and control the entire process of production. Nonetheless, commercial success was still associated with those places where a more hierarchical putting-out system was able to develop. Places such as Moià, where, in 1765, production was in the hands of 53 clothiers, divided between 23 'major' and 30 'minor', failed to capture distant markets in the way that Igualada and Terrassa did.[48] In Terrassa, by 1764, five clothiers controlled 80 per cent of production.[49] In Igualada, by 1752, 32 of the 39 looms recorded were under the control of three clothiers: Torelló, Borrull and Lladó.[50] These were the only three manufacturing cloths of 30 and 32 threads. The four others mentioned by name, each with only one or two looms, were producing cloths of 22 and 26 threads. There were doubtless other clothiers producing lower quality cloths not included in this survey.

The emergence of this particularly hierarchical putting-out system in Igualada can be clearly traced over the course of the eighteenth century. It took the form of a clear differentiation among the ranks of the clothiers and, more importantly,

[43] García Sanz, *Competitivos en lanas pero no en paños*, pp. 421–2, 427–9.

[44] Thomson, 'Variations in the Industrial Structure of Pre-Industrial Languedoc', pp. 83–4; id., *Clermont-de-Lodève*, pp. 313–5 (where success for clothiers is defined by ability to respond to markets by organising labour).

[45] Johnson, 'Capitalism and the State', pp. 44–5.

[46] Muset, 'Protoindustria e industria dispersa', 51–6; Cobos, *Pagesos, paraires i teixidors*, pp. 277–81.

[47] Deyá, 'La industria rural textil'.

[48] Ferrer, 'Moianès', pp. 82–5.

[49] Benaul, 'Los orígenes de la empresa textil lanera en Sabadell y Terrassa en el siglo XVIII', *Revista de historia industrial*, 1 (1992), pp. 39–61 (p. 53).

[50] API *caixa* 793, survey of manufacturing (1752).

Table 3.1   Textile equipment in clothiers' inventories, 1680–1716

Name	Year	Carding equipment	Spinning wheels	Wool (*lliures*)	Cloths	Dye-house
Josep Santasusanna	1684	Yes				
Alexandre Puig	1684	Yes		520	8	Yes
Josep Bergadà	1684					
Agustí Figueres	1685					
Isidro Domingo	1688		3			
Josep Samsot	1691	Yes		1 sack	9	
Josep Lafarga	1691					
Caterina Roca	1692		1			
Caterina Estruch	1692					
Agustí Miquel	1692					
Francesc Anglès	1693	Yes	2			
Gaspar Figueres	1693	Yes	2	320		
Joan Lafarga	1698					
Josep Samsot	1701					
Pau Francolí	1705		3		1	
Josep Anglès	1707					
Ramon Estruch	1709					
Lluís Francolí	1709	Yes	4	130		Vat only
Jacinto Pujol	1710		2			
Valentí Borrull	1711					
Joan Estruch	1712	Yes		31		
Fèlix Novell	1713	Yes		104		

Sources: Santasusanna: ACA, NI 780, fos 32r–33r; Puig: ACA, NI 780, fos 35r–39r; Bergada: ACA, NI 780, fos 49–51; A. Figueres: ACA, NI 780, fos 52r–57r; Domingo: ACA, NI 780, fos 137–8; Samsot (1691): ACA, NI 780, fos 162r–163r; Roca: ACA, NI 780, fos 177r–178r; C. Estruch: ACA, NI 780, fo. 185; Miquel: ACA, NI 780, fos 191r–193r; F. Anglès: ACA, NI 780, fos 209r–210r; G. Figueres: ACA, NI 780, fos 216–19; Lafarga: ANI 207, fos 143–4; Samsot (1701): ANI 207, fos 188–9; P. Francolí: ANI 207, fos 247r–248r; J. Anglès: ANI 254, fo. 63; R. Estruch: ANI 791, fos 166–8; L. Francolí: ACA, NI 791, fos 170r–177r; Pujol: ACA, NI 791, fos 191–5; Borrull: ANI 254, fos135r–136r; J. Estruch: ANI 208, fos 69r–70r; Novell: ANI 208, fos 112r–114r.

a marked differentiation among the 38 master clothiers recorded in the town.[51] Eleven of these accounted for two-thirds of all cloths produced, with the foremost, Lluís Francolí, accounting for 12 per cent. A similar degree of differentiation existed in Esparreguera, however; Igualada does not stand out particularly at this

---

[51]   J. Torras, 'Gremio, familia y cambio económico: Pelaires y tejedores en Igualada, 1695–1765', *Revista de historia industrial*, 2 (1992), pp. 11–30 (p. 18).

date.[52] Most clothiers at this time had fairly modest operations, compared with what was to follow. Significantly, Segimon Borrull and Josep Torelló Mas were ranked only thirteenth and fourteenth respectively among the 38 clothiers. Twenty-two inventories have been located for clothiers and clothiers' widows for period 1680–1713. They are listed in Table 3.1. Only 12 clothiers had equipment and they were mostly confining their activities to the preliminary stages of spinning, carding and distributing wool. Only two clothiers had finished cloths in their possession. Significantly, no clothier owned a loom. The only two who stand out are the two with dyeing facilities: Alexandre Puig and Lluís Francolí.

Differentiation was to become more marked, however, after the War of the Spanish Succession, although a lack of sources makes the origin of this process hard to pinpoint.[53] The 1724 *cadastre* gives some idea, in that clothiers who were household heads are described as either master or journeyman, since this affected the amounts of poll tax paid. Tax was also paid for apprentices and for certain types of capital equipment such as dye-houses. There were 25 clothiers listed as household heads, of whom 15 were journeymen, working on commission for others. By this date, the Torelló and Borrull families were already the most prominent: paying the most tax, including on their own dye-houses. Segimon Borrull paid the most tax, 190 *rals*, in part because he had three apprentices, as well as a dye-house and press. Josep Torelló Mas was second, paying 157 *rals* tax, also including a dye-house, though no apprentices. Only three other clothiers had apprentices and dye-houses or part ownership of a dye-house. The others were far behind, with six paying the minimum contribution.

In part, the differentiation that can be discerned was due to the vicissitudes of war, mortality and other life-cycle factors affecting some clothiers to a greater extent that others. For the most part, however, the differentiation was due to the commercial success of the three clothiers already mentioned: Torelló, Borrull and Lladó. Josep Torelló's success, far better documented, consisted of making strategic investments, in particular, a dye-house of his own in the 1720s.[54] He also cemented a strong professional relationship with Segimon Borrull through marriage.[55] In one generation, there were four Torelló--Borrull marriages, including the eldest sons of both clothiers. In 1726 Josep set up the company mentioned above with his second son, Josep Torelló Galofré, a move necessitated by the death of his eldest son, Joaquim, who left only a daughter, Josepa.[56] At this point, he invested all his capital in the company, while his son invested only 400 *lliures*, with the agreement that on the father's death, a fifth of the company would go to Josep junior, on top of his initial investment. New contracts were drawn up in 1733 and 1735 in which

[52] Cobos, *Pagesos, paraires i teixidors al Llobregat montserratí*, pp. 179–81. The figures for Esparreguera are for 1686 and 1688.

[53] Only one clothier's inventory has been found for 1713–44, with no equipment.

[54] Torras, *Fabricants sense fàbrica*, pp. 86–7.

[55] Ibid., pp. 97–126.

[56] ACA, NI 799, fos 189r–190r.

the son's share of the profits had greatly increased, in recognition of the fact that most of the work, particularly selling and buying away from Igualada, fell to him.[57]

In 1745 both Torelló and Borrull were granted, alone among the Igualada clothiers, the title of *Fabricante real* (royal manufacturer).[58] The privileges this title conveyed included various tax exemptions and, perhaps most importantly, enhanced rights to bid for wool anywhere in the kingdom, to take their cloths to fulling-mills outside the parish and to set up looms in any houses they wished for the following 8 years. While the title was worth having as a mark of status and quality, as Torras comments, the privileges would have made little difference to manufacturing costs. More significantly, the business had already reached considerable dimensions in order to achieve such recognition in the first place. Between them, Torelló and Borrull had 19 looms, 340 spinning wheels, 2 presses, dyeing vats and a fulling-mill.[59] They employed over 500 people. The concession of the title treats the two concerns as one, but the accounts drawn up by the Torellós that same year, described above, mention Borrull only as a debtor, albeit it for a substantial sum, 5,848 *lliures*, entrusted to him in order to purchase wool. By 1750 a rupture seems to have taken place between the two families.[60] In that year, Josep Torelló bought his brother-in-law out of his share in the jointly owned fulling-mill.

Less evidence survives for Borrull after the split from the Torelló family, as no inventories have been found for the Borrull family. The rupture does not appear to have affected his success, however. By 1756 Segimon father and Segimon son had acquired another fulling-mill in nearby Orpí, as evidenced by the contract they signed with Josep Alegre to work the mill for them for the next 12 years.[61] As for Lladó, he was the son of a glassmaker from Esparreguera, whose mother remarried an Igualada clothier. Lladó did not inherit from his stepfather but presumably learned the business from him. At Lladó's death in 1769, he was running a substantial operation, combining all stages of the production process, mostly under one roof. In his house, specific rooms are described as 'the carding workshop', 'the room with the spun wool', 'the shearing workshop'. He had 147 cloths in various stages of production and large stocks of wool, including some that had been put out to other carders and, significantly, to two other clothiers. He was owed 82 *lliures* by other clothiers for the use of his fulling-mill. Most importantly, he owed 15 looms, set up in seven houses, for which the weavers owed him 66 *lliures* rent.

By the mid-eighteenth century various surveys testify to the differentiation among the Igualada clothiers.[62] In the 1760s and 1770s, there were 20 to 30

---

[57]   ANI 245, fos 25–6; ANI 247, fos 105–6.

[58]   Torras, *Fabricants sense fàbrica*, pp. 127–31.

[59]   ACA, *Audiència, Diversorum*, 220, fols 366v–372v.

[60]   Torras, *Fabricants sense fàbrica*, p. 138.

[61]   ANI 397, fols 400–1.

[62]   AHCB, FJC, vol. 81, fos 24v, 74r–75r; API, *caixa* 4, 'Relación de las fabricas y telares de la villa de Igualada' (9 Feb. 1764), unfol.; API, *caixa* 4, 'Relación ... de las

clothiers in operation in Igualada, but with just three controlling the lion's share of production: around 60 per cent of looms and employing 1,200 of the 1,900 estimated employees of the woollen industry.[63] Even these figures do not convey the full extent of the differentiation that existed by this date. The 1765 *cadastre* lists 87 clothiers in total. Only 66 were household heads, however, the remainder being sons or younger brothers who would probably not be included in the surveys. Of the 66, 46 (70 per cent) were of journeyman status, an increase of 10 per cent from 1724. By contrast, in Olesa in 1756, only 31 per cent of the 16 clothiers were of journeyman status.[64] The 20 or so counted in the manufacturing surveys were thus only those still with their own workshops and some degree of independence.

Twenty-one inventories of clothiers have been found for these decades, spanning from 1744 to 1779, including those already discussed. They are listed in Table 3.2. That the woollen industry was in a better state compared with the earlier period is evident in that only four of these clothiers had no kind of equipment or stocks of wool recorded in their inventories. Most clothiers were still restricted to the initial stages of production, carding and spinning, though there are signs here of some tendency towards expansion, especially when compared with elsewhere in Catalonia. In Esparreguera and Olesa, four spinning wheels seems to have been the maximum for any clothier's inventory.[65] A modest commercial expansion can be seen in some cases, such as Macià Vila, who had a Miquel Carrica of Saragossa among his debtors, along with four clothiers from Capellades, Sant Pere de Riudebitlles and Olesa, although this modest credit of 126 *lliures* was all but cancelled out by the 100 *lliures* he owed Joan Badia and Lladó for fulling and pressing his cloths. Nonetheless, few clothiers owned looms or dye-houses, not to mention fulling-mills.

From an early date, therefore, differentiation among clothiers became more marked in some locations than in others, with some better able than others to exploit their favourable position in the production process. The situation was rather different for other producers, particularly weavers. More technically specialised, weavers tended to form a smaller and more tightly knit group. The main point of differentiation among them was ownership of their own looms or not. In 1695–6 seven master weavers, along with an unknown number of journeymen and

---

diferentes fabricas se hallan existentes en esta villa y corrientes en el dia' (30 Apr. 1779), unfol.; surveys from 1770 and 1779 reproduced in Torras Ribé, *La comarca de l'Anoia*, pp. 261–72.

[63]   Similar patterns of concentration of production, though not to quite the same hierarchical extent, have been identified by Thomson for Clermont-de-Lodève compared with neighbouring textile industries (*Clermont-de-Lodève*, pp. 305–15).

[64]   Cobos, *Pagesos, paraires i teixidors al Llobregat montserratí*, pp. 195–6 (my calculation from the figures in table 3.10).

[65]   Ibid., pp. 253–67, apps 1, 2. Again, only three clothiers in Esparreguera and none in Olesa had dyehouses.

Table 3.2   Textile equipment in clothiers' inventories, 1740–79

Name	Year	Carding equipment	Spinning wheels	Looms	Wool[a]	Cloths	Dye-house
Francisco Biosca	1744						
Francisco Borrull	1744	Yes	3	2	Yes	34	Yes
Pere Bergadà	1744		1				
Josep Torelló[b]	1745	Yes	3	1	74		Yes
Jacinto Estruch	1749	Yes	5				
Jacinto Barnola	1749	Yes	11	1	Yes	7	Shared
Maria Elias	1751				58		
Josep Estruch	1753	Yes	1				
Tomàs Torras	1760						
Josep Montaner	1761		5				
Josep Coca	1767	Yes	3				
Joan Castells	1767		2				
Anton Gramunt	1768	Yes			Yes	5	
Francesc Novell	1768	Yes	4				
Josep Ciurana	1769						
J.A. Lladó	1769	Yes	15	15	Yes	147	Yes
Macià Vila	1769	Yes	12	1	Yes	18	
Jacinto Bover	1775						
Agustí Olivella	1776						
Sebastià Planas	1776	Yes	2		Yes	Yes	
Tomàs Castelltort	1779	Yes	7		Yes	9	

Notes: [a] 'Yes' means quantity not given. [b] Josep Torelló's inventory appears to be limited to what was on the premises and to his share of the business only.

Sources: Biosca: ANI 344, fos 103r–104r; Borrull: ANI 344, fos 80–2; Bergadà: ANI 344, fos 77r–78r; Torelló: ANI 344, fos 90–4; Jacinto Estruch: ANI 394, fos 45–6; Barnola: ANI 344, fos 168–9; Elias: ANI 316, fos 111–13; Josep Estruch: ANI 344, fos 221–3; Torras: ANI 401, fos 29v–30v; Montaner: ANI 394, fos 118–20; Coca: ANI 477, fos 39–42; Castells: ANI 477, fos 166r–167r; Gramunt: ANI 409, fos 252r–255r; Novell: ANI 478, unfol.; Ciurana: ANI 394, unfol.; Lladó: ANI 394, fos 205–18; Vila: ANI 479, unfol.; Bover: ANI 485, unfol.; Olivella: ANI 417, fos 320–1; Planas: ANI 486, unfol.; ANI 487, unfol.; Castelltort: ANI 482, unfol.

apprentices, wove all the cloths produced in Igualada.[66] The distribution ranged from the 21.5 per cent of the total value of the cloths woven by Miquel Simorra to the 8 per cent woven by Pere Riba. There were thus fewer weavers than clothiers, and less differentiation among them at this date. Only four weavers are listed in the 1724 *cadastre*, of whom only one had master status. Over the period 1680–1729 there were only eight marriages of woollen weavers in Igualada.

---

[66]   Torras, 'Gremio, familia y cambio económico', pp. 21–3.

Table 3.3   Textile equipment in woollen weavers' inventories

Name	Year	Spinning wheels	Carding	Looms	Wool	Cloths
Josep Llambert	1713	1		1		
Josep Millet	1744			1		
Maria Rosa Termes	1756	1				
Francisco Casals	1760					
Francesc Serra	1761	1		1		
Josep Colom	1766			2 combs		
Agnès Castells	1767					
Pau Casals	1770	2		1	52 lliures	4
Magí Prats	1785					
Josep Llimona	1792	1	1	1[a]		
Francisco Balaytó	1799					
Josep Casals	1809	1[a]				
Pau Colomer	1827			1		

Note: [a] For cotton.

Sources: Llambert: ANI 208, fos 168–9; Millet: ANI 344, fos 99r–100r; Termes: ANI 397, fo. 296; F. Casals: ANI 438, fos 287v–288v; Serra: ANI 402, fos 3v–4v; Colom: ANI 445, fos 665–6; Castells: ANI 477, fo. 217; P. Casals: ANI 411, fos 20–3; Prats: ANI 426, fos 25–6; Llimona: ANI 502, unfol.; Balaytó: ANI 628, fos 204r–205r; J. Casals: ANI 649, fos 234–5; Colomer: ANI 698, fo. 16.

As the woollen industry expanded, however, the number of weavers increased hugely. From 1730 to 1779, there were 150 marriages of woollen weavers. In the 1765 cadastre, there were 64 woollen weavers, of whom only four had master status. What stands out, however, is how many were journeymen. Of the 58 household heads, 55 were journeymen. What this meant in practice is hard to determine, given how few inventories survive for woollen weavers. For the entire period, there are only 13, listed in Table 3.3. Four, including the wife of a weaver, recorded no textile equipment at all, a higher proportion than in Esparreguera and Olesa, where only one out of 15 and none out of 13 weavers respectively did not have textile equipment.[67] The remainder show little differentiation. Guild regulations limited weavers to two looms each in any case, but none had a second loom, implying that they probably had neither the space nor the need for a journeyman or apprentice.[68] A few had spinning wheels or similar, but only one had modest wool stocks and any finished cloths. Only one had carding equipment, suggesting much more specialised and restricted production than for clothiers.

[67]   Cobos, Pagesos, paraires i teixidors, tables 4.2 (p. 261), 4.3 (p. 265).

[68]   Deyá finds similar patterns for Mallorca in 1784, with a mean of 1.13 looms per weaver. Deyá, 'La industria rural textil', pp. 28–9.

What matters most for understanding relations of production in Igualada and the success of certain clothiers is not just the differentiation among clothiers on the one hand and among weavers on the other, but the extent to which clothiers had the upper hand over weavers when it came to control over production. In this regard, Igualada looks very much like any other dynamic proto-industrial community in Europe, such as Lodève.[69] Weavers had always worked for clothiers, which was logical, given the access of the latter to the raw materials and the nature of the production process. What was changing was the increasing dependence of weavers upon clothiers and the loss of ownership of the means of production for the former. In 1695–6 the seven weavers listed all wove for a range of clothiers: Simorra for twenty, the others for nine to twelve each, a wider range than the two to six identified by Cobos for the Esparreguera weavers.[70] While each weaver clearly had a clothier from whom he received a large share of his work, the significance of the relationship varied widely, from the 63 per cent share that Benet Valls had from the most important of the nine clothiers who gave him work, to the 20 per cent share Josep Llambert had from the most important of his. Of the weavers in Table 3.3, however, only Pau Casals demonstrates a modest degree of independence. Among his debtors were three Igualada clothiers, another Igualada weaver and one from Esparreguera. None of the other inventories reveal anything about the relationship of the weavers to clothiers or other weavers, except for the inventory of Magí Prats, one of those with no textile equipment, who lived in a rented house described as being part of Josep Torelló's manufacture. As mentioned above, Josep Anton Lladó also rented out both houses and looms to weavers.

As these last examples highlight, what distinguished Torelló, Borrull and Lladó from other clothiers was their ownership not just of dye-houses and fulling-mills, but also of looms. Differentiation was thus in part determined by the extent to which weavers worked directly and, we can assume, exclusively for them. Even when an exact relationship cannot be ascertained, the fact that the majority of weavers in 1765 were effectively, if not officially, working as journeymen is a significant indication of their decline in status. Weavers still claimed master status, but what that meant in terms of ownership of the means of production is increasingly hard to determine. Master weavers are described as working both on their own looms and those owned by others.[71] Another master weaver, Mateu Casals, had his loom set up in the house of Joan Aragonés, for whom he worked.[72] In 1773 and 1774 the weavers' guild submitted a series of complaints to the Junta

---

[69]   Thomson, *Clermont-de-Lodève*, pp. 315–8, 325–8, 348–53; Johnson, 'Capitalism and the State'.

[70]   J. Torras, 'From Craft to Class: The Changing Organisation of Cloth Manufacturing in a Catalan Town', in Safley and Rosenband, *The Workplace Before the Factory*, pp. 165–79, table 8.2 (p. 170); Cobos, *Pagesos, paraires i teixidors*, p.182.

[71]   ANI 445, fos 947–8, inspection of looms carried out on behalf of the Junta de Comerç (13 Nov. 1766).

[72]   AHCB, FJC, vol. 55, fos 132r, 133r–135r.

de Comerç against certain journeymen weavers who worked as if they were master weavers, but 'in rented houses'.[73] By the 1780s there were even signs that many weavers were becoming resigned to their subordinate status or, at least, willing to recognise themselves as journeymen, if they could claim advantages in so doing. In 1780 the weavers claimed exception from a tax on trade: 'our only daily work consists of weaving cloths, as journeymen that we are of the master clothiers, who provide us with the wool, looms and other necessary equipment, and paying us for the simple labour we expend on each cloth, leaving us exempt from all type of purchasing'.[74]

What lay behind these differences in control over production and the rapid emergence of a hierarchical putting-out system was the early breakdown of guild regulations in Igualada, compared with elsewhere.[75] In this regard, the survival of a *Kaufsystem* may owe much, as Duplessis has suggested, to the protection offered by guilds and similar institutions.[76] As described above, Catalan proto-industry did not emerge in rural areas as a means of bypassing guild restrictions; on the contrary, proto-industry initially used guild regulations to guarantee quality control.[77] Over the eighteenth century, however, several proto-industrial Catalan communities experienced conflict between guilds and independent producers. In Igualada, as Torras has shown, it was the success of the clothiers' guild, or, more correctly, a small group of prominent clothiers, in establishing control over production that ultimately determined commercial success.[78] Similar arguments can be made for the success of the woollen industry in Terrassa and Sabadell.[79] In Esparreguera, however, the commercial expansion of the clothiers was checked by the continuing strength of the weavers' guild.[80] In Igualada, as early as 1723, the clothiers were able to sidestep many of the obstacles to freedom of production created by the weavers' guild by negotiating an agreement that any master clothier prepared to pay a substantial amount could be admitted as a member of the weavers' guild. As for their own guild, it had ceased to perform many functions that clothiers' guilds performed elsewhere, such as purchasing wool on behalf of guild members. Most Igualada clothiers, as we have seen, remained reliant on guild facilities for dyeing and fulling, but those such as Torelló and Borrull who could afford their own were obviously at an advantage.

---

[73] AHCB, FJC, vol. 66, fos 21r–55r.

[74] AHCB, FJC, vol. 57, fos 68r–79r.

[75] Sheilagh Ogilvie argues that proto-industry was ultimately most dynamic in areas where it escaped guild control, and cites Igualada as an example ('Guilds, Efficiency and Social Capital: Evidence from German Proto-Industry', *Economic History Review*, 57 (2004), pp. 286–333 (pp. 312–14)).

[76] Duplessis, *Transitions to Capitalism in Early Modern Europe*, pp. 124–6.

[77] J. Torras, 'Small Towns, Craft Guilds and Proto-Industry in Spain', *Jahrbuch für Wirtschafts Geschichte*, 1998/2 (1998), pp. 79–96.

[78] The most detailed account is Torras, 'From Craft to Class'.

[79] Benaul, 'Los orígenes de la empresa textil lanera'.

[80] Cobos, *Pagesos, paraires i teixidors*, pp. 235–43, 263.

Ultimately, however, what mattered, as already argued, was control over all stages of production but especially weaving. Grievances are expressed about spinning and carding, noticeably in a complaint of 1772 that 'illegitimate manufacturers' were a bad influence on carders and spinners by paying them wages in advance.[81] 'No carder returns the amount of wool entrusted to him, which is lost because badly carded. ... Frequently the owners are left without carders or money, and with considerable work to get their wool back.' The solution advocated by the clothiers, in line with a recent Royal Ordinance of 1769, was twofold: 'to choose their workers freely and to give them orders as they wish' and 'that women be prohibited from carding wool, as not being their proper task'. Similarly, in response to a survey on spinning by the Junta de Comerç in 1786, the cloth manufacturers and weavers, here for once presenting a united front, advocated a ban on spinners and carders working for more than one clothier or weaver at a time.[82] It is an interesting but unanswerable question whether any clothiers sought to tie spinners to them through the loan of spinning wheels, as appears to have been the case with weavers and looms. The only evidence in this regard is the statement by the Junta de Comerç in 1745 that Torelló and Borrull reportedly owned 340 spinning wheels, suggesting that there may have been some attempt to control putting-out networks of spinners by these clothiers at least.

In general, however, the struggle over production came down to control of weaving. Although a 1769 ordinance granted manufacturers the right, among other privileges, to employ as many weavers and other workers as they wished, the Igualada clothiers had long claimed this right in theory and in practice. Not only is this evident in the number of weavers working for Torelló, Borrull, Lladó and one or two other clothiers, but also in the frequent complaints by the weavers' guild that these clothiers were bypassing guild members to employ weavers from outside the guild and the town. The weavers were increasingly likely to be immigrants, thus lacking the family ties that had previously underlined their solidarity within the guild. Whereas 8 out of the 12 weavers married in Igualada during the period 1680–1729 were born in the town, of the 150 who married between 1730 and 1779, 89 were not.

Conflict continued, with the weavers mounting legal challenges to the 1723 agreement in 1742 and 1758.[83] The resulting suit dragged on until ordinances in the 1780s finally rendered it null and void. Against this background of legal strife, the weavers tried unsuccessfully to defend their own interests by creating an entirely separate guild of their own in 1754 (formerly they had been part of an amalgamation of several guilds) and by going on strike in 1757 in protest at attempts to impose a new width of cloth. In their representations to the Junta de Comerç, the clothiers continued to speak in name of a guild, but a new capitalist

---

[81]   AHCB, FJC, vol. 55, fos 49–51.

[82]   AHCB, FJC, vol. 80, fos 38–65.

[83]   ACA, *Audiència, Plets civils*, 8297.

mode of thinking emerges clearly in their view of themselves and their role. In one statement in 1762, the clothiers defined a cloth manufacturer as someone with 'a true intelligence in the art [of manufacturing]', whereas a weaver's intelligence did 'not go beyond weaving a cloth after a fashion, whilst being ignorant of absolutely everything else necessary to run a manufacturing concern'.[84] The clothiers went on to make a significant comparison between their manufacturing concerns and the large-scale enterprises such as the royal factories at Guadalajara:

> In all the manufactures of the kingdom ... there is a director, who rules, governs and orders everything necessary to the factory ... Without any interference in the running of these concerns from any dependent individuals within them, such as weavers, and what a Director is to the royal factories, so is a manufacturer in his own manufacturing concern, since he takes an interest in the quality of the cloths in order to sell them well afterwards, and obtains the necessary credit without which no enterprise can survive.

Equally significant is the reply from the weavers:

> The clothiers who style themselves manufacturers are no such thing, rather, they practise one of the four crafts involved in the manufacture of a cloth [apart from weaving] these are the clothier, dyer and cropper ... and although it would be more fitting to describe the weaver as a cloth manufacturer than the clothier, there is no reason for one to dominate the other, and raise himself up to be a master, for each is only master of the work that falls to him.[85]

The weavers were clinging here to a traditional, artisan way of thinking, which was increasingly unable to withstand the new, market-orientated mentality emerging among the clothiers. How general this mentality was is hard to determine. Torelló, Borrull and Lladó were certainly the leaders in the dispute and the ones most frequently blamed by the weavers, as in a complaint in 1767 that Segimon Borrull had convinced other clothiers not to give work to weavers who refused to weave the narrower width.[86]

Whether the majority of clothiers went along with Torelló, Borrull and Lladó willingly or not, however, remains an unanswerable question, given the lack of evidence. Not all clothiers were in the same position when it came to responding to commercialisation and the insertion of capital into the production process. As has been demonstrated, the most successful clothiers were those able to be flexible in responding to demand through a variety of strategies. Once a certain degree

---

[84] AHCB, FJC, *caixa* 2, 13/7. For a similar struggle, voiced in similar language, between *marchands-fabricants* and weavers for control of production in the Lyons silk industry, see Poni, 'Fashion as Flexible Production', pp. 47–50.

[85] AHCB, FJC, *caixa* 2, 13/18.

[86] AHCB, FJC, *caixa* 2, 12.

of commercial success had occurred, however, the reorganisation of production in order to meet demand became much easier. The successful clothiers were able to bypass guild controls and subordinate other producers. As differentiation increased among the clothiers, so the ability of smaller clothiers to compete decreased, thus reinforcing the dominance of the few still further. Interestingly, however, the situation in Igualada was to change with the advent of the cotton industry, which offered new opportunities once more, opportunities which in this case were exploited not by the leaders of the woollen industry but by a new set of producers from within and without the textile industry.

The cotton industry

The cotton industry was well-established in Catalonia for most of the eighteenth century, but it was based in Barcelona, and expansion into rural areas was later than in the woollen industry. From its origins in the 1730s until the 1780s, the industry was limited on the whole to the specialised branch of calico-printing, with weaving, bleaching and printing all incorporated into the same manufactures. Much more so than the woollen industry, the development of the cotton industry, as James Thomson and Alex Sánchez have shown, was heavily conditioned by state intervention in the form of tariffs and privileges and by the turbulent political events of the end of the eighteenth century and first decades of the nineteenth.[87] A first important shift can be identified after 1783, when both the cotton industry and Catalan viticulture became more integrated into a wider Atlantic economy, as a result of favourable tariff policies that promoted trade with America.[88] A new market emerged in the form of demand for printed linens by the colonies. At the same time, a ban on the import of many manufactured cotton goods encouraged a process of import substitution in order to satisfy domestic demand. By 1789 the records of 37 calico manufactures in Barcelona show an almost even split between colonial and interior markets, though with production for colonial markets much more the preserve of larger manufacturers.[89]

---

[87]   J.K.J. Thomson, *A Distinctive Industrialization: Cotton in Barcelona 1728–1832* (Cambridge, 1992); id., 'Explaining the Take-Off in the Catalan Cotton Industry', *Economic History Review*, 58 (2005), pp. 701–35; A. Sánchez, 'La empresa algodonera en Cataluña antes de la aplicación del vapor, 1783–1832', in F. Comín and P. Martín (eds), *La empresa en la historia de España* (Madrid, 1996), pp. 155–70; id., 'Crisis económica y respuesta empresarial: Los inicios del sistema fabril en la industria algodonera catalana, 1797–1839', *Revista de historia económica*, 18 (2000), pp. 485–523.

[88]   Thomson, 'Explaining the Take-Off in the Catalan Cotton Industry'; J.K.J. Thomson, 'Technological Transfer to the Catalan Cotton Industry: From Calico Printing to the Self-Acting Mule', in Farnie and Jeremy (eds), *The Fibre that Changed the World*, pp. 249–82; Sánchez, 'Crisis económica y respuesta empresarial', pp. 491–4.

[89]   Sánchez, 'Crisis económica y respuesta empresarial', p. 492.

One effect of changing demand was that many established manufactures abandoned weaving to concentrate on the printing stages. This left the way open for the establishment of independent weaving concerns. A much more important effect, however, was the stimulus to spinning. Prior to 1783 the disincentives to spinning in terms of an inadequate supply of good quality raw cotton and a lack of skilled labour were such that manufacturers preferred to import spun yarn from Malta. The new colonial market for printed linens, however, also opened up access to supplies of raw cotton from America. The 1780s thus saw the establishment of spinning concerns for the first time, an important factor to which this chapter will return. The impact of war with England in cutting off colonial trade between 1797 and 1808 did not reverse this trend towards spinning. Although the industry as a whole was forced to reorientate itself towards domestic markets with a return to calicoes, competitiveness here required manufacturers to improve quality and reduce costs in spinning, acting as a spur to mechanisation and the concentration of production. The incorporation of spinning, particularly the diffusion of technology, received a further boost during the Napoleonic wars, which cut off traditional supplies of spun yarn from Malta. Domestic spinning was finally firmly established by a 1802 ban on the import of spun yarn.

What this chapter is concerned with is the expansion of the cotton industry into rural areas from the 1780s onwards and the continuities that can be seen in terms of the labour force and scale of production from the established woollen industry through these early phases of cotton manufacturing, despite the change of fibre. Rural expansion took the form of spinning and weaving, particularly the former, rather than the spread of calico-printing concerns, though these were founded outside of Barcelona as well. Once spinning and weaving cotton became profitable, the Barcelona calico manufacturers who had hitherto dominated the industry attempted to control these operations through the formation of a monopoly company, the Real Companyia de Filats, which tried to put out cotton spinning to rural areas.[90] The putting-out networks of the woollen industry were an obvious source of cheap and skilled labour. By the 1780s there were complaints from many areas of Catalonia, including Igualada, that cotton was displacing wool.[91] It was claimed that many spinners in Igualada preferred spinning cotton to wool, because the former was cleaner.[92] Another set of complaints from different areas of Catalonia, though not including Igualada, makes clear that wages were considerably better in cotton than in wool.[93] Moreover, in terms of demand, cotton quickly displaced the cheaper, coarser woollens that had been the staple product of the textile industry in many

---

[90] A. Garcia Balañà, *La fabricació de la fàbrica: Treball i política a la Catalunya cotonera (1784–1884)* (Barcelona, 2004), pp. 71–89; Y. Okuno, 'Entre la llana i el cotó: Una nota sobre l'extensió de la industria del cotó als pobles de Catalunya el darrere quart del segle XIII', *Recerques*, 38 (1999), pp. 47–76.

[91] Okuno, 'Entre la llana i el cotó', pp. 49, 53–4.

[92] AHCB, FJC, vol. 80, fos 38–65.

[93] AHCB, FJC, vol. 79, fos 131r–218r. These are discussed in more detail in Chapter 5.

areas: these traditional woollens could not compete with a cheap and much more desirable product such as cotton.[94]

In areas where the woollen industry was well-established, some clothiers recognised the opportunities offered by the new fibre, and switched themselves to putting out cotton.[95] Initially they often did so as agents (*filadors*) for the Barcelona manufacturers, but soon moved to set up their own initiatives. The Real Companyia de Filats was unable to compete for long with these local ventures. Eventually, many members of the company abandoned attempts to control spinning and weaving and switched to buying woven cloths from local independent manufacturers instead.

In Igualada, only one individual can be identified as a *filador*, Gabriel Galí, who makes a few brief appearances in the Real Companyia de Filats accounts and papers for 1786–8.[96] Instead, independent cotton manufactures were soon set up. According to one source, cotton manufacturing was introduced in 1783, and within a year there were 16 manufacturers with 126 looms in operation and numerous carders and spinners.[97] As elsewhere in Catalonia, while cotton offered new opportunities to some from commercial or other artisan backgrounds, these manufacturers were overwhelmingly from textile backgrounds, usually wool.[98] Of ten such cotton manufacturers listed in a 1789 survey, all but two can be identified as being of textile origins, mostly weavers.[99] Mobility between wool and cotton is evident both over the life-cycle of individuals and between generations.[100] In terms of life-cycle mobility, 78 combinations of wool and cotton

[94]   J.M. Benaul and E. Deu, 'The Spanish Wool Industry, 1750–1935: Import Substitution and Regional Relocation', in Fontana and Gayot (eds), *Wool*, pp. 845–84.

[95]   A similar process of rapid emancipation of local initiatives from urban control is described by Béatrice Veyrassat for the Saint-Gall and Appenzeller regions of Switzerland (*Négociants et fabricants dans l'industrie cotonnière Suisse 1760–1840* (Lausanne, 1982), pp. 173–5).

[96]   BC, FEG, 59/1, 56/9, 56/3.

[97]   See the account by the mayor, Bonaventura Clarís in 1784, reproduced in Torras Ribé, *La comarca de l'Anoia*, pp. 279–92 (pp. 287–90).

[98]   The extent to which cotton manufacturing was taken up by merchants and artisans with a non-textile background is discussed in Chapter 5.

[99]   Reproduced in Torras Ribé, *La comarca de l'Anoia*, pp. 293–300 (p. 295). Whereas Okuno attempts to link these individuals to the 1765 *cadastre* ('Entre la llana i el cotó', p. 59), I preferred to link them to the marriage register in the first instance or to a baptism or burial record. In this way, links were more likely to be to the individual in question rather than to a father with the same name. Individuals that Okuno identifies as clothiers, I have thus identified as weavers, but the fundamental point about their textile origins remains the same.

[100]   Life-cycle mobility was analysed using an algorithm devised by Peter Kitson, whereby changes in occupational title are counted for men over the course of the life-cycle captured by family reconstitution, that is, from marriage to baptisms and burials of children, to their own burials or those of spouses. Only individuals with at least two appearances in the parish registers can thus be included, though not all will be in observation for the same length of time. See P.M. Kitson, 'Family Formation, Male Occupation and the Nature of

occupations could be identified.[101] The most frequent of these were woollen weaver and cotton weaver, which appeared 21 times just in this format and more frequently in combination with other occupations, such as clothier.[102] Of the 39 grooms identified in the Igualada marriage register as cotton manufacturers (*fabricants de indianes* or *fabricants de cotó*), 64 per cent were the sons of textile workers.[103] Among the 564 grooms identified unambiguously as cotton weavers, 30 per cent had fathers in textile professions. This is a high proportion for an industry that was never guilded and was thus open to everyone.

Inventories provide further evidence of the overlap between wool and cotton in terms of the number of those described as clothiers or cloth manufacturers yet whose inventories included equipment related to cotton production as well as wool. Table 3.4 lists the 23 inventories of clothiers and cloth manufacturers from 1780 onwards. Cotton appears in inventories alongside wool as early as 1790 in the inventory of Magí Soler. By a later date, some clothiers seem to have abandoned wool altogether, as in the cases of Francesc Vila and Ignasi Simon and the woollen weaver Josep Llimona in Table 3.3.

Not all clothiers went over to cotton, but the fortunes of those who did not varied sharply. The three families who had dominated the woollen industry in its heyday neither continued their success in wool nor went over to cotton. Josep Torelló Borrull died in 1794, leaving the business still in a healthy state, as far as can be judged. His eldest son had died childless in 1793, however, leaving the inheritance in the hands of the youngest son, Isidro, trained as a lawyer and with other interests. Under his headship, the family fortunes eventually went in a different direction.[104] Similar demographic accidents saw the end of the Lladó

Parochial Registration in England, c.1538–1837' (PhD thesis, University of Cambridge, 2004), apps 5, 6. Intergenerational mobility is measured by a straightforward comparison of grooms' occupations with those of their fathers as stated in the marriage registers.

[101] Quantifying the extent of change between the two sectors over the life-cycle is difficult. On the one hand, these 78 combinations are earlier than the standardisation of occupations, so, for example, *cotoner* and *fabricant de cotó* appear as separate occupations, though in reality there was no difference between them. On the other hand, the frequent unspecific use of 'weaver' means that other instances of wool and cotton in combination go unidentified as such.

[102] The most common combinations were 'weaver / calico weaver / woollen weaver' (10), 'calico weaver / woollen weaver' (8), and 'cotton weaver / calico weaver / woollen weaver' (3).

[103] For similar examples elsewhere in Catalonia, see L. Ferrer, 'Les primeres fàbriques i els primers fabricants a la Catalunya central', in M. Gutiérrez (ed.), *La industrialització i el desenvolupament economic d'Espanya: Homenatge al Dr Jordi Nadal* (2 vols, Barcelona, 1999), vol. 2, pp. 1038–56; A. Solà, *Aigua, indústria i fabricants a Manresa (1759–1860)* (Manresa, 2004), p. 69.

[104] Isidro became involved in liberal politics during the 1820s and in managing a large estate inherited by his wife Teresa (Pere Pascual, *Els Torelló: Una família igualadina d'avocats i propietaris* (Barcelona, 2000)).

Table 3.4 Textile equipment in clothiers' inventories, 1780–1829

Name	Year	Carding equipment	Spinning wheels	Jennies	Looms	Wool (*lliures*)	Cotton (*lliures*)	Cloths	Dye-house
Onofre Biosca	1788		2						
Magí Soler	1790		2 (W), 1(C), 1		3 (C)		180	1 (C)	
Josep Barral	1791		3						
Josep Torellób	1794		7 (W)		9 (W)	Yes[a]		35 (W)	Yes
Josep Amigó	1794	Yes	8 (W), 1 (C)				35		
Macià Creus	1798	Yes				480		1 (W)	
Anton Mestre	1798		2 (W)						
Joan Lafarga	1802								
Josep Francolí	1803	Yes							
Francesc Vila	1806	Machine (C)	4	2	2 (C)		156	7 (C)	
Josep Ciurana	1808		1						
Joan Planas	1808	Yes				Yes		(W)[c]	Shared

Name	Year							
Josep Cendrad	1808	Yes			2 (W)	1 (W)	60 (W)	Shared
Agustí Santasusanna	1808							
Agustí Bas	1808	Yes	260			1 (W)	5 (W)	
Ignasi Simon	1809	Machine (C)	26		3 (C)	2 (C)	5	
Joan Codina	1809	Yes	572		7 (W)	6 (W)		
Manuel Planas	1813	Yes		14		1		Shared
Pere Ferrer	1816	Yes						
Joan Cendra	1816	Yes						
Isidro Badiae	1819	Machine (W)			1 (W)	5 (W)	Machine (W)	

Notes: W: wool; C: cotton; if neither, unspecified. ^a 'Yes' means quantity not given. ^b Also owned a machine for packaging woollen cloths and a fulling-mill. ^c The cloths are not itemised but totalled 14,000 *lliures* along with his petty cash. ^d Also owned a third share in a fulling-mill. ^e Also owned a machine for spinning wool.

Sources: Biosca: ANI 498, unfol.; Soler: ANI 542, fos 228v–230v; Barral: ANI 580, fos 39–42; Torelló: ANI 482, unfol.; Amigó: ANI 546, fos 197–9; Creus: ANI 527, fos 39–41; Mestre: ANI 627, fos 251–2; Lafarga: ANI 639, fo. 52; Francolí: ANI 640, fos 236–40; Vila: ANI 593, fos 21–2; Ciurana: ANI 636, fos 42–6; J. Planas: ANI 579, fos 49–54; Josep Cendra: ANI 646, unfol.; Santasusanna: ANI 646, unfol.; Bas: ANI 536, fos 128–3; Simon: ANI 649, fos 284r–285r; Codina: ANI 595, fos 214–15; M. Planas: ANI 600, fo. 615r; Ferrer: ANI 602, fos 67r–71r; Joan Cendra: ANI 602, fos 847v–848r; Badia: ANI 605, fos 636–8.

fortunes, with Josep Anton's son and heir Pau Anton also dying childless. The fate of the Borrull family is unknown.

As regards other clothiers who continued to limit their activities to wool, most show evidence of only small-scale production: one or two spinning wheels, some carding equipment or modest stocks of wool, though the picture here is distorted by the nine inventories from the war years. A few did continue substantial production in the woollen industry alone, as in the case of Joan and Manuel Planas, father and son, who had considerable capital invested in trade with Madrid, Cadiz and the colonies. Manuel and Isidro Badia were the only clothiers known to have invested in machinery for wool. On the whole, however, cotton seems to have offered better routes to financial success than wool, as evidenced by how few clothiers followed the example of their Terrassa and Sabadell counterparts by investing in the mechanisation of woollen production.[105]

The failure of the Igualada woollen industry to follow the route taken by Terrassa and Sabadell is perhaps surprising, given the similarities in terms of products and industrial structures. As Benaul has commented, it was the finer woollens in which these areas had specialised that enabled the industry to continue in Terrassa and Sabadell and made mechanisation worthwhile, since such products were not as vulnerable to competition from cotton.[106] Similar arguments can be made for the woollen industry in Béjar, which also mechanised. The explanation may lie simply in the demographic accidents which befell the leading Igualada clothier families: other producers were not manufacturing the same cloths with the same degree of investment and organisation and thus probably stood to benefit more from a switch to cotton than from remaining with wool.

This continuity in terms of those employed in textiles is worth stressing, given that it has been argued that proto-industrial labour did not form the basis of factory labour and that artisans and domestic workers were frequently the most reluctant to submit to the discipline of the factory.[107] In Catalonia, by contrast, the proto-industrial origins of factory workers are clear.[108] The early phases of factory manufacturing in Igualada, Terrassa and Sabadell drew their labour force in part from local proto-industry and in part from areas covered by the putting-out

---

[105]   Similarly, there was only one attempt at mechanised woollen production in Manresa, which failed (Solà, *Aigua, indústria i fabricants*, pp. 113–23). On the mechanisation of the woollen industry in Sabadell and Terrassa, see J.M. Benaul, 'Cambio tecnológico y estructura industrial en los inicios del sistema de fábrica en la industria pañera catalana, 1815–1835', *Revista de historia económica*, 13 (1995), pp. 199–226.

[106]   Benaul and Deu, 'The Spanish Wool Industry', pp. 850–4.

[107]   Hudson, *The Genesis of Industrial Capital*, pp. 81–4; Tessie Liu, *The Weaver's Knot: The Contradictions of Class Struggle and Family Solidarity in Western France, 1750–1914* (Ithaca, 1994), pp. 123–7.

[108]   J.R. Rosés, 'Measuring the Contribution of Human Capital to the Development of the Catalan Factory System (1830–61)', *European Review of Economic History*, 2 (1998), pp. 25–48.

networks of the eighteenth century.[109] In the case of Igualada, many immigrants were drawn from the putting-out areas to the west: the Conca de Barberà and the Segarra. Later, the factory industry of Barcelona in turn drew on the labour force of places such as Igualada, rather than recruiting unskilled labour from rural areas.[110] Thus, among the workers of La España Industrial, one of the leading factories of the Catalan industrial revolution, 86 per cent were from textile backgrounds, with the Igualada region being the most significant in terms of recruitment after Barcelona itself.[111] A large proportion of those employed as managers of larger manufacturing concerns, both in Barcelona and in Sallent, were of textile backgrounds, often former *fabricants* of smaller concerns.[112]

With the transition to steam power and large factories from the 1830s onwards, there was a break to some extent with the proto-industrial past among entrepreneurs. Garcia Balañà has found little continuity in Sallent between the owners of 1830s and 1850s manufacturing concerns.[113] The increase in fixed capital costs pushed many smaller manufacturers out of business though, as already stated, many progressed to managing factories instead. The break should not be exaggerated, though. Solà has shown that the picture for Manresa was more mixed: a wave of new manufacturers appeared in the 1840s, but many older families continued to flourish.[114] Solà suggests that what new entrepreneurs brought was not so much capital in many cases as technical skills, particularly those associated with calico-printing and the construction of new machinery. Many still came from proto-industrial backgrounds, often with a period spent in Barcelona. Sánchez has stressed the dynamism of many of these arrivals on the Barcelona scene.[115] Some of Igualada's proto-industrial families also went on to become the entrepreneurs of the new generation, albeit in different locations. Indeed, two of the new manufacturing families in Manresa were the Vives and Aguilera families, originally cotton manufacturers from Igualada.[116] The founders of La España Industrial were the Muntadas brothers from Igualada, sons

---

[109] E. Camps, *La formación del mercado de trabajo industrial en la Cataluña del siglo XIX* (Madrid, 1995), pp. 58–91, apps (pp. 279–91); Benaul, 'Industrialització', pp. 51–2.

[110] N. Mora-Sitjà, 'Labour Supply and Wage Differentials in an Industrialising Economy: Catalonia in the Long Nineteenth Century' (DPhil thesis, University of Oxford, 2006), pp. 90–9.

[111] Camps, *La formación del mercado de trabajo industrial*, pp. 86–8, app. (p. 290). The figure of 86% is my calculation from table 9, assuming, as Camps does, that *jornalero* (labourer) indicates an unskilled textile worker.

[112] Garcia Balañà, *La fabricació de la fàbrica*, pp. 331–7 (Barcelona), 405–11 (Sallent).

[113] Ibid., pp. 368–77.

[114] Solà, *Aigua, indústria i fabricants*, pp. 128–45.

[115] Sánchez, 'La empresa algodonera', p. 169.

[116] Solà, *Aigua, indústria i fabricants*, pp. 152–3, 163.

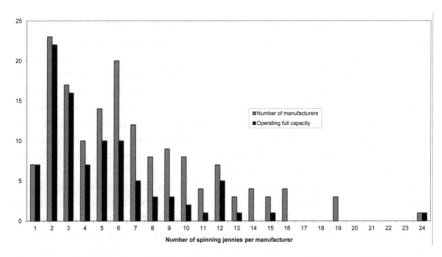

Figure 3.2   Distribution of spinning jennies across manufacturers, 1820

of a clothier.[117] Another *igualadí*, Macià Vila, also the son of a clothier, founded short-lived concerns in Igualada and more successful factories in Reus.[118] As in France and Switzerland, many of the first factories of the Catalan cotton industry were joint ventures between commercial and proto-industrial capital.[119]

Local capital, local knowledge and technical skills were thus crucial in the foundation of the first phase of cotton manufacturing and continued to be important throughout the transition to the factory in the mid-nineteenth century. Another of the important continuities between the woollen and cotton industries, however, was the persistence of small-scale production up until the middle years of the nineteenth century. In contrast to calico-printing manufactures, which were large-scale and capital-intensive, even though those founded outside Barcelona were more modest than those of the capital, spinning and weaving concerns remained small-scale and required relatively little in the way of start-up capital. Sánchez gives an average for the period 1797–1807 of 7,380 *lliures*, compared with approximately 41,000 *lliures* for a calico manufacture.[120] The initial phases of mechanisation, that is, the introduction of the spinning jenny or its local, improved variant, the *bergadana*, did little to alter this pattern.[121] Even in areas such as Manresa, Sallent and Cardona,

[117]   Garcia Balañà, *La fabricació de la fàbrica*, p. 266, n. 30.

[118]   P. Pascual et al., *Macià Vila i el 'vapor cremat'* (Vic, 2004).

[119]   Sánchez, 'Crisis económica y respuesta empresarial', p. 512; Solà, *Aigua, indústria i fabricants*, tables 4.6 (p. 101), 7.9 (pp. 221–2). For French comparisons, see Terrier, *Les deux âges de la proto-industrie*, pp. 155–61; for Switzerland, see Veyrassat, *Négociants et fabricants*, pp. 198–203, 257–63, app. 8, tables A, B.

[120]   Sánchez, 'La empresa algodonera', p. 161.

[121]   A. Solà, 'Filar amb berguedanes: Mite i realitat d'una màquina de filar cotó', in *La indústria tèxtil: Actes de les V Jornades d'Arqueologia Industrial de Catalunya, Manresa,*

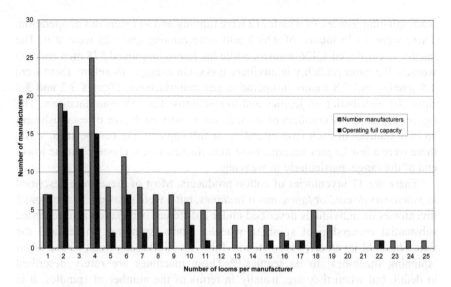

Figure 3.3   Distribution of looms across manufacturers, 1820

where waterframes were introduced as early as 1801 and mule-jennies in 1807, manufacturing concerns were still modest.[122] The largest concerns rarely exceeded 50 units in terms of machines.[123] Even as late as the 1840s, when mechanised weaving was introduced to Catalonia, along with the use of self-acting mules and throstles in spinning, Solà has stressed the co-existence of smaller and larger concerns in Manresa, rather than any sudden or rapid shift.[124]

The dominance of small-scale production in Igualada can be illustrated using two sources. The first is a list of the cotton manufactures in 1820, the second is the inventories of cotton producers, which can be analysed in a similar manner to that done above for wool. The list of cotton manufactures is a rough document drawn up in response to a survey by the Junta de Comerç.[125] There were 158 manufacturers listed, with a total of 1,056 'machines', almost certainly in the

16–28 octubre, 2000 (Barcelona, 2002), pp. 143–68; id., 'Màquines tèxtils i lexicografia en la història de la llengua catalana', Miscellània d'estudis Bagencs, 10 (1997), pp. 153–86'; on mechanisation generally, see Sánchez, 'La empresa algodonera', pp. 160–5.

[122]   J.K.J. Thomson, 'Olot, Barcelona and Ávila, and the Introduction of the Arkwright Technology to Catalonia', Revista de historia económica, 21 (2003), pp. 297–334; Ferrer, 'Primeres fàbriques'; Solà, Aigua, indústria i fabricants, pp. 71–107.

[123]   Sánchez, 'La empresa algodonera', p. 164

[124]   Solà, Aigua, indústria i fabricants, pp. 128–45.

[125]   AMI lligall 28.1. The manufacturers are listed by name, along with the number of 'machines' and looms each had in operation and not in operation. The numbers do not add up to the totals given at the bottom: I count 600 looms instead of 578. A summary follows in the form of responses to questions asked by the junta, including numbers employed. The

main spinning jennies, of which 712 were running and 344 were out of operation. There were 1,125 looms, of which 600 were running and 525 were still. The machines employed 1,406 women, while the looms employed 578 men and 480 women, the latter probably in auxiliary tasks. On average, therefore, there were 4.5 jennies and 3.8 looms in operation per manufacturer. Figures 3.2 and 3.3 show the distribution of jennies and looms across the 158 manufacturers. The figures are given as numbers of manufacturers with each size of establishment and the number in each case operating at full capacity. As can be seen, while there were a few larger concerns, most manufactures were clustered at the lower end of the range, particularly in weaving.

There are 17 inventories of cotton producers. Most of these were described as *fabricants de cotó* or *fabricants d'indianes*, but 6 were weavers. In addition, 5 inventories of individuals described under a different occupation also recorded substantial ownership of spinning wheels, looms, spinning jennies and the like. These 22 inventories are listed in Table 3.5. Following Solà, I have taken 'spinning machines' to be jennies.[126] These machines are rarely described in detail, but when they are, usually in terms of the number of spindles, it is clear that they are jennies. The term *bergadana* occurs only once, in the 1818 inventory of Anton Amigó. Amigó's inventory also records Arkwright machinery, presumably animal-powered.[127] The possible reference to an Arkwright machine in the inventory of Miquel Galtés is surprising, given the lack of water power and since it would represent a very early usage in the Catalan context.[128]

The 18 inventories with equipment show similar patterns to those in the 1820 survey, namely a mean of 4.6 spinning wheels, 3.5 looms and 4.6 spinning machines per manufacturer. Overall, both the 1820 listing and the inventories show that differentiation was much less marked among cotton manufacturers, however they

---

number of men employed on looms is probably also 600 rather than 578, since the figures appear to work out as one weaver per loom.

[126]   Solà shows that the term *màquina* was usually used at this date for the spinning jenny in its various forms ('Màquines tèxtils i lexicografia', pp. 173–9). The term *bergadana*, used for an improved Highs jenny with 100–120 spindles, comes into usage relatively late, as here.

[127]   The inventory records six 'English machines with 48 spindles each', fitting the usual description of Arkwright technology at this date (Thomson, 'Olot, Barcelona and Ávila', p. 304). The machines are located on the ground floor, in the *quadra*, the term usually used for the stable so presumably could have been driven by mules, though this is not made clear.

[128]   Thomson, 'Olot, Barcelona and Ávila', pp. 320–1. Animal power was used in Barcelona factories for Arkwright machinery, but was both less efficient and more costly than water. Outside of Barcelona, the only references are to Arkwright machines powered by water, with the earliest being for Manresa in 1801. See L. Ferrer, 'Bergadanas, continuas y mulas: Tres geografías de la hilatura del algodón en Cataluña (1790–1830)', *Revista de historia económica*, 22 (2004), pp. 337–86 (pp. 373–9); id., 'Primeres fàbriques', pp. 1047–51; Sánchez, 'La empresa algodonera', table 1 (p. 162).

styled themselves, than among clothiers. They also tended to cover most aspects of the production process within the same manufacturing concern, a more unusual feature. In Manresa in particular most establishments were dedicated exclusively to spinning. In the 1820 Igualada listing, only one concern was limited to weaving alone, and seven to spinning. Even the three inventories of those described as weavers had spinning wheels and two of them had machines. The only exception to this are the calico manufacturers Josep Anton Fàbregas and Jaume Mas, who both restricted production to the printing stages. Fàbregas in fact appears in the inventory of Miquel Galtés as owing Galtés 1,017 *lliures*, 8 *sous*, 6 *diners* for two batches of calicoes. In the other cases, however, some aspects of spinning and weaving were incorporated alongside printing.

In part, this difference between Igualada and other locations lies in energy sources: most concerns in Manresa were founded to take advantage of water power for the new spinning technology. In Igualada, this incentive to specialise was not present. Indeed, occupational titles in cotton at this stage were fairly imprecise, reflecting the fluidity of roles within the sector. The analysis of life-cycle mobility in Igualada bears this suggestion out in the frequent shifts between occupational titles, not just between cases such as *fabricant de cotó* or *cotoner* (cotton manufacturer) and *fabricant d'indianes* or *indianaire* (calico manufacturer) where the differences in practice are likely to have been minimal if they existed at all but, more significantly, between terms denoting 'manufacturer' and weaver.[129] If occupations are standardised, then the most frequent combination of occupations over the life-cycle within the entire dataset is cotton manufacturer / weaver, occurring 144 times, far ahead of 'clothier / woollen weaver' at 59.

A similar fluidity appears to characterise relations of production in the early stages of the industry, though the sources are patchier than for the woollen industry. In some places, manufacturers did not own the *berguedanes* or looms in their workshops and worked on a putting-out basis for Barcelona manufacturers.[130] In Igualada, the cotton manufacturers do appear to have owned the means of production in most cases. Their relationships with other manufacturers and with merchants are hard to reconstruct but do not appear to have been exclusive or binding. Reconstructing wider commercial networks for cotton manufacturers is difficult, given how short-lived many concerns were and how few long-run series of accounts survive. No accounts have been found for any of the Igualada manufacturers, so their contacts have to be worked out from inventories and from appearances in the surviving Barcelona accounts.[131] While the sources are biased towards capturing one-off appearances, rather than long-run relationships,

---

[129] Veyrassat finds a similar fluidity in occupational titles in Saint-Gall (*Négociants et fabricants*, pp. 159–60).

[130] For examples, see Garcia Balañà, *La fabricació de la fàbrica*, pp. 189–200.

[131] All documentation for calico or cotton manufacturers or for merchants dealing in textiles up to 1830 was examined for references to Igualada producers. In many cases, however, the origins of creditors and debtors are not given.

Table 3.5 Inventories of cotton producers

Name	Year	Occupation	Carding machines	Spinning wheels	Machines	Looms	Printing equipment	Cotton (*lliures*)	Cloths
Miquel Galtés	1800	wood carver	1	4	4 (J), 1 (A)[a]	4		156	20
Isidro Prat	1806	merchant	1	5		8	8 tables, 3 dyeing vats, 1 cylinder		
Bartomeu Canals	1808	cotton manufacturer		8	10 (J)	6		52	168
Anton Mussons	1809	smallholder	1	5	3 (J)[b]	3			
Salvador Mimó	1810	cotton weaver	1		7 (J)	2		208	
Pau Boix	1811	calico manufacturer	1	7	4 (J)	5		56	4
Joan Camps	1812	calico weaver							
Francisco Oller/ Eulàlia Comas[c]	1815	weaver		3		1			
Joan Badia	1817	calico weaver							
J.A. Fàbregas	1817	calico manufacturer					14 tables, 1 cylinder		352
Anton Amigó	1818	hat manufacturer	2	14	7 (J), 8 (A)[d]	6		210	
Magí Borras	1818	shoemaker		3	2 (J)				
Jaume Mas	1819	calico manufacturer					12 tables, 2 meadows,[e] 2 dyeing vats		250

	Year	Occupation							
Josep Llobet	1820	calico manufacturer	1	7	6 (J)	705	Wood for 2 looms	4 tables, 200 moulds	3
Jaume Vallès	1822	cotton weaver							
Anton Casas	1823	weaver/cotton manufacturer	1	9	6/7 (J)[f]	181		5	57
Albert Vallès[g]	1824	cotton manufacturer	3		1 twisting cotton	1,045	2 ribbons	Dyeing equipment	94
Josepa Rius	1824	widow cotton manufacturer		5	4 (J)				
Antònia Riera	1825	widow calico manufacturer							
Ramon Camps	1829	cotton manufacturer	1	2	10 (J)	416			6
Joan Soler[h]	1829	cotton weaver	1	4	5 (J)				
Josep Thomas	1829	calico manufacturer	2	4	4 (J)	2		3 (out of use)	

Notes: J: spinning jenny; A: Arkwright machine. [a] Also had a 'machine for working cotton, property of one Bernabé'. [b] One spinning jenny not in the house. [c] Joint inventory of husband and wife. [d] Two Arkwright machines under construction. [e] One owned, one rented. [f] One machine unspecified. [g] Specialised in ribbon-weaving. [h] Equipment all in a workshop in Capellades.

Sources: Galtés: ANI 588, fos 78–84; Prat: ANI 643, fos 302–6; Canals: ANI 646, unfol.; Mussons: ANI 647, unfol.; Mimó: ANI 650, fos 164r–165r; Boix: ANI 651, fo. 31; J. Camps: ANI 598, fo. 494; Oller/Comas: ANI 601, fos 208–209r; Badia: ANI 603, fo. 522v; Fàbregas: ANI 663, fos 49r–58r; Amigó: ANI 663, fos 57–68; Borras: ANI 558, fo. 108; Mas: ANI 605, fos 190r–191r; Llobet: ANI 607, fos 228r–231r; J. Vallès: ANI 695, fo. 48; Casas: ANI 610, fos 21–2; A. Vallès: ANI 666, fos 44r–47r; Rius: ANI 666, fos 76v–77r; Riera: ANI 612, fos 152–5; R. Camps: ANI 681, fos 103–5; Soler: ANI 668, fos 87r–88r; Thomas: ANI 560, fos 57–68.

it nonetheless appears that commercial relationships were often brief, rarely exclusive and tended to be flexible. The 4 years of surviving accounts for Francisco Puig's Barcelona company show that he purchased calicoes once from Miquel Galí.[132] The strongest relationship detected is that between the Sirés company and Francisco Anton Matoses.[133] Okuno has shown that between 1785 and 1806, Igualada accounted for 15.2 per cent of all cloths purchased by Sirés from outside Barcelona, slightly less than Manlleu (17.2 per cent) and Cardona (16.2 per cent).[134] The bulk of these supplies came from Matoses, with other Igualada manufacturers appearing only once or twice. Matoses's relationship with Sirés was not exclusive, however, since he also appears in the accounts of Arnaldo Salas and Jacinto Martí.[135] Moreover, he only purchased raw cotton from Sirés once, suggesting that this was not usually a two-way relationship. I have only found one instance where an Igualada manufacturer purchased raw cotton from a Barcelona supplier to whom he then sold the finished product, a relationship that might be seen as approximating the putting-out relationships of the woollen industry.[136]

Quantifying the extent to which a putting-out network of domestic spinning and weaving operated alongside these small manufactures is similarly difficult. Of the weavers in Table 3.5, presumably Francisco Oller and Eulàlia Comas had continued to work in their home on a putting-out basis, as did Josep Llimona (see Table 3.3). Miquel Galtés, aside from the cloths on his own looms, had two that were being woven outside, though the weavers are not identified. By contrast, three weavers' inventories do not record looms. Either they rented them, or worked outside the home in one of the workshops. Only one of the 188 weavers identified in the 1824 *cadastre* as heads of household was paying the higher rate of *personal* tax that would indicate more substantial and independent status.

The sources available for the Igualada cotton industry thus confirm the predominance of small-scale production, even when a certain degree of mechanisation is evident, that has been described for other places.[137] Capital investment was also small-scale. None of the concerns in the 1820 listing are described in terms of joint ownership, which is somewhat surprising given how common this was within the sector. By contrast, the inventories offer some clues in this regard. Half the value of Jaume Mas's cylinder and the mule required to drive it had been invested by Pere Fàbregas, another manufacturer. At the same time, Mas owned a third share in another house and workshop in Espluga de Francolí. Miquel Galtés had a machine for

---

[132]   AHCB, FC, B922, Francisco Puig, 'Llibre mayor' (1802–6), fo. 104.

[133]   AHCB, FC, Joan Batista Sirés, B232, B263, B265–8, B271–2, B275–6, B279, B281, B285.

[134]   Okuno, 'Entre la llana i el cotó', p. 52.

[135]   AHCB, FC, Arnaldo Salas y Jacinto Martí, A99, 'Llibre mayor'.

[136]   ANI 646, inventory of Bartomeu Canals (11 June 1808), unfol., which reproduces a letter from Anton Ribé of Barcelona, outlining the outstanding debt.

[137]   Veyrassat gives a figure of 6 or 7 weavers per cotton manufacturer in the Saint-Gall region for the period 1800–40 (*Négociants et fabricants*, pp. 179–80).

working cotton owned by a certain Bernabé. Anton Amigó's cotton manufacturing workshop was in a separate building and appears to have been under the direction of one Josep Codina and Amigó's son Josep.

As Thomson has pointed out, small-scale production represents something of a discontinuity within the cotton industry itself, given the tendency towards larger units in the first stage of calico-manufacturing.[138] It was, however, as this chapter has shown, a continuity within textiles as a whole and in terms of the shift from wool to cotton. Sánchez sees small-scale production, particularly investment in more than one workshop by the same manufacturer or partnership, as less risky in the face of low levels of domestic demand and continuing political and economic instability.[139] Small-scale production was often better able than the factory to withstand the vagaries of the trade cycle, a suggestion made by Pat Hudson with reference to the *Kaufsystem* in Yorkshire in particular, but one more generally applicable to other forms of small-scale production and in other areas.[140] Sánchez also points out that traditional energy sources, including water power, were often too limited or irregular to make large-scale capital investment worthwhile.[141] Only with steam power did large factories make sense. Similarly, the flexibility of the early types of machine used in cotton gave few advantages to larger-scale concerns. The *bergadana* was seen as being highly suited to domestic use, as will be discussed in Chapter 5. Likewise, one of the advantages of Crompton's mule was that its low energy demands meant it could be adapted to any production unit. There were thus few economies of scale to be had in spinning or weaving, compared with printing. More importantly, this continuity in small-scale production up until the 1830s or so was one of the ways in which the early phases of the cotton industry adapted best to the realities of the existing proto-industrial structures. Underpinning small-scale production was the importance throughout of the household economy and family labour, an aspect that will be discussed in detail in subsequent chapters, though it is worth noting here that the use of family labour also reduced running costs, compared with waged spinners and weavers.

This chapter has sought to show that the success of Catalan proto-industry, in particular that of Igualada, relied on the ability to capture distant markets and respond quickly to changes in demand. In turn, the ability to respond quickly was determined by the flexibility of small-scale family production, a key feature of both the woollen and the cotton industries. For the woollen industry, success involved the imposition of new, hierarchical relations of production within a putting-out system that turned most producers, particularly weavers, into dependent workers. By contrast, the cotton industry, at least in the initial stages witnessed here, allowed

---

[138] Thomson, *Distinctive Industrialization*.

[139] Sánchez, 'La empresa algodonera', p. 163; id., 'Crisis económica y respuesta empresarial', pp. 512–4.

[140] Hudson, *The Genesis of Industrial Capital*, pp. 73–4; see also Veyrassat, *Négociants et fabricants*, pp. 43–4.

[141] Sánchez, 'La empresa algodonera', p. 170.

considerable independence to smaller producers, though survival in difficult years was by no means guaranteed. Family ties and family discipline created a flexible workforce and also may have provided some protection against the risks and uncertainties posed by unprecedented involvement in national and international markets. At the same time, however, proto-industry and the related changes on the land described in the previous chapter were altering the basis for family formation, whilst also having serious consequences for welfare. This is the subject of the next chapter.

Chapter 4
Family Formation and Population Growth

Introduction

One of the most salient features of the era of transition through which much of European society was passing in the eighteenth century was a rise in population. This growth represented a new trend, the first phase of what has been identified as a modern demographic cycle, whereby growth would eventually surpass previous known levels before being checked for the first time in the twentieth century by the conscious control of fertility within marriage, rather than either Malthus's preventative check of restricted marriage or his positive check of increased mortality.[1] The change can also be characterised as a shift from a 'high pressure' demographic regime, where high mortality was balanced by high fertility, to a 'low pressure' regime, where low mortality allowed for correspondingly low fertility. Only the first phase of the demographic transition, however, namely, the rapid population growth of the eighteenth century, concerns us here.

Such rapid and sustained growth could obviously not occur without increased output and productivity in other sectors. Population pressure on the land and declining real wages could only be avoided through increases in agricultural output and productivity and the growth of other sectors to absorb labour. Seen from this perspective, sustained population growth was a product of growth elsewhere enabling previous resource constraints to be removed. From another perspective, however, population behaviour could be what enabled productivity growth in the first place: as discussed in Chapter 1, the ability of European society to keep population growth below a theoretical ceiling permitted the accumulation of capital. The demographic structures viewed as important here are Hajnal's 'north-west European marriage pattern' and the corresponding preference for neo-local nuclear household formation. However, in associating different family forms and the relative strength of family ties with economic growth, some careful distinctions need to be made. Following Hajnal and Reher, de Vries associates weak family ties with the nuclear family and strong ties with the extended family, viewing the former as promoting the individualism required for economic growth. Reher, however, is very careful not to associate his distinction between 'weak' and 'strong' family ties with specific family forms, pointing out that such an association is impossible given the geographical diversity of such forms. The earlier idea that the western or north-western European family was predominantly nuclear or

---

[1]   John Landers, *The Field and the Forge: Population, Production and Power in the Pre-Industrial West* (Oxford, 2003), pp. 20–6.

simple in form, compared with extended or joint family structures elsewhere has been undermined by subsequent scholarship.[2] For Reher, the strength of family ties matters more than structure. What is important, therefore, is how the family conditioned the behaviour of different members; in particular, the capacity or otherwise to take advantage of changing market opportunities. Catalan family forms and relationships, as discussed below, have traditionally been regarded as extremely strong, yet permitting a dynamic response to economic opportunities when these arose.

This chapter is therefore concerned with explaining population growth in terms of how the family responded to economic change, specifically, how the changes on the land and the growth of proto-industry described in previous chapters could lead to population growth by altering the basis for family formation. Given the emphasis on marriage in most accounts, explaining population behaviour usually entails explaining what factors determined the age at marriage and the propensity to marry. In the English case, the operation of labour markets through changing real wages has been singled out as the prime cause.[3] For a time, proto-industrialisation was also believed to have enabled early marriage and rising fertility by permitting opportunities for household formation based partly or wholly on resources other than access to land.[4] Subsequent empirical work has made it clear that the idea of a specific type of proto-industrial demographic behaviour cannot be sustained.[5] Nonetheless, although the relationship between population and proto-industry varied from place to place, the Catalan experience shows that the former could still be strongly affected by the latter. Moreover, the relationship was not limited solely to marriage. Though mortality and fertility have received scant attention by comparison with marriage, there is evidence that the effects of proto-industrialisation may be as or more evident in mortality rates as they are in marriage.

---

[2]   While the nuclear or simple family does appear to have been predominant in northern and western Europe since at least the medieval period, it was also far more common in other areas of Europe and the wider world than was initially recognised (Tamara Hareven, 'The History of the Family and the Complexity of Social Change', *American Historical Review*, 96 (1991), pp. 95–124).

[3]   E.A. Wrigley and R.S. Schofield, *The Population History of England, 1541–1871: A Reconstruction* (2nd edn, Cambridge, 1989).

[4]   Mendels, 'Proto-Industrialization'; Hans Medick 'The Proto-Industrial Family Economy: The Structural Function of Household and Family During the Transition from Peasant Society to Industrial Capitalism', *Social History*, 3 (1976), pp. 291–315; Levine, *Family Formation*.

[5]   For an overview of the debate and some of the most recent contributions, see Ogilvie and Cerman, *European Proto-Industrialization*. Many of the criticisms are answered in Kriedte, Medick and Schlumbohm, 'Proto-Industrialization Revisted'; J. Schlumbohm, '"Proto-Industrialization" as a Research Strategy and a Historical Period: A Balance Sheet', in Ogilvie and Cerman, *European Proto-Industrialization*, pp. 12–22.

More generally, mortality trends were the background against which the preventative check operated. As suggested in the Introduction, if the preventative check were the most influential factor in English population trends over the long-term, this may have been because the weight of the positive check was comparatively light. In Spain, by contrast, as Jordi Nadal has remarked, 'the weight of excessive mortality' continued to be felt well into the twentieth century.[6] Within Spain, Catalonia is often viewed as being the first region to have escaped the constraints of the positive check, with some historical demographers positing a decline in infant and child mortality rates from as early as the eighteenth century.[7] Certainly, mortality rates were always lower than in the interior, but the experience of Igualada, described below, suggests the decline in infant and child mortality may not be general to the whole region. Instead, rather, high mortality may in fact have been the inescapable penalty of economic growth.

Indeed, part of the value of this particular case study of Igualada is its contribution to explaining Catalan population growth. All of Spain enjoyed population growth over the eighteenth and nineteenth centuries, with Catalonia standing out as one of the regions with the fastest growth rate. The most recent estimates yield growth rates of 0.6 to 0.7 per cent per annum between 1717 and 1787, the years for which population counts are available.[8] While a wealth of studies based on parish registers now exists to provide the basis for reliable population estimates, there has been little attempt to go beyond the description of population trends to examine deeper underlying causes.[9] The small size of many of the communities studied also limits the amount of information that can be extracted from the parish registers or censuses and the degree to which such information might be representative of broader trends.

Igualada, by contrast, represents a large study in demographic terms. As mentioned in the Introduction, population grew from a minimum total of 1,630

---

[6] Jordi Nadal, *La población española (siglos XVI a XX)* (4th revd edn, Barcelona, 1991), p. 138.

[7] Jordi Nadal, 'Demografía y economía en el origen de la Cataluña moderna: Un ejemplo local: Palamós (1705–1839)', in id., *Bautismos, desposorios y entierros: Estudios de historia demográfica* (Barcelona, 1992), pp. 149–73; Àngels Torrents, 'Transformacions demogràfiques en un municipi industrial català: Sant Pere de Riudebitlles, 1608–1935' (PhD thesis, Universitat de Barcelona, 1993); Francesc Muñoz, 'Creixement demogràfic, mortalitat i nupcialitat al Penedès (segles XVII–XIX)' (PhD thesis, Universitat Autònoma de Barcelona, 1992); id., 'Nivells i tendències de la mortalitat a les localitats del Penedès (segles XVII–XIX)', *Estudis d'història agrària*, 9 (1992), pp. 181–202; M.A. Martínez, *La població de Vilanova i la Geltrú en el segle XVIII* (Vilanova i la Geltrú, 1987).

[8] L. Ferrer, 'Una revisió del creixement demogràfic de Catalunya en el segle XVIII a partir dels registres parroquials', *Estudis d'història agrària*, 20 (2007), pp. 17–68.

[9] Ferrer lists these studies, most of which are unpublished PhD theses or undergraduate dissertations (ibid., pp. 38–41).

in 1717 to 4,925 in 1787 to 7,731 in 1830.[10] Unlike the majority of parishes in Catalonia, the registers survive virtually complete from 1513 to the present. The dataset includes 25,887 baptisms, 6,133 marriages and 21,814 burials, from which 8,700 families have been wholly or partly reconstituted. To my knowledge, this dataset represents the largest reconstitution carried out to date for Catalonia and one of the largest for Spain.[11] It compares favourably with reconstitutions carried out elsewhere in Europe.[12] Catalan registers record much more information than English registers, and information increases over time.[13] In Igualada, the information given includes male occupations, allowing demographic results to be broken down by occupational groups.

Catalan family forms

Of all the Spanish regions, Catalonia practised the most impartible form of inheritance.[14] Initially, the testator had complete freedom to dispose of his or her property at will.[15] This freedom was gradually eroded by the institution during the Middle Ages of rights known as *drets de llegítima*, whereby 25 per cent of the property belonged by rights to the testator's children. The remaining 75 per cent was still at the disposal of the testator, however, and by custom it was bestowed upon one heir alone, usually the eldest son, known as the *hereu*. In the absence of sons, the property went to the eldest daughter, known as the *pubilla*. In practice, the

---

[10] Iglésies, *Evolució demogàfica de la comarca d'Igualada*, pp. 12–14. Ferrer argues that the 1717–18 census figures underestimate the total population by as much as 50–70 %, while the 1787 census does so by about 10–26% ('Una revisió del creixement demogràfic de Catalunya', pp. 23–6). For a discussion of the censuses, see Marfany, 'Proto-Industrialisation and Demographic Change', pp. 19–21, 41–5.

[11] Of Catalan reconstitutions that span a similar time period, the largest is that of Vilanova i la Geltrú, which had a population of 6,161 in 1787, although only one of two parishes has been reconstituted.

[12] Of the 26 parishes in the Cambridge Group reconstitutions, for instance, only Birstall was larger, with a population in 1801 of over 14,000; Gainsborough, the second largest, having a population of over 5,000 (E.A. Wrigley et al., *English Population History from Family Reconstitution, 1580--1837* (Cambridge, 1997), pp. 22–3).

[13] For a discussion of Catalan parochial registration, the Igualada registers and the methodological issues involved in their reconstitution, see Marfany, 'Proto-Industrialisation and Demographic Change', pp. 45–55. Nominal linkage was done using Microsoft Access 2000, following the Cambridge Group methodology, as described in E.A. Wrigley, 'Family Reconstitution', in id. (ed.), *An Introduction to English Historical Demography* (London, 1966), pp. 96–159.

[14] For different regional patterns of inheritance, see David Reher, *Perspectives on the Family in Spain, Past and Present* (Oxford, 1997), pp. 48–59.

[15] On the legal history of Catalan inheritance customs, see Ferrer, *Pagesos, rabassaires i industrials*, ch. 7.

hereu could therefore end up inheriting 80 per cent or more of the family property. Younger daughters received their *llegítima* at marriage as their dowry. Younger sons might receive it at marriage or at the legal age of majority (25). At marriage, the couple and their parents or other relatives drew up contracts known as *capítols matrimonials*, in which various transfers of property and legal agreements were brought together in a single document.[16] In the case of the marriage of an eldest son, the first transaction was the transfer of the property from parents to son, although the parents retained the full use of it until their deaths. If the father died first, his widow had usufruct of the property, provided she did not remarry. Until the deaths of the parents, the new couple would live in the same house, forming a classic extended or 'stem' family. The second transaction was the settling of the bride's dowry, which was usually in the form of cash and a trousseau, determining both the amount and the timetable for payments. A woman's dowry remained her property after marriage, though her husband and his family administered it for her. If she had children, they had rights to a quarter of it, the remainder being hers to dispose of in the same way as men. If she died childless, the dowry reverted to her family. If she were left a widow and wished to remarry, her first husband's family was obliged to pay her dowry to her new in-laws. In return for her dowry, the bride renounced all further claims on her parents' property.

In addition to the clauses which dealt strictly with the marriage, the couple often added further clauses, in which they made provision for the future against the possibility that either might die intestate. Usually they agreed that one of their children would inherit, reserving the right to choose which child at a later date, but stipulating that primogeniture should be followed in the event of their failing to do so. Marriage contracts thus effectively tied three generations of a family to the property, ensuring that questions of inheritance were rarely left unsettled by the premature death of an eldest son.

Marriages of younger children were simpler, in that there were no questions of inheritance to settle. Ideally, parents hoped to marry their daughters to *hereus* from other families, though this often involved downward social mobility for women. Younger sons might, if they were lucky, marry a *pubilla*, in which case the roles were reversed and the son moved in with his parents-in-law, with his *llegítima* becoming the equivalent of a dowry. Since there were far fewer *pubilles* available than *hereus*, younger sons were usually in the position of either not marrying at all, in which case they had the right to continue living in the parental home, or of marrying a woman who was not a *pubilla* and forming a separate household on the basis of their two *llegítimes*. Traditionally, families who could afford to do so placed their younger sons in the church. Aside from the benefits of status associated with the priesthood, such placements usually represented an investment for families. Beneficed positions and their role as creditors within communities

---

[16]   Jaume Codina, *Contractes de matrimoni al delta del Llobregat (segles XIV a XIX)* (Barcelona, 1997); Rosa Congost, *Notes de societat (La Selva, 1768–1862)* (Santa Coloma de Farners, 1992).

allowed priests to accumulate an income, which usually devolved back to the family of origin eventually, either through bequests in wills or other forms of provision for kin.

The system of impartible inheritance described here was almost universally practised in early modern Catalonia, despite the testator's legal freedom to testify. As a result, Catalan inheritance practices have achieved almost mythical status in the writings of novelists, political economists, historians and anthropologists. The system has been viewed above all as providing stability through the transfer of property undivided down through the generations, with families securely tied to the land, guaranteeing continuity of property holding and social relations.[17] At the same time, younger sons were free to take their portions and seek their fortunes elsewhere, pursuing careers in the church, urban professions or, later on, industry or colonial trade. In so doing, they provided a dynamic element within Catalan society. Perhaps the most often cited expression of this idealisation of Catalan inheritance practices is that of the historian Jaume Vicens Vives:

> The industry and commerce of Catalonia have been created by the efforts of younger sons, and by their eldest brothers, who watch over them from the distant farm. ... Every Catalan has his family ... born from the land on which his first ancestor laid the stones of the farmhouse which was to govern it.[18]

That the stem family could be a force for stability in rural Catalonia is not in doubt, though there is now more scepticism as to the absence of conflict between *hereus* and their younger brothers. More important for the purposes of this argument are the implications of these family formation patterns for different individuals. For eldest sons, their marriage opportunities were determined by inheritance: it was incumbent upon them to marry and ensure the succession of the household and, depending upon mortality rates, they were likely to spend at least part of their adult married lives as part of an extended family of which they were not the head. The marriages of younger children, however, and in particular those between younger sons and younger daughters, depended on the ability to command some kind of 'niche' in the local economy sufficient for the formation of a new, independent household. For one generation at least, this would be a nuclear household headed by the couple themselves, even though they would usually revert back to impartible inheritance customs and a stem-family model for the next generation.

Marriage

Studies for Catalonia and the rest of Spain lend some weight to Hajnal's suggestion that 'significant departures from the European pattern may probably be found not

---

[17]   Andrés Barrera, *Casa, herencia y familia en la Cataluña rural* (Madrid, 1990).

[18]   J. Vicens Vives, *Notícia de Catalunya* (2nd edn, Barcelona, 1984), pp. 30, 40.

only as one proceeds eastwards but on the southern edge of Europe as well'.[19] Mean ages at marriage calculated from the 1787 census and from family reconstitutions range from 21 to 27 for men and 20 to 26 for women, with Catalonia at the lowest end of the spectrum.[20] At their highest, therefore, Spanish ages at marriage were in keeping with Hajnal's 'north-west European marriage pattern', but, at their lowest, they were a 'significant departure'.

The attempts that have been made to explain such variation have usually been in terms of the different inheritance practices in different regions, but with a greater degree of comparison across space than across time. What is of interest here is whether in Catalonia the tie binding inheritance and reproduction was broken over the eighteenth century by economic change or whether family ties continued to be strong yet adaptable as suggested by Vicens Vives. So far, those studies that argue for the continuity of impartible inheritance customs until well into the twentieth century have focused on rural, more isolated areas of Catalonia, such as the Pyrenees. One hypothesis would be that a rapid decline in the importance of inheritance in determining family formation would be more visible in areas of proto-industry and commercial viticulture and in the family formation rates of younger sons, as new niches in the economy became available.[21]

In fact, for Igualada and elsewhere in Catalonia, there is evidence in support of changing marriage practices and family formation rates for both eldest and younger children in response to proto-industrialisation and changes on the land. Contemporaries already believed that the growth of labour markets promoted marriage. In 1762 Bernardo Ward, a government minister, bemoaned what he perceived as the stagnation of the Spanish population. His solution was to 'remove all obstacles from marriage, so that any woman who wishes to work may be able to earn one or two *reales* a day, and any man five or six, and they will thus be able to marry at the right age'.[22] The Catalan political economist, Francisco Romà Rossell made a similar argument in 1786, but with specific reference to proto-industry:

---

[19]   Hajnal, 'European Marriage Patterns', p. 103.

[20]   Robert Rowland, 'Sistemas matrimoniales en la Península Ibérica (siglos XVI–XIX): Una perspectiva regional', in V. Pérez Moreda and D.S. Reher (eds), *Demografía histórica en España* (Madrid, 1988), pp. 72–137; M. Livi-Bacci, 'Fertility and Nuptiality Changes in Spain from the Late 18th to the Early 20th Century', *Population Studies*, 22 (1968), pp. 83–102, 211–34; A. Moreno, J. Soler and F. Fuentes, 'Introducción al estudio socio-demográfico de Cataluña mediante el Censo de Floridablanca (1787)', *Actes del Primer Congrés d'Història Moderna de Catalunya* (2 vols, Barcelona, 1984), vol. 1, pp. 23–38; David Reher, *Town and Country in Pre-Industrial Spain: Cuenca, 1550–1870* (Cambridge, 1990), p. 75; Torrents, 'Transformacions demogràfiques', p. 207.

[21]   I have discussed this idea, with comparative data, in R. Congost, L. Ferrer and J. Marfany, 'The Formation of New Households and Social Change in a Single Heir System: The Catalan Case, 17th to 19th Centuries', in P. Pozsgai and A-L. Head-König (eds), *Inheritance Practices, Marriage Strategies and Household Formation in European Rural Societies* (Brussels, 2012).

[22]   Cited in Nadal, *La población española*, p. 98.

> As soon as industry is introduced into a country, there can be no doubt that
> people will marry if they wish [for] any girl with twenty-five *ducados* for a
> dowry, and even more so with fifty, will find a husband, for to a journeyman this
> small income can be the basis of a fortune, by providing him with some means
> by which to live, or at least the tools most necessary for his craft.[23]

Unfortunately, the data give little insight into how the proportions never marrying
may have changed over time, since family reconstitution excludes those who
do not marry. One proxy that is frequently used is the proportion of those aged
over 50 who are described as single in census listings. In the household listing
of 1716 for Igualada, the proportions were 4.9 per cent for men and 0.4 per cent
for women. In the 1787 census, the proportions were 7.3 per cent and 2.9 per
cent respectively, but may include the population of religious houses, which
were definitely not included in 1716. A different proxy, namely, the proportions
of single men and women among burials of those aged over 50 (where ages are
recorded), match the figures here at around 4–6 per cent for men and 1–2 per
cent for women.[24] Consistent recording of male marital status at burial did not
begin until the mid-eighteenth century, however, and too few adult burials provide
accurate age information before 1780 for any real assessment of change over time
to be possible.

   Nonetheless, by the late eighteenth century, Igualada shows remarkably
low proportions of men and women never marrying by European standards.
Moreover, these proportions are associated with clear evidence of falling ages at
first marriage, presented in Table 4.1. The first few cohorts are subject to varying
degrees of truncation bias, depending on sex, so are likely to be underestimates.[25]
Nonetheless, from the 1760s and 1770s, there is a clear drop in age at first marriage
for both sexes. For women, the pattern is less clear, and the fall less spectacular,
but there is still a fall of over 2 years to the lowest mean age of 21 years in 1810–
19. More striking, however, is the trend in male ages at first marriage. The mean
age falls 3 years from 25.5 to 22.5 years in 1810–19. The median and modal ages
experience even more dramatic falls, from 25.0 to 21.6 years, and from 25 to 19
years respectively.

---

[23]   Francisco Romà Rossell, *Los señales de la felicidad de España*, ed. E. Lluch
(Barcelona, 1989; 1st edn, Madrid, 1768), pp. 16–21.

[24]   See J. Marfany, 'Choices and Constraints: Marriage and Inheritance in Eighteenth-
and Early Nineteenth-Century Catalonia', *Continuity and Change*, 21 (2006), pp. 1–34.

[25]   Truncation bias refers to the fact that, for marriages taking place before 1730,
according to the rules of family reconstitution, the ages of those marrying late are more
likely to be excluded, since the baptisms of the individuals concerned will have taken place
before 1680. On truncation bias and other methodological issues involved in calculating
ages at marriage through family reconstitution, see Marfany, 'Proto-Industrialisation and
Demographic Change', pp. 121–9.

Table 4.1   Age at first marriage in Igualada

Years	Mean	Median	Mode	N
Women				
1700–9	20.3	20.2	20	90
1710–19	21.9	21.4	21	103
1720–9	22.6	22.3	21	50
1730–9	21.3	20.6	18	103
1740–9	22.4	21.0	18	136
1750–9	22.3	22.2	23	168
1760–9	23.2	22.4	21	159
1770–9	22.4	21.4	21	241
1780–9	21.8	21.0	21	286
1790–9	21.4	20.7	19	313
1800–9	21.7	21.0	19	366
1810–19	21.0	20.3	19	547
1820–9	22.2	21.5	18	508
Men				
1700–9	21.8	21.9	23	49
1710–19	24.7	24.1	25	79
1720–9	26.3	25.8	22	56
1730–9	23.8	23.3	21	66
1740–9	25.1	24.4	22	135
1750–9	25.0	24.3	22	123
1760–9	25.5	25.0	25	121
1770–9	24.8	24.1	24	196
1780–9	24.7	24.5	24	227
1790–9	23.7	22.9	22	256
1800–9	24.2	23.3	21	304
1810–19	22.5	21.6	20	437
1820–9	22.7	21.9	19	425

Source: Igualada reconstitution.

In some ways, that male ages should show a greater degree of change is not surprising. Given that women were already marrying young by European standards at the start of the period, there was more scope for male ages to fall, although the number of teenage brides still increased. By the 1810s and 1820s, there were more first-time brides aged 15 than there were aged 30. More importantly, however, the change in male ages suggests that proto-industrialisation and other economic changes were loosening traditional constraints on marriage, constraints that had hitherto been greater for men than for women, and especially for younger sons.

The first feature that can be cited in support of such a statement is the difference in ages at first marriage according to occupation. Figure 4.1 gives mean ages at first marriage for men according to the occupations given in the marriage registers.[26] To avoid issues of truncation bias, only the figures for 1730 onwards are presented.[27] Ages for women show no meaningful pattern according to fathers' occupations and are thus not reproduced here, though they are available elsewhere.[28] While most occupations show a fall in age at first marriage for men, for many groups, the numbers are too small to be relied upon. The most dramatic apparent fall, for those in the professions and commerce, is based on an extremely small sample (16 in the first period, 24 in the second). Where the numbers are robust, however, the fall is undeniable. Above all, Figure 4.1 points to a significant proto-industrial effect upon marriage, with those in textiles marrying younger than those in any of the other larger occupational groups, with an average age of 24.1 in the second period and 22.6 in the last 50 years. Given the size of this group within the population, much of the overall fall in male marriage ages may be attributed to early marriage in the textile sector. More importantly, within textiles, weavers married nearly 2 years younger on average than clothiers, at 22.5 and 24.1 years respectively.[29] A similar association between rural industry and early marriage, particularly for weavers, has been found for other areas of Catalonia.[30] Given the evidence discussed in Chapter 3 that weavers were increasingly proletarianised, the effect of proto-industry here appears to be one of allowing for household formation with fewer means than were required by other occupations within and without the textile sector. Increasingly, as has been shown, weavers did not even need to own their own looms in Igualada. That women's ages should show no discernable pattern according to either their fathers' or their husbands' occupations is unsurprising, since neither would necessarily influence the earning capacities of the women themselves. Proto-industry may nevertheless still be partly responsible for the fall in women's ages at marriage by providing them with the means to earn a dowry sooner. The previous chapter has already presented evidence that spinning, especially in cotton, offered women higher wages than in other sectors.

Catalonia therefore resembles the proto-industrial regions in the earlier studies by Mendels, Medick and Levine, which found a fall in age at first marriage and increase in nuptiality rates. Subsequent studies challenged the idea of a proto-

---

[26]   The groupings reflect similarities between occupations and associations within guilds, but also attempts to see if occupations with a particularly strong presence in the town, such as textiles and leather, displayed differences in demographic or consumer behaviour. For a fuller discussion, see ibid., pp. 68–72, 111–14.

[27]   Figures for the period 1680–1729 are presented in Marfany, '"Casarse en edad apropriada": edat al matrimoni i estratègies matrimonials a Igualada, 1680–1829', *Miscellanea aqualatensia*, 11 (2004), pp. 13–44

[28]   Marfany, 'Choices and Constraints', p. 82; ead., 'Is it Still Helpful to Talk about Proto-Industrialisation?', p. 961.

[29]   Sample sizes were 1,084 for weavers and 250 for clothiers.

[30]   Llorenç Ferrer et al., 'Edat de casament i celibat definitiu a la Catalunya central (1803–1807)', *Manuscrits*, 10 (1992), pp. 259–86; Torrents, 'Transformacions demogràfiques', pp. 217–20

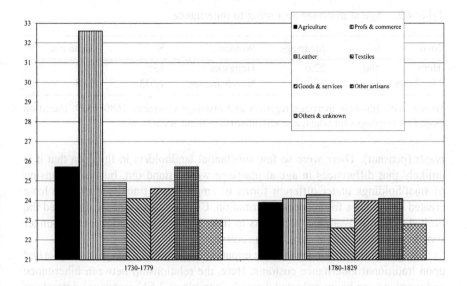

Figure 4.1   Men's ages at first marriage according to occupation

industrial effect on marriage by providing empirical evidence to the contrary, including for Mendels's own case study of Flanders.[31] The tendency has been to account for these differences in terms of relative proletarianisation and size of landholdings. Where the transmission or acquisition of property continued to play an important role in household formation, marriage behaviour was less affected by proto-industrialisation. By contrast, where property was losing importance relative to proto-industrialisation, sometimes in conjunction with other changes, then marriage behaviour was affected, as in the case of English proto-industrial communities. What is most striking about the Catalan case, however, is the greater effect upon the age at which men married. In part, this reflects the fact that women were already marrying young but, as will be argued, it is also the result of the particular constraints of inheritance customs upon Catalan men.

Proto-industrialisation was not, however, the only force operating upon marriage ages. Also significant in Figure 4.1 is the fall of 2 years in age at first marriage in the agricultural sector. Elsewhere in Catalonia, smallholders, *rabassaires* and labourers married at earlier ages than substantial peasants.[32] Unfortunately, the Igualada registers refer to all these under the generic heading

---

[31]   C. Vandenbroeke, 'Le cas flamand: Évolution sociale et comportements démographiques au XVIIe–XVIIIe siècles', *Annales ESC*, 39 (1984), pp. 915–39; F. Hendrickx, *In Order not to Fall into Poverty*; Isabelle Devos, 'Marriage and Economic Conditions since 1700: The Belgian Case', in I. Devos and L. Kennedy (eds), *Marriage and Rural Economy* (Turnhout, 2005), pp. 101–32.

[32]   Ferrer et al., 'Edat de casament i celibat definitiu', p. 266.

Table 4.2　Age at marriage according to inheritance

Men	N	Mean age	Women	N	Mean age
Heirs	480	22.6	Heiresses	135	19.2
Non-heirs	569	25.1	Non-heiresses	1,033	21.8

Source: API, Igualada marriage registers and marriage contracts, 1680–1829. Based on those first marriages for which age and inheritance status were known.

pagès (peasant). There were so few substantial landholders in Igualada that it is unlikely that differences in age at marriage would stand out, but the expansion of smallholdings under different forms of emphyteutic transfer may well have created new niches for household formation. Chapter 2 has already discussed the limited evidence available that points to links between the marriages of younger sons in particular and *rabassa morta* contracts.

The question still remains as to the impact such economic changes may have had upon traditional inheritance customs. Here, the relationship between inheritance and marriage can be investigated through a sample of 2,542 marriage contracts of the type described above. These represent all the contracts that could be located in the archives. Since marriage contracts usually make clear the status of the bride and groom as either *hereus/pubilles* or younger children, where marriage ages can be calculated for the individuals in question, it is then possible to see if differences exist in mean age at marriage according to inheritance status.

The results are presented in Table 4.2. They contradict the traditional assumption that heirs would marry later than their younger siblings as the family would need to settle all other marriage portions first.[33] Although the number of siblings to be married off did affect age at marriage for men, the tendency was still for heirs to marry at earlier ages than their younger siblings.[34] While families did require time to accumulate resources in order to pay marriage portions, dowries and *llegítimes* were usually paid in instalments over several years rather than all at once. Moreover, a compelling reason in this regard to marry the heir off quickly was that the dowry of the incoming bride was frequently used to pay the dowries of outgoing sisters. Finally, given high mortality rates, there was the concern to ensure the reproduction of the family. With heiresses, there was the added dimension of guaranteeing there would be an adult male to administer the property, especially when parents were already deceased. Many of the very young ages at first marriage for women correspond to *pubilles* in this situation.[35]

Of more interest here, however, is the way in which this traditional relationship between inheritance and marriage was breaking down in Igualada over this period. The first point is the declining frequency with which marriage contracts were

---

[33]　See Barrera, *Casa, herencia y familia*, pp. 208–13.

[34]　See Marfany, 'Choices and Constraints', pp. 86–8.

[35]　For examples, see ibid, pp. 87, 91–2.

Table 4.3   Declarations of marriage contracts in the Igualada marriage register

	In Igualada		Signed elsewhere		Not stated[a]		Not signed[b]		Total
	N	%	N	%	N	%	N	%	
1688–99	360	92	11	3	10	3	11	3	392
1700–9	178	89	2	1	16	8	5	2	201
1710–19	164	78	3	1	40	19	3	1	210
1720–9	71	61	2	2	36	31	7	6	116
1730–9	87	45	3	2	60	31	45	23	195
1740–9	155	54	3	1	37	13	92	32	287
1750–9	157	50	3	1	33	11	120	38	313
1760–9	106	34	1	0	98	32	106	34	311
1770–9	158	37	3	1	110	26	157	37	428
1780–9	156	32	8	2	160	33	168	34	492
1790–9	212	36	2	0	45	8	327	56	586
1800–9	196	30	4	1	76	12	374	58	650
1810–19	205	21	4	0	545	55	229	23	983
1820–9	186	19	6	1	658	68	119	12	969
Total	2,391	39	55	1	1,924	31	1,763	29	6,133

Notes: [a] There is no explicit statement that the couple had not signed a contract, which could mean that the priest did not ask or that there was no contract [b] There is an explicit statement that the couple had not signed a contract

Source: API, Marriage registers of Santa Maria d'Igualada.

signed. From 1688 onwards, the marriage registers record whether or not the couple had signed a marriage contract. Table 4.3 shows the steady decline in the numbers signing contracts before marriage, from 94.6 per cent of couples in 1688–99 to 19.8 per cent by 1820–9. The issue is complicated, since many couples who had not signed a contract at the time of marriage subsequently went on to sign one later. Nonetheless, the increasing lack of urgency in drawing up such documents is also significant. Either marriage was becoming detached from considerations of property, or the amounts of property to be transmitted were not felt to warrant a lengthy legal contract. Moreover, where contracts did continue to be drawn up, the nature of the document was changing. Increasingly, the clauses dealing with the inheritance of future generations are dropped, while more immediate concerns come to the fore, such as the maintenance of younger siblings or widowed elderly parents or the payment of debts.[36]

Further evidence of the declining importance of inheritance and property transfers emerges when those who signed contracts are compared with those who did not. Here, the presence of a marriage contract can be taken as a rough proxy

---

[36]   For examples, see Marfany, 'Choices and Constraints', pp. 91–9.

Table 4.4   Male age at marriage according to wealth and birth order

Age rank	Marriage contracts			No marriage contracts		
	Mean	Median	Mode	Mean	Median	Mode
Eldest	23.6	23.1	23	23.5	22.6	20
Younger	24.9	24.3	24	24.2	23.4	21

Source: API, Igualada marriage registers and marriage contracts, 1680–1829. Based on those first marriages for which age and inheritance status were known.

for wealth or, at least, as a sign that inheritance customs continued to influence marriage. Table 4.4 shows differences in age at marriage for men (again, there is no clear pattern for women) according to whether or not they signed a marriage contract and according to their status as eldest or younger sons. The results are striking, particularly the 3-year gap between the modal ages of those signing contracts and those not. Inheritance continued to hold some sway, as evidenced by the continued difference in terms of age rank in both groups. Even among less wealthy families, there still appears to have been some preference for eldest sons when it came to transmitting what few goods there were. Nonetheless, while younger sons were still at some disadvantage compared with their eldest brothers, proto-industrialisation and easier access to land were creating new opportunities for them to marry and form households.

The breaking down of traditional constraints on marriage did not, however, necessarily mean a breakdown in the strength of family ties. Marriage continued to be a process that involved the extended family, certainly in the provision of dowries, where a wide range of relationships can be discerned, including siblings, aunts and uncles, grandparents and godparents. We should be wary, though, of assuming that familial involvement was necessarily at the cost of independence or, more importantly, that independence and leaving home early were essential in order to respond to changing market opportunities. By providing financial assistance, kin could enable the consumer expenditure required to set up households, as will be discussed in Chapter 6. Moreover, as de Vries himself concedes, evidence from Japan shows that 'strong' families could also provide a flexible, yet disciplined labour force when required. The importance of family labour to Catalan industrialisation is discussed in Chapter 5. Idealised visions of the rural past aside, Catalan historians may have been right that the strength of Catalan family forms allowed for dynamism as well as stability.

Migration

Stability is also germane to another aspect of household formation practices: namely, whether proto-industry and changes on the land were creating niches

Table 4.5   Place of birth and residence of brides and grooms in Igualada

	1680–1729		1730–79		1780–1829		1680–1829	
	N	%	N	%	N	%	N	%
Men								
Born and resident in Igualada	446	57.5	701	54.4	1,742	56.7	2,889	56.2
Born in Igualada, resident elsewhere	2	0.3	20	1.6	30	1.0	52	1.0
Born elsewhere, resident in Igualada	147	18.9	366	28.4	802	26.1	1,315	25.7
Born and resident elsewhere	181	23.3	202	15.7	498	16.2	881	17.1
Total	776		1,289		3,072		5,137	
Women								
Born and resident in Igualada	515	67.4	899	65.0	2,170	67.3	3,584	66.7
Born in Igualada, resident elsewhere	1	0.1	8	0.6	22	0.7	31	0.6
Born elsewhere, resident in Igualada	108	14.1	283	20.5	800	24.8	1,191	22.2
Born and resident elsewhere	140	18.3	193	14.0	231	7.2	564	10.5
Total	764		1,383		3,223		5,370	

Source: API, Marriage registers of Santa Maria d'Igualada.

for younger sons who would previously have emigrated from the community altogether and, indeed, attracting migrants from elsewhere. Of all demographic variables, migration has been the most neglected in studies of proto-industrial regions. What discussion there has been, however, has focused on the idea that proto-industry broke down the traditional patterns of rural migration into the cities by providing new opportunities for work in the countryside.[37] Rates of urban growth may even have been relatively modest in the early stages of the modern demographic cycle precisely because of the growth of the rural non-

[37]   Braun, *Industrialization and Everyday Life*, pp. 14–16, 34; P. Hudson and S. King, 'Two Textile Townships, c. 1660–1820: A Comparative Demographic Analysis', *Economic History Review*, 53 (2000), pp. 706–41 (pp. 716–7, 735); Vandenbroeke, 'Le cas flamand', pp. 934–5.

agricultural sector.[38] Proto-industry and easier access to land might also be expected to encourage immigration from poorer agricultural regions.

Capturing migration flows is difficult, but parish registers yield some evidence in the form of information on place of birth and residence. This information is most consistently recorded in the marriage registers. Table 4.5 shows that, over the period studied, the percentages of grooms and brides born outside the parish remained stable at around 45 per cent of grooms and 35 per cent of brides.[39] Similar patterns have been found back as far as 1615 by Assumpta Fabré.[40] The geography of immigration did shift, however, with a rise in the numbers drawn in from the areas to the west: especially the Segarra and Conca de Barberà districts, which were traditionally poor areas and, as mentioned in Chapter 3, covered by the putting-out networks of the Igualada textile industry, while districts that were also proto-industrial, such as the Bages, sent fewer immigrants to Igualada.

Immigration after marriage appears to have remained equally stable, although it is harder to assess. One way of approaching the question is to compare the ratio over time of dummy marriages (marriages created as part of the family reconstitution process to account for couples who only appear in the registers at the moment of baptising or burying their children) to observed marriages.[41] The years prior to 1710 have to be excluded, as many dummy marriages for this period are created not for immigrants but for those marrying before 1680. After 1710 the ratio of dummy marriages to actual marriages is remarkably stable. The overall ratio of dummy to actual marriages, 0.4:1 is very close to the average for individual years, 0.5:1. There were only 8 years in which the ratio of dummy marriages to observed marriages rose above 0.7:1, all except one of which belonged to periods of war.[42] Over the short-term, migration of married couples into the parish could fluctuate sharply, but over the long-term, there was no sign of an increase in this regard. By the mid-nineteenth century, this appeared to be changing. Enriqueta Camps has shown that much factory labour by the 1850s consisted of a floating population of families with young children.[43] This phenomenon, however, was not yet evident in Igualada by 1829.

---

[38] Jan de Vries, *European Urbanization 1500–1800* (London, 1984), pp. 231–46; Landers, *The Field and the Forge*, pp. 40–2.

[39] As elsewhere, the custom was to marry in the bride's parish, so fewer women should appear as immigrants.

[40] A. Fabré, 'Aproximació a l'estudi de la immigració i de l'ocupació a Igualada, Manlleu i Centelles, segles XVII i primera meitat del XVIII' (Postgraduate diss., Universitat Autònoma de Barcelona, 1991).

[41] Observed marriages here include some marriages which did not take place in the parish, but which can be dated from the evidence of a marriage licence or marriage contract.

[42] Dummy marriages exceeded observed marriages in 1711, 1758, 1808 and 1814, and were above 0.7:1 in 1810, 1811, 1815 and 1816.

[43] Camps, *La formación del mercado*, pp. 91–8.

Emigration is almost impossible to capture, yet, as outlined above, this may be the more important factor where proto-industrialisation is concerned. Over the long-term, the only measure of emigration available is rather crude, namely, the proportion of baptisms that could not be linked to a marriage or a burial. In other words, the lack of a marriage or of a burial in infancy or childhood suggests that the individual left Igualada at some stage prior to marriage. Given how few people never married, it is reasonable to take this proportion as corresponding to migration in childhood or young adulthood. Marriages that cannot be linked to burials may also suggest emigration, though here it is difficult to distinguish those who were resident in the parish for a time from those who simply married in the parish but did not reside there afterwards ('residence' in the registers is that prior to marriage). For this reason, perhaps, no pattern could be found.

The percentage of baptisms that could not be linked to a marriage or burial fell from 40 per cent in the 1680s to 15–20 per cent in the 1760s, the last decade that could be used without encountering truncation bias.[44] Although the combined effects of a falling age at marriage and rising infant mortality must be taken into account, a fall of 20–25 per cent is still considerable and suggests there may have been a greater propensity over time for individuals to remain in Igualada. Those baptised in the 1760s would be entering work over the 1770s and 1780s, the peak of the woollen industry and the establishment of cotton. Unfortunately, truncation bias prevents what would have been a valuable comparison with later decades. Nonetheless, it can be tentatively concluded that Igualada fits the picture presented above whereby proto-industry proved a means of retaining individuals who would previously have been forced to emigrate in search of a niche elsewhere, while also exercising a certain 'pull' factor over immigrants from poorer areas.

Marital fertility

Earlier marriage and the formation of a greater number of new households in each generation, coupled with the likelihood of declining emigration are in themselves sufficient to explain rapid population growth in Catalonia. In addition, however, there is some evidence that fertility also rose within marriage in Igualada. Direct associations between marital fertility and economic change are hard to make. Although early historians of proto-industrialisation often claimed that proto-industrial workers had larger families than other occupational groups, this phenomenon tended to be viewed as the result of earlier marriage.[45] Where marital fertility levels were found to be high regardless of marriage age,

---

[44] For a discussion, see Marfany, 'Proto-Industrialisation and Demographic Change', pp. 90–1. A similar method is used by Hudson and King, 'Two Textile Townships', pp. 715–17.

[45] See the discussion in Ogilvie, *State Corporatism*, pp. 257–61.

it has been assumed that proto-industrial couples chose to have more children because child labour was an asset in such occupations, but the mechanisms whereby this choice was exercised, such as shorter birth intervals, have rarely been specified.

Such vagueness is unsurprising given the methodological difficulties with the analysis of fertility. A technical point is that the most precise measures of marital fertility, namely, age-specific marital fertility rates (ASMFR) are restrictive in terms of which women in any given study can be included.[46] More importantly, determining what constitutes conscious choice in fertility is fraught with difficulties. It is easier to see choice being exercised to limit family size, though even here historians have been reluctant to consider behaviour affecting the length of the intervals between birth ('spacing' behaviour) as deliberate, compared with the limitation of family size before the end of the biological reproductive span, once a desired number of children have been born ('stopping' behaviour). While some studies have suggested that spacing might have been a deliberate response to difficult circumstances, long birth intervals are most usually attributed to the contraceptive effect of breastfeeding, but with the assumption that breastfeeding was not consciously used as contraception.[47] Where marital fertility appears to be rising, this could be the result of an active desire to have more children, exercised through greater coital frequency, for example. It is, however, equally likely that it could be the result of a decline in the length of time spent breastfeeding.

Marital fertility does appear to have risen in Igualada, as far as can be measured from ASMFRs. These are presented in Table 4.6. The sample sizes are small, for the reasons adduced above, but those age groups for which sample sizes are more robust do show a rise over the eighteenth century.[48] These meagre figures can be supplemented with much more satisfactory evidence, derived from over 10,000 birth intervals for all women with at least two births, which can shed light on the kind of 'spacing' behaviour described above.

---

[46]   ASMRFs require that the woman's age at marriage and at each birth be known, that she have no children outside of marriage and that her marriage be completed, that is, that the couple remain married until the woman reaches 45, sometimes 50. In a reconstitution of a historical population, the sample will therefore be limited to those women baptised and married in the parish who survive and whose husbands survive until they reach 45 years of age.

[47]   For examples of deliberate spacing behaviour, see J. Landers, 'Fertility Decline and Birth Spacing among London Quakers', in J. Landers and V. Reynolds (eds), *Fertility and Resources* (Cambridge, 1990), pp. 92–117; E. Garrett, 'The Trials of Labour: Motherhood Versus Employment in a Nineteenth-Century Textile Centre', *Continuity and Change*, 5 (1990), pp. 121–54. For evidence that breastfeeding was not used as contraception in rural Spain, see D.S. Reher, *Familia, población y sociedad en la provincia de Cuenca, 1700–1970* (Madrid, 1990), p. 105 n. 36.

[48]   See Marfany, 'Proto-Industrialisation and Demographic Change', pp. 196–203.

Table 4.6   ASMFRs in Igualada: bachelor–spinster completed marriages, rates per 1,000 women per year

Age at marriage	15–19	20–4	25–9	30–4	35–9	40–4	45–9	TMFR20
1700–49								
<15	320.0ᵃ	402.8	291.2	271.9	200.0	300.0	—	
15–19	417.2	383.7	360.7	381.1	295.2	123.1	8.1	
20–4		382.3	400.6	383.4	310.3	165.1	15.9	8.29
25–9			429.6	320.5	229.9	179.7	—	
30–4				575.3	300.0	150.0	—	
35–9					—	—	—	
40–4						408.3	200.0	
45–9							—	
1750–99								
<15	400.0	386.5	311.8	474.6	300.0	223.2	—	
15–19	464.4	430.8	375.6	358.4	334.2	208.3	6.1	
20–4		422.6	379.2	368.9	327.5	189.8	18.0	8.53
25–9			506.1	373.5	354.2	182.7	23.9	
30–4				426.7	357.9	172.2	52.1	
35–9					251.7	250.0	150.0	
40–4						225.3	—	
45–9							1,189.7	

Note: ᵃ Italicised figures are based on fewer than 30 births.
Source: Igualada reconstitution.

What has to be determined first is whether an apparent rise in marital fertility is real or simply the result of rising infant mortality. In other words, if infant mortality rises in a society in which most women are breastfeeding for prolonged periods, the contraceptive effect of breastfeeding will be curtailed by infant deaths, and birth intervals will be correspondingly shorter as women conceive again. In Igualada, as will be seen, infant mortality was rising over the period, and birth intervals curtailed by the death of the first child under one year of age were on average five to six months shorter than birth intervals where the first child survived. This supports the anecdotal evidence that most Igualada women were indeed breastfeeding their children and, more importantly, that the effects of infant mortality need to screened out in order to see a real rise in marital fertility.[49]

Table 4.7 shows the results of such an exercise. Only those birth intervals where the first child survived to at least its first birthday are included, to filter out the effects of infant mortality. The length of the birth interval is therefore more likely to reflect

[49]   The anecdotal evidence is a question posed by Zamora as to whether or not women usually breastfed their children. All the surviving returns state that women usually did.

Table 4.7   Trends in mean birth intervals (months)

Period	N	Mean birth interval
1680–9	244	31.3
1690–9	443	33.0
1700–9	413	33.1
1710–19	401	31.8
1720–9	536	32.5
1730–9	588	32.0
1740–9	699	30.5
1750–9	884	30.3
1760–9	1,037	31.9
1770–9	1,220	30.4
1780–9	1,356	29.9
1790–9	1,943	29.3
1800–9	1,826	30.0
All	11,590	30.7

Source: Igualada reconstitution.

the duration of breastfeeding than any other factor. Over the reconstitution period, the tendency was for mean birth intervals of this type to fall, from a maximum of 33.1 months at the start of the eighteenth century to a minimum of 29.3 months by the last decade of that century, a fall of just under 4 months. Aside from a blip in the 1760s, this fall was fairly consistent throughout. Wrigley et al. argue that a fall of two months in mean birth intervals (the fall observed in the English data), if solely due to breastfeeding practices, would mean a shortening on average of breastfeeding by two to three months.[50] Although the Igualada data are based on smaller numbers, the sample sizes are still substantial, implying a potentially greater reduction in the average length of breastfeeding over the period.

The implications of these findings are highly significant. Not only is it clear that marital fertility in Igualada was indeed rising, but a decline in the mean duration of breastfeeding points to other demands on the time of married women. No other explanation occurs for why women would have chosen to breastfeed for less time. Here is indirect evidence of an 'industrious revolution' in terms of an intensification of labour within the family economy. As will be discussed in the next chapter, there is reason to be sceptical that proto-industrial activities could be as easily fitted in alongside domestic tasks and other types of work as some commentators have suggested. Instead, as will be seen below, this kind of self-exploitation of female labour was one that had deleterious consequences for infant and child health.

---

[50]   Wrigley et al., *English Population History*, pp. 445–9.

Penalties of growth: infant and child mortality

Questions of choice and behaviour become less evident once attention is turned to mortality. Traditionally, mortality was viewed as beyond human influence, whether it resulted from harvest failure in a context of low agricultural output and market integration or from the exogenous shocks of epidemic disease.[51] More recent work, however, has bestowed a degree of human influence upon mortality. The effects of rising prices and harvest failure could be either exacerbated or mitigated by family organisation and structure, by community support or state intervention, but often with different outcomes depending on gender and age.[52] The work of historical geographers on the spatial patterns of epidemic and endemic disease has also showed a degree of influence, albeit indirectly through improvements in trade and transport links that facilitated the spread of pathogens and the worsening disease environment associated with urban growth.[53] In a similar vein, the most recent work on proto-industry posits a strong association with worsening mortality. Even if different areas of Europe were able to escape from the Malthusian constraints on growth traditionally imposed by falling real wages, all, to some extent, paid a penalty for growth in the form of high mortality.

The study of mortality in Igualada shows a clear penalty in terms of welfare. Most revealing, and easiest to reconstruct are patterns of infant and child mortality, shown in Figure 4.2, where a distinct rise can be detected over the eighteenth and early nineteenth centuries. These rates follow the typical profile of infant and child mortality to be found in Mediterranean countries whereby mortality in the 1–5 age group (4q1) is much higher than infant mortality proper (1q0), in contrast to northern Europe, where the first year of life tended to be the most dangerous.[54]

The significance of this rise in infant and child mortality emerges most clearly from a comparison of the rates in Figure 4.2 with rates for other locations. As shown in Table 4.8, Igualada stands in contrast to most other Catalan localities studied, where both infant and child mortality rates were lower and falling over time. However, these localities were mostly rural, and many were on or near the coast. The Penedès sample includes two medium-sized towns: Vilanova i la Geltrú and Vilafranca del Penedès. The other localities were all villages with populations of under 3,000. Palamós is on the north-east coast. Given small size and location, it is unsurprising that the picture derived from such case studies should be more optimistic as regards the experience of mortality than that suggested by Igualada. The addition of more studies from the Catalan interior and for urban locations is likely to provide a corrective to the optimistic picture of falling mortality, as the

[51] Le Roy Ladurie, pp. 422–8, 549–58.

[52] T. Bengtsson, C. Campbell, J.Z. Lee, *Life under Pressure: Mortality and Living Standards in Europe and Asia, 1700–1900* (Cambridge, MA., 2004).

[53] Landers, *The Field and the Forge*, pp. 28–35.

[54] For a detailed discussion of mortality during the first year of life, see Marfany, 'Proto-Industrialisation and Demographic Change', pp. 160–83.

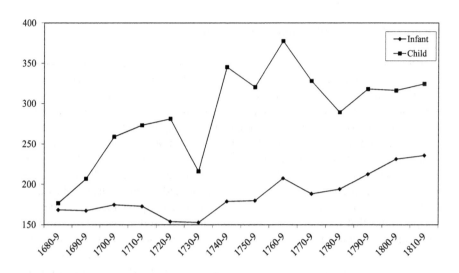

Figure 4.2   Infant and child mortality rates in Igualada

extremely high infant and child mortality rates reported for Barcelona almost a century later suggest.[55]

More important, however, is that the findings for Igualada fit with a broader tendency for proto-industrialisation to be associated with worsening mortality. Despite the claims made by some historians for improved living standards and nutrition as a result of higher incomes, where mortality rates have been calculated for proto-industrial communities, they more often show an upwards trend.[56] In England, the manufacturing parishes included in the Cambridge Group reconstitutions: Birstall, Gedling and Shepshed, bucked the national trend of declining infant mortality over the eighteenth century, as did Calverley and particularly Sowerby.[57] Infant mortality also rose sharply in Wildberg and also to some extent in Auffay.[58]

---

[55]   For the severity of mortality in central Spain, see David Reher, Vicente Pérez Moreda and Josep Bernabeu-Mestre, 'Assessing Change in Historical Contexts: Childhood Mortality Patterns in Spain During the Demographic Transition', in C.A. Corsini and P.P. Viazzo (eds), *The Decline of Infant and Child Mortality* (1997), pp. 35–56.

[56]   For claims that proto-industrialisation improved living standards, see Braun, *Industrialization and Everyday Life*, pp. 62–80. For a more direct link to mortality decline, see U. Pfister, 'Proto-Industrialization and Demographic Change: The Canton of Zürich Revisited', *Journal of European Economic History*, 18 (1989), pp. 629–62 ; and references in id., 'The Proto-Industrial Household Economy: Toward a Formal Analysis', *Journal of Family History*, 17 (1992), pp. 201–32 (pp. 210–14).

[57]   Wrigley et al., *English Population History*, pp. 215, 274; Hudson and King, 'Two Textile Townships', pp. 726–9.

[58]   Gullickson, *Spinners and Weavers*, pp. 152–7; Ogilvie, *Bitter Living*, p. 197.

Table 4.8   Infant and child mortality rates, selected Catalan locations

Place	Period	1q0	4q1
Penedès (15 parishes)	1675–90	219.4	347.2
	1784–90	196.2	312.4
Palamós	1751–60	202.7	81.2
	1771–80	237.0	60.2
	1801–10	204.1	75.7
	1811–20	144.7	51.5
Barcelona	1861–4	204.6	330.8

Sources: Muñoz, 'Creixement demogràfic', p. 113; id., 'Nivells i tendències de la mortalitat', p. 192 (Penedès and Barcelona); Nadal, 'Demografía y economía', p. 153 (Palamós).

The effect of proto-industrialisation in driving up infant mortality is attributable to a number of factors, all difficult to disentangle. Ogilvie argues above all for a decline in breastfeeding and childcare as a result of the pressures of married women's work. As discussed above, Igualada women were also spending less time on average breastfeeding over this period. Hudson and King show that rising mortality rates in Sowerby and Calverley were concentrated to a large extent in a core group of families and were due to a complex set of economic and social factors, including poverty and proletarianisation, but also residence in unhealthy areas of the parish, a lack of kin within the same community and illegitimacy. In general, rapid growth of communities could create its own hazards in the form of overcrowding, poor sanitation and greater exposure to disease.

In terms of the precise environmental effects at work in Igualada, overcrowding cannot be measured, but there is some evidence for other worsening conditions. Although the main streets of the town were paved by the late eighteenth century, the inhabitants were still living in close proximity to the slaughterhouses and tanneries. More importantly, population growth pressed heavily on scarce water resources. During the eighteenth century, the town was served by only two public fountains. The inadequacy of the water supply dominated discussions among the town council for decades, with numerous attempts to regulate the use of both fountains, but it was not until 1831 that four new fountains were built.[59]

Finally, Igualada witnessed several years of severe mortality, as illustrated in Figure 4.3.[60] Twelve years can be identified as crisis years, half of which correspond to war years, either the War of the Spanish Succession or the Napoleonic invasion. The other years coincide with high prices, such as 1764 and 1769, or epidemic disease, as in 1783. Rather than being exceptional, such crisis years represented an

[59]   J. Segura, *Història d'Igualada* (facs. edn, 2 vols, Igualada, 1978; 1st ed., Barcelona, 1907), vol. 2, pp. 316–17.

[60]   See J. Marfany, 'Las crisis de mortalidad en una comunidad catalana, Igualada, 1680–1829', *Revista de demografía histórica*, 23 (2005), pp. 13–41.

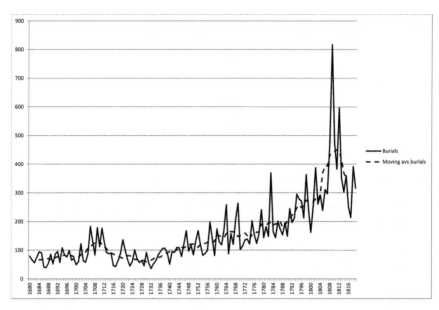

Figure 4.3   Annual totals of burials in Igualada, 1680–1829

intensification of the conditions prevailing in 'normal' years. Despite the increasing integration of Catalan grain markets over this period, prices rose and decades of higher prices were still correlated with higher mortality.[61] More importantly, the severity of the climate ensured a harsher disease environment than in northern Europe, particularly in contexts of rising population density. It is unsurprising that the second most intense episode of crisis mortality in Igualada was in 1783, when an epidemic of 'putrid fevers' swept across the peninsula. According to a contemporary doctor, out of all Catalan towns affected, the disease was 'most malignant' in Igualada.[62]

Involvement with markets through commercialised viticulture and particularly proto-industry therefore had a profound impact on Igualada in terms of family formation and thus population growth. Viewed in one light, the changes were

---

[61]   On grain markets, see R. Garrabou, E. Tello and A. Roca, 'Preus del blat i salaris agrícoles a Catalunya (1720–1936)', in M. Gutiérrez, *La industrialització i el desenvolupament econòmic d'Espanya: Homenatge al Dr Jordi Nadal* (2 vols, Barcelona, 1999), vol. 2, pp. 422–60; R. Garrabou and E. Tello, 'Salario come costo, salario come reditto: il prezzo delle giornate agricole nella Catalogna contemporanea (1727–1930)', *Meridiana*, 24 (1995), pp. 173–203; on the (statistically significant) correlation between grain prices and mortality in Catalonia, see F. Muñoz, 'Fluctuaciones de precios y dinámica demográfica en Cataluña (1600–1850)', *Revista de historia económica*, 15 (1997), pp. 507–43.

[62]   Josep Masdevall, *Relación de las epidemias de calenturas putridas y malignas* (Madrid, 1786), p. 47.

extremely positive: many men and women, younger sons above all, benefited from new opportunities to make a living locally that freed them from the constraints of inheritance customs. They could set up households sooner than previous generations had done. Viewed in another light, however, growth brought negative consequences: the worsening environment that resulted from population growth had a clear welfare penalty in terms of higher infant and child mortality, and continued crisis episodes. The following chapters continue to examine what market involvement meant for households and what the gains and losses were.

PART II
Industrious Consumers?

Chapter 5

Production in the Household Economy

Introduction

The second part of this work examines the extent to which households reoriented themselves towards the market as part of the dual changes of commercial viticulture and proto-industrialisation described in previous chapters. It has been shown that the household economy and family structure underpinned the nature of production in both sectors, particularly in terms of scale, and gave it the flexibility necessary to respond to changing market demand. What remains to be explored is how and to what extent households combined the activities of sharecropping and proto-industrial production and how far commercialisation was changing the nature of the household economy as well as being dependent upon it. In particular, the aim is to test the extent to which the reorientation of the household economy towards the market in Catalonia took the forms of specialisation or diversification of production and of a shift from production for consumption to production for exchange. This involves both identifying which activities households were choosing to engage in and an assessment of the scale of such activities.

More importantly, this chapter also seeks to examine whether such reorientation involved an intensification of labour within the household economy. The capacity for self-exploitation seen by many historians as intrinsic to the proto-industrial household economy could be viewed as an 'industrious revolution'. Indeed, as mentioned, de Vries himself suggests that the proto-industrial household may have been one context in which the industrious revolution was most likely to operate.[1] Both in more general terms and in the specific case of proto-industry, women's work has been highlighted as central to the industrious revolution. The introductory chapter has already highlighted the controversy surrounding the claims made for women's participation in these contexts and for the implications of this participation in terms of their status. This controversy is a question that this chapter will also seek to address as far as the sources permit, trying to identify changes in women's work and to develop the suggestions made in the previous chapter concerning the allocation of their time.

The effects on family formation of a shift towards market production have already been described to a considerable extent in the previous chapter. One question left outstanding is the extent to which the rapid population growth identified for Igualada, in common with elsewhere in Catalonia, resulted in greater proletarianisation for households at the bottom of the social scale and a

---

[1] De Vries, *Industrious Revolution*, pp. 96–104.

commensurate increase in social differentiation within the community. The final area considered by this chapter is precisely that of changes in the ownership of the means of production, insofar as these can be gauged from the sources, and how far these indicate a growing social polarisation over the period. The question of social differentiation is taken up again from the point of view of consumption in the following chapter.

Measuring production from inventories

De Vries's argument that households devoted more of their labour to producing for markets than for home consumption is not based for the most part on individual household-level data. Instead, he takes the trend towards specialisation, both in agriculture and proto-industry, in different regions of Europe as evidence of specialisation at the household level. He suggests rather than demonstrates that the areas that witnessed such specialisation were also those of greatest consumer demand. In so doing, he ignores the findings of the study by Overton et al., which set out to test at the household level the hypothesis that changing consumer behaviour led to the specialisation of production. These historians used inventories to measure the number and scale of productive activities undertaken by households in two regions: Kent, which saw rising levels of wealth and consumer expenditure, and Cornwall, which remained poorer and less commercialised. Their findings do not support the existence of an industrious revolution in either county. In particular, a rise in the number and variety of material goods, including new goods, in the inventories from Kent was not accompanied by specialisation of production or a decline in production for home use but quite the opposite.

While inventories are a blunt tool for measuring production in some ways, Overton et al. have shown that a considerable amount can still be done with them. First is the issue of what counts as a productive activity and how it reveals itself through the inventories. Households could generate income through certain activities, such as the extension of credit or renting out of property, which are hard to view as productive activities in the sense that is implied by the industrious revolution, with its emphasis on the allocation of labour. For the purposes of this analysis, production activities are classed under the following headings: agricultural production, proto-industrial production, artisan production, provision of goods and services, retailing, professional services and food production for use. Agricultural production was usually indicated by ownership of land or of agricultural tools. Livestock was rarely found in the absence of either land or tools, except in the case of mules, donkeys or horses for transport. These instances are not included here, but one case of sheep owned on a sharecropping basis and pastured on someone else's land is, as are two cases of poultry ownership. Proto-industrial production was indicated by ownership of equipment such as looms and spinning-wheels. Artisan production included all types of crafts not covered by proto-industry, mostly building, carpentry and metalwork. In a few instances, households were counted twice if there was evidence of more than one craft. Provision of goods and services included transport (muleteers and carters), food on a commercial scale, that is, by bakers and butchers, and clothing and shoes. Retailing covered all cases of commercial activity by merchants, shopkeepers and the like, but also retail activities as a by-employment. In other words, a cobbler selling his shoes was counted under goods and services only, but a smallholder running an inn was counted under both agriculture and retailing. Professional services included doctors, notaries and the like, where professional activity was usually evidenced by ownership of books. Finally, food production for use was indicated by ownership of equipment for bread-making, wine-making, distilling spirits or preserving meat. References to sums of money invested in any of these activities were also counted as indicative of production.

The Igualada inventories nearly always give the occupations of the deceased or the deceased's husband, unlike English inventories.[2] The occupation given on the inventory was, by itself, not sufficient as evidence of production: tools or other goods relating to that occupation also had to be present. Insisting on positive evidence of productive activities in this way allows for discussion of the extent to which households continued to own the means of production or not, a question largely absent from other studies.

The findings presented in this chapter and the next are based on the sample of 522 inventories *post mortem* used to examine landholdings in Chapter 2. They represent all the inventories found in the archives that appeared to be both complete and legible. There were undoubtedly more that have either not survived or have not yet been located, since the chronological coverage of the sample is not even. There are very few inventories in the Igualada archives for the 1720s and 1730s.[3] The key feature to be stressed is that these inventories represent a very small fraction of the total population. There were 8,030 adult burials in Igualada between 1680 and 1819. The inventory sample thus covers about 6.5 per cent of adult burials, compared with 8–9 per cent in other Catalan studies.[4] The number of inventories also does not keep step with population growth, instead continuing to fluctuate around 40–50 per decade from the 1740s onwards.

Ages could be calculated for 152 cases through links to the family reconstitution. The average age was 53.8 years for all inventories, 53.6 for men and 56.6 for women. While the biggest concentration of inventories was to be found in the age groups 50–9 and 60–9, there was a reasonable spread across the life cycle between the ages of 30 and 80. Unsurprisingly, only nine individuals were under 30. If households might be expected to be at the peak of productive activity when the household head was in his or her forties, the average age of the inventoried population was thus fairly close to this. In terms of occupations

---

[2]   Only two inventories of men had no occupation, compared with almost half the Cornwall and Kent inventories (Overton et al., *Production and Consumption*, p. 34).

[3]   Papers seem to be missing for at least one notary, Vicens Cots.

[4]   Moreno, *Consum i condicions de vida*, p. 13.

Table 5.1   Productive activities recorded in inventories

	1680–1754		1755–1829	
	N	%	N	%
Agriculture	145	84.8	278	79.2
Proto-industry	50	29.2	150	42.7
Crafts	39	22.8	74	21.1
Provision of food, clothing or transport	13	7.6	54	15.4
Retailing	21	12.3	44	12.5
Professional activities	12	7.0	24	6.8
Food production for use	136	79.5	291	82.9

covered, the inventories are reasonably representative. The liberal professions and merchants are overrepresented in the inventory sample relative to their weight among the overall population of household heads given in the *cadastres*.[5] This overrepresentation reflects not just the greater wealth and status of this group, but also the presence of priests, who are not recorded in most *cadastres*. Conversely, 'weaver' was the most frequent occupation by 1824, with 188 households (11 per cent), yet there are only 28 (5.7 per cent) inventories of weavers and the widows of weavers for the entire 150 year period.

Forms of production

Table 5.1 shows how many households had evidence of the productive activities listed above, also expressed as a percentage of all inventoried households. They show little change over time in the types of activities in which households were engaged, with the exception of proto-industry and goods and services. The majority of households were engaged in agricultural or viticultural production of some kind and in food production for use. Other activities, as discussed below, were mainly practised in accordance with the designated occupation in the inventory. The increase in households with evidence of clothing, food provision or transport, subsumed here under goods and services, is simply a reflection of the growth of this group within the population as a whole. No inventory had evidence of such activities being practised alongside a different designated occupation. By contrast, the increase in proto-industrial activity is the result of households other than those headed by individuals with textile occupations taking it up. Of the 200 households with evidence of proto-industrial production in their inventories, only 91 (45.5 per cent) had textile occupations in the inventory header.

Table 5.2 gives a classification of inventories according to the number of productive activities recorded in each, in an attempt to assess whether there was

---

    [5] For occupations in the *cadastres*, see Marfany, 'Proto-Industrialisation and Demographic Change', pp. 68–77.

Table 5.2 Number of productive activities in inventories

Activities	1690–1759		1760–1829	
	Inventories	%	Inventories	%
0	9	5.3	7	2.0
1	18	10.5	38	10.8
2	53	31.0	107	30.5
3	71	41.5	142	40.5
4	20	11.7	49	14.0
5	0	0.0	8	2.3
Total	171		351	

a decline in by-employments as de Vries's model of the industrious revolution would predict. What is striking is how little change there was over time. Most households continued to practise two or three activities throughout, with a mean of 2.5 and mode of 3. Since productive activities for most households included some form of food provisioning, as discussed below, the picture is essentially one of dual economy households. There is a very slight increase in the later period in the number of households that appear to be diversifying their activities, mainly through some form of retailing or commercial investment, but otherwise there is little sign of either the specialisation of production suggested by de Vries or the entrepreneurial behaviour found by Overton et al. in their Kent study.[6]

The more important questions to answer, however, are how, on what scale and in what combinations these activities were being practised. As Overton et al. point out, there is a considerable difference between the weaver with a smallholding, for whom by-employments were a form of risk-avoidance and highly seasonal, and the more entrepreneurial farmer or craftsman who sought to increase his income through diversifying into other areas.

Agriculture and viticulture

In terms of agricultural or viticultural production, the main difference in terms of scale was how much land households held. Other indications are provided by ownership of livestock, which could offer commercial possibilities, self-provisioning or, in the case of mules and oxen, freedom from the constraints of interlocking markets discussed in Chapter 2. Chapter 2 has shown that most holdings were below the 10 *jornals* or 5 hectares considered the minimum for subsistence and that few owned much livestock, but what that meant in practice needs further examination.

To start with the biggest landowners: the small group of 20 who held more than 50 *jornals*. The difficulty here is knowing how far this group was still involved in direct cultivation. With one exception, all had a combination of one or more *masos*

---

[6] Overton et al., *Production and Consumption*, pp. 65–78, esp. table 4.5 (p. 76).

and several small plots. The *masos* were cultivated by tenant farmers, though no inventory states if on a sharecropping contract or for fixed rent. For the small plots, inventories never state that these are farmed directly, with or without hired labour, and only sometimes that they have been ceded on *subestabliments* such as *rabassa morta* contracts. Where nothing is mentioned about cultivation, the plots may still have been cultivated by others. The inventory of Anton Riera Roger, for example, does not mention the tenure of any of his 77.25 *jornals*, but does record that some of the wine stored in his cellar belonged to his sharecropper (*parcer*) Rafel Valls.[7]

Similarly, six households recorded neither ploughs nor livestock, suggesting that their land was cultivated by others. Some households had tools and ploughs, not always in combination with draught animals, but may simply have loaned these to cultivators, rather than using them themselves. Only two, Josep Anton Fàbregas, the calico manufacturer described in the Introduction and Josep Anton Lladó, the clothier described in Chapter 3, kept livestock (sheep and goats) on a commercial scale. Fàbregas owned grazing rights on another family's *mas*. In short, this group had mostly a *rentier* relationship to the land. Certainly none of them described themselves as *pagesos*. Most belonged to the category of professionals and minor nobility, with a few merchants and clothiers or cotton manufacturers. This is a marked contrast to the Penedès district, where 56 of the 75 households owning one or more *masos* in Moreno's sample from 1770–90 were described as *pagesos*.[8]

The relationship to the land begins to be more mixed in the next group, those owning between 10 and 50 *jornals*. At the upper end of the scale were eight owners of *masos*. At the other end, there was one *rabassaire*, Pere Borràs, whose 12 *jornals* included two held *a rabassa morta*. In between were various combinations of small to middling plots. While some of these were still ceded to other cultivators through different forms of *subestabliment*, there are more indications here of direct cultivation. To begin with, ten of this group were described as *pagesos*. Nearly two thirds (62 per cent), owned tools, including 35 with ploughing equipment, and nearly half (40) owned livestock. Four had sheep, goats and pigs on a commercial scale. Self-sufficiency, however, is hard to assess: holdings may have been large enough to produce sufficient foodstuffs and, in some cases, to surpass the labour capacities of the family unit, as evidenced by the concessions to other cultivators, but the absence of tools and livestock in many of these inventories is difficult to interpret. There is no relationship between size of holding and absence of livestock or tools. For some larger landowners who had ceded some land to other cultivators, the assumption is that they were not cultivating their own land directly. At the other end of the scale, however, this lack suggests a dependence upon hiring or borrowing similar to that of smaller cultivators.

---

[7]   ANI 661, fos 17–30.

[8]   B. Moreno, 'Pautas de consumo y diferenciación social en la Catalunya preindustrial' (PhD, European University Institute, Florence, 2002), my calculation from table 3.7 (p. 185); see also id., *Consum i condicions de vida*, pp. 62–73. It is clear that continued use of the label *pagès* here indicates owner-occupation.

Below the threshold of self-sufficiency, conditions still varied considerably. Between 5 and 10 *jornals*, there were still plots conceded to other cultivators, suggesting that even at this level, holdings could outstrip the labour capacity of the family. For the first time, however, such concessions were outnumbered by those holding land through *subestabliments*, mainly *rabassa morta* contracts (12 in total). There were still two cases of commercial livestock farming, both with sheep, and, on a more modest scale, three cases of poultry, goats and pigs in numbers that would allow for some production for exchange. Fourteen still owned ploughs, but fully a third had neither tools nor livestock

Below 5 *jornals*, however, there was no question of holdings being too great and ownership of land was more precarious still. Among the most numerous group of landowners, those with between 2 and 5 *jornals*, the only two cases where land may have been conceded to other cultivators are inventories of women. By contrast, there were nineteen *rabassaires* in this group, another two with land ceded by *establiment*, three with other types of sharecropping or fixed rent contract and four whose land was mortgaged. There were 12 ploughs and one individual with a flock of 60 sheep, but otherwise livestock consisted of mules, poultry and two cases of bee-keeping. In 41 per cent of cases, no livestock or tools were recorded, suggesting these households were subjected to interlocking markets.

Finally, the small group with plots of under 2 *jornals* are interesting, given that their holdings were below even the average dimensions of a single plot. The obvious assumption might be that these plots were *horts* (vegetable plots) and that these households were therefore no more than the equivalent of English cottagers. In fact, only one of the plots was an *hort*. One plot was planted with cereals, one with vines and olive trees and the remainder were vineyards. Seven of the 29 were *rabassaires*. Only one had a plough, and 16 (55 per cent) had neither livestock nor tools. Clearly nearly all were reliant on hiring or borrowing draught animals and tools to cultivate their land, yet even such miniscule plots could be a worthwhile part of an 'economy of makeshifts'.

The question of what access to land meant in the overall context of the household economy will be returned to below. From the above description, what becomes clear is that self-sufficiency is hard to gauge. The situation of households varied enormously with regard to investment in livestock and tools. While there was clearly some correlation between size of holdings and the presence in inventories of livestock and tools, especially ploughs, the relationship is by no means straightforward. Larger landowners might choose to place the obligation to provide tools and livestock firmly upon the cultivators, whereas for smaller landowners, the need to borrow or hire these could be another example of the way in which cultivators could be trapped in interlocking markets.

What is clear is that households were specialising in one way, by choosing to focus on viticulture. As discussed in Chapter 2, it is unclear what the real extent of cereal production was, given the ambiguity as to whether grain was sown alongside vines or not. Nonetheless, it is clear that many cultivators were dependent upon markets for their own foodstuffs, an issue further explored below. Unsurprisingly, few households saw commercial livestock farming as a worthwhile investment, given the lack of sufficient grazing in Igualada itself. All who did own livestock had it pastured elsewhere under the care of other households, and nearly half (5 out of 11) were clustered in the years up to and including 1710.

Proto-industry

Setting aside food production for the time being, proto-industry was the next most important productive activity after agriculture. As mentioned above, it was the activity that showed the most spectacular increase and an increase that went beyond the growth of the sector in terms of occupations of household heads. Table 5.3 shows to which occupational sector households with evidence of proto-industrial production belonged. There was no occupational group that did not have members engaged in proto-industrial production, and the extent to which households in different occupational sectors were involved in such production was fairly similar, around a third in most cases. The exceptions to this were textile households, unsurprisingly, with almost three-quarters of inventories recording textile equipment or other evidence of production, leatherwork and the provision of goods and services. In the case of leather, the highly specialised and relatively capital-intensive nature of production may have excluded or discouraged investment in other activities, with the exception of land. Certainly, inventories of leather producers never recorded evidence of any other craft, and there were only four instances of retailing activity in this group. In the case of goods and services, the low proportion may be an underestimate resulting from caution when it came to classing the equipment of tailors, haberdashers and the like as proto-industrial equipment.

A more important question is the scale and nature of production undertaken by these households. Chapter 3 has already shown that production among those with textile occupations was small-scale and has highlighted the differences among clothiers, on the one hand, and between clothiers and weavers, on the other. The expectation would be that production would be equally small-scale if not smaller among those households for which proto-industrial production was clearly a by-employment.

The figures confirm this expectation. The majority, 84 or 77 per cent of the 109 households in Table 5.3 that were not headed by someone with a textile occupation had evidence of spinning. In all but six of these, spinning was the only activity. Most households had only one or two spinning wheels or other spinning equipment. Only six households not headed by someone with a textile occupation were engaged in weaving, but on a larger scale than spinning, with 24 looms amongst them. Unsurprisingly, only four households with non-textile occupations had invested in machinery for spinning or carding. These cases of more substantial investment were all limited to the later decades of the period and to cotton. They are included in Table 3.5 and show combinations of spinning, weaving and other stages of manufacture under one roof. The picture is therefore one of a tiny group

Table 5.3   Households with evidence of proto-industry

Occupational sector	Number	Percentage of households with proto-industrial production	Percentage of households in sector
Textile	91	45.5	74.0
Agriculture	22	11.0	29.3
Professionals	18	9.0	34.0
Commerce	13	6.5	31.0
Leather	9	4.5	16.1
Goods and services	23	11.5	24.2
Crafts	20	10.0	30.3
Other	4	2.0	33.3
Total	200		

of households that invested in cotton in a more entrepreneurial fashion, set against the vast majority that were engaged solely in spinning and for whom therefore this was almost certainly women's work, done alongside other activities, including agricultural or viticultural production.

Other activities

There is little that needs to be said about other types of artisan activity, including the provision of goods and services or what I have here termed professional activities: medicine, legal services and the like. The latter were practised exclusively by those with designated professional occupations in their inventories. In the case of doctors of law, as opposed to notaries, it is questionable how far they made any kind of an income from legal activities, rather than simply living off land, money lending and commercial investment. The most that can be said is that they all owned law books. Similarly, evidence of craft production was rarely found in inventories without the corresponding occupation mentioned. There were only eight cases where households had goods relating to a form of artisan production other than that given, and four of these were more in the form of commercial investment: two owned tanneries, possibly rented out, and another two had workshops for manufacturing soap. In the other four cases, the goods were possibly inherited or belonged to another member of the household. Given continued guild restrictions on access to most crafts, it is unsurprising that crafts were rarely found as a by-employment. The type of crafts most commonly practised varied little over the period: clothing and footwear, building, woodwork and metalwork, with leatherwork as a more specialised local sector.

Retailing or some other form of commercial investment was slightly more common as a by-employment, especially among the few instances of households with evidence of four or five productive activities. Twenty-three households had evidence of retailing or commercial investment alongside other activities. Sixteen of these were engaged in forms of food provisioning, including three inn-keepers, but all on a fairly modest scale. In some cases, such provisioning did not go beyond a market stall. Three had purchased municipal rights to the sale or provisioning of either grain or meat. Of the others, one sold iron and another had invested in a company selling wool and cloths. Only two recorded investments in overseas trade. Pere Regordosa, a haberdasher by trade, had modest shares in a boat with the captain, Josep Parés of Sitges.[9] Josep Cendra, a cloth manufacturer, had invested in a company that purchased cocoa.[10] As far as can be judged, small-scale retailing was the norm even among those who described themselves as merchants. The 15 whose inventories included details of the money owed to them were trading on a small scale both in terms of the volume of credit and the geographical range of their creditors. Josep Riera's 27,775 *lliures* worth of credit was made up entirely of small sums of under 10 *lliures* owed to him by households in Igualada and the surrounding villages.[11] All the other merchants and shopkeepers for whom credits were listed had under 15,000 *lliures* in total.

Finally, despite the slight increase noted here in food retailing, most households were not following the pattern suggested by de Vries and others of reducing the time spent on self-provisioning of foodstuffs in order to increase time on other activities. In his study of a French proto-industrial region, the Perche Ornais, Claude Cailly found that it was the richest and poorest groups that showed most evidence of purchasing foodstuffs from the market, with the obvious difference being that the latter group did so out of necessity, the former out of choice.[12] In Igualada, however, it was the richer households that showed most evidence of food production, at least in terms of having equipment to process certain foods. Wine-making has already been discussed in Chapter 2. Similarly, only 47 households (0.9 per cent) had equipment for curing meat. There are no references to dairy products at all. The only food-related equipment possessed by the majority of households was for making bread. Baking at home appears to have been extremely rare in Igualada: almost all households, regardless of status, relied on municipal ovens or took their dough to a baker, but 80 per cent of the inventory sample had equipment and often designated rooms for making the dough, with no change in this proportion throughout the period. Absence of equipment for making bread does not seem to correlate with poverty in the inventories.

Equipment, though, can only tell us about food processing. It cannot tell us if the ingredients were still home produced. In the case of meat, only 11 inventoried households owned pigs and 35 poultry or rabbits, as shown in Table 2.4. All of

---

[9]   ANI 454, fos 61r–72r.

[10]   ANI 646, unfol.

[11]   ACA, NI 791, unfol.

[12]   C. Cailly, 'Structure sociale et consommation dans le monde proto-industriel rural textile: le cas du Perche Ornais au XVIIIe siècle', *Revue d'histoire moderne et contemporaine*, 45 (1998), pp. 746–74; see also Aymard, 'Autoconsommation et marchés'.

these were better-off households. The remainder, if they were consuming meat at all, had to be purchasing it from the market. In the case of staples such as grain and wine, particularly the former, an increasing number of households would have had to resort to the market to meet some if not all of their needs, as discussed above and in Chapter 2. The difference between Igualada and the Perche Ornais, however, is that richer households in Igualada, rather than choosing to purchase foodstuffs, were able to avoid markets by extracting grain and wine from their tenants and sharecroppers instead. The next chapter will also consider the extent to which households chose to buy ready-made clothing, as opposed to making their own.

Time allocation, women's work and proletarianisation

Combining production activities

More important perhaps than the scale of production to assessing the extent of an 'industrious revolution' is the time allocated by households or individual members of households to different activities and the implications for the household economy of combining certain activities. While proto-industry was a source of income for all types of family economy, what is significant is the extent to which it was combined with landholding. Of the 200 households with evidence of proto-industrial production, 156 (78 per cent) had land. A further 16 had other evidence of agricultural production in the form of tools. As discussed in previous chapters, while there is no clear relationship between the type of landholding and agriculture in a given area, on the one hand, and the emergence of proto-industry in that same area, on the other, there is nonetheless usually a direct correlation between some measure of land-poverty and proto-industry. Indeed, the small size of holdings in this area, as elsewhere in the Catalan viticulture zone, made some form of alternative employment a necessity for the family economy. Josep Colomé has estimated the monetary outputs that would be yielded by a plot of land of fewer than 5 hectares in the nineteenth century and has concluded that families with holdings of such a size would not be able to cover more than 20 per cent of their reproduction costs, leaving aside savings and such extra payments as dowries.[13] At the same time, he estimates that, except perhaps during the vine harvest, such holdings would not occupy even one man full-time, let alone an entire family. Even assuming higher outputs than Colomé's, the combination of proto-industry with smallholdings is still noticeable.[14] While proto-industry

---

[13]   J. Colomé, 'Pequeña explotación agrícola, reproducción de las unidades familiares campesinas y mercado de trabajo en la viticultura mediterránea del siglo XIX: el caso catalán', *Revista de historia económica*, 8 (2000), pp. 281–307.

[14]   Deyá also finds a greater concentration of proto-industry, including more looms per weaver, in viticultural areas of Majorca ('La industria rural textil', pp. 22–4).

was to be found across the entire hierarchy of landowning, 40 per cent of those households with under 10 *jornals*, the supposed threshold for subsistence, were engaged in proto-industry, as were 43 per cent of the 35 *rabassaires*. Given that households with smaller holdings, especially *rabassaires*, are underrepresented in the inventory sample, these figures are certainly an underestimate. As discussed in Chapter 2, proto-industry may have facilitated the emergence of a rural proletariat, evidenced by the fact that nearly a third (30 per cent) of those households with no land recorded in inventories were engaged in proto-industry, a much higher proportion than that for other activities, with the exception of agricultural labour (as evidenced by tools), which accounted for 32 per cent of these inventories. More typical, however, at least within the inventory sample, was the attempt to combine both. The holdings of households with evidence of proto-industry were actually slightly larger than for those with no evidence of such activity. The mean size for the former was 14.7 *jornals*, the median size 6 *jornals* and the mode 4 *jornals*, compared with equivalent figures for non-proto-industrial households of 12.5, 4.5 and 2 *jornals* respectively. The average figures among proto-industrial households, though, mask huge variation. While cloth and cotton manufacturers had mean holdings of 27.3 *jornals*, clothiers had a mean size of 9.4 and weavers only 2.6 *jornals*.

Proto-industry in Catalonia was thus essential to ensuring the survival of households with insufficient land, though, as discussed in previous chapters, both commercial viticulture and proto-industry also enabled many Catalans to participate in markets in new ways. In this regard, the Catalan pattern appears more dynamic than the 'commercial-survival economy' of inland Flanders, where proto-industry was more of a 'safety-first' response to the relentless sub-division of existing holdings.[15] As mentioned in Chapter 3, Pat Hudson and others have suggested that the eighteenth-century woollen proto-industry could remain competitive with the factory for a long time, since artisans were protected by landholdings from the volatility of the trade cycle in a way that factories, with higher overhead costs, could not be. It was thus landholding that enabled the flexibility and adaptability of the family economy that in turn made proto-industrial production viable.

While the flexibility of the workforce often enabled proto-industry to survive better, it required a similar flexibility on the part of the manufacturers who employed such workers. As Marta Vicente and Albert Garcia have shown, early attempts by Barcelona cotton manufacturers to set up centralised spinning manufactures soon encountered difficulties in imposing factory discipline on their mainly female workforce, as women moved in and out of the factories according to the needs of the family economy and the possibilities of alternative employment.[16] The manufacturers either had to adapt their factories to artisan

---

[15]   Thoen, '"Commercial Survival Economy"'.

[16]   M.V. Vicente, 'Artisans and Work in a Barcelona Cotton Factory (1770–1816)', *International Review of Social History*, 45 (2000), pp. 1–23; Garcia Balañà, *La fabricació de la fabrica*, pp. 166–89.

working patterns, mainly by assigning irregular work to women, or abandon centralised production altogether.[17] With many of the small-scale concerns founded subsequently, the distinction between domestic and centralised was blurred. Many small manufactures essentially used the labour of an extended family and even the larger concerns relied on the recruitment of family labour: thus, mule-jenny spinners recruited their own sons and daughters as auxiliaries, and factory managers brought in family members.[18] While no documentation has been uncovered that would permit a similar analysis of the use of family labour in the Igualada cotton industry, the ratio described in Chapter 3 of four spinners or three weavers to manufacturer, often fewer, suggests a unit of production that need not have extended much beyond the family. The same patterns of flexible employment found for elsewhere in Catalonia were thus almost certainly a feature of the Igualada economy.

Flexibility was undoubtedly easier within extended families, despite de Vries's reluctance to see the extended family as dynamic. Though hard to test, it is reasonable to suppose that the more members a household could call upon, the easier it would be to allocate labour optimally across the whole range of activities. Moreover, keeping the family as the core of the production unit, whether in viticulture or proto-industry, provided incentives for discipline and maximisation of output. Such is the claim made for Asian households, for example, while Italian historians have seen 'the richness of relations' within extended family groups as 'a flexible structure even in the most difficult situations'.[19]

Underlying this flexibility and discipline, however, was the 'self-exploitation mechanism of the proto-industrial family economy compared with the greater rigidities of wage labour', a mechanism that was the key to the persistence of the household as unit of production and, in turn, to the persistence of proto-industry.[20] Given both the vagaries of proto-industrial production for distant, unpredictable markets and the cyclical nature of wine prices, self-exploitation was the only way in which many families could hope to survive. The small-scale nature of production was both a blessing and a curse: it allowed easy access to land and to industry, but offered little margin of protection against a fall in demand for

[17]   Similar problems and solutions have been described for other European regions (see P. Caspard, 'The Calico Painters of Estavayer: Employers' Strategies Toward the Market for Women's Labour', in D.M. Hafter (ed.), *European Women and Preindustrial Craft* (Bloomington, 1995), pp. 108–36; S.D. Chapman and S. Chassagne, *European Textile Printers in the Eighteenth Century: A Study of Peel and Oberkampf* (London, 1981), pp. 171–82.

[18]   Garcia Balañà, *La fabricació de la fabrica*, pp. 199–200, 380–97.

[19]   Sugihara, 'The East Asian Path of Economic Development', pp. 86–8; M. Breschi, R. Derosas and M. Manfredini, 'Mortality and Environment in Three Emilian, Tuscan and Venetian Communities, 1800–1883', in Bengtsson, Campbell and Lee, *Life Under Pressure*, pp. 209–51 (pp. 240–2).

[20]   Hudson, *The Genesis of Industrial Capital*, pp. 73–4.

products. The vulnerability of many households is clear from the example of Joan Badia, a calico weaver, whose single vineyard, only 1 *jornal* in dimension, was to be sold at public auction to pay his debts and those of his parents.[21] Similarly, the family of Joan Soler, a cotton weaver, had already mortgaged their shares of the crops from the 2 *jornals* they held on a *rabassa morta* contract.[22]

Labour intensification

Self-exploitation is key to the greater industriousness evident in eighteenth-century Catalonia. Quantifying the length of the working day or the number of days worked over the course of the year is impossible.[23] There is, however, considerable anecdotal evidence of longer working hours. Edicts against shops staying open on Sundays and feast days, such as that issued by the authorities in Barcelona in 1785, were not new in the eighteenth century.[24] What was new was a growing number of voices arguing in favour of greater industriousness, including calls to reduce the number of religious feast days as a spur to greater industry, though it seems that in practice, working on Sundays and religious holidays was already often tolerated.[25] Arthur Young was surprised, on attending mass at Calaf, 'to see great numbers of men going out of the town with their reap hooks to cut their corn, the same as on any other day; this must be with the leave of their priests, and to give that leave argues a liberality I had not been taught to expect'.[26] Navarro-Mas comments approvingly that, in the Barcelona area, people 'were more likely to sin by working on holidays than by not working on weekdays'.[27] In Igualada, the parish priest, Francisco Davesa, left money in his will for 270 masses a year which, winter and summer alike, were to be held before sunrise, so that labourers and artisans could attend mass without missing any working time.[28] According to Gálvez's reply to Zamora, 'there are few days on which people do not work' and 'no man, woman or child is idle at any time of year'.[29] The replies

---

[21]   ANI 603, fo. 522v.

[22]   ANI 668, fos 87r–88r.

[23]   Too few accounts specify numbers of days worked in a year for changes to be identified.

[24]   R. d'Amat i de Cortada (Baró de Maldà), *Calaix de sastre (1769–1819)*, ed. R. Boixareu (11 vols, Barcelona, 1987–2005), vol. 1, pp. 171, 152.

[25]   On transferring certain feast days to Sundays, see e.g. M. Barba i Roca, *El corregiment i partit de Vilafranca del Penedès a l'últim terç del segle XVIII* (Vilafranca del Penedès, 1991), p. 82.

[26]   Young, 'Tour in Catalonia', p. 227.

[27]   J. Navarro-Mas, 'Respuesta al interrogatorio del sr. D. Francisco de Zamora por lo concerniente al corregimiento de Barcelona'; repr. in Zamora, *Diario de los viajes hechos por Cataluña*, pp. 462–3.

[28]   ACA, NI 825, fos 140r–149r.

[29]   Torras Ribé, *La comarca de l'Anoia*, pp. 365–6.

from the surrounding villages were more eloquent on this score: 'All work until they can work no more in order to earn their bread, and none are idle', 'the only custom is to work and eat'.[30]

Women's work

This greater industriousness in the form of self-exploitation was arguably most evident in women's work. It has long been recognised that women's work in the past was central to the household economy and therefore to the economy as a whole. This recognition does not, however, imply any consensus on the meanings that should be attached to women's work. Some historians have claimed that the domestic location and supposedly unskilled nature of proto-industry allowed for higher participation rates by married women in particular, though the absence of apprenticeships facilitated entry for all women.[31] At the same time, the additional earnings provided by proto-industry are claimed to have enhanced women's status within the household and increased their power as consumers.

The underlying assumptions behind these claims are that skill was conferred only through formal guild training and thus could not be acquired by women and that women's participation in labour markets was constrained above all by reproductive demands. Neither assumption has much basis in fact. As Sheilagh Ogilvie has pointed out, the most powerful argument against the importance of apprenticeships in conferring skill is that guilds allowed widows to continue running their husbands' workshops, thereby tacitly conceding that skills could be acquired through on the job training.[32] Similarly, while reproductive demands undoubtedly could be a constraint, many European women were not subject to this constraint for much or often all of their working lives, given relatively late ages at marriage and high celibacy rates. Moreover, the extent to which reproductive demands constrained women's work varied and certainly did not preclude women working outside the home. The type and location of the work done by women was determined by numerous factors, of which reproduction was only one and arguably one that was less important than institutional constraints. As discussed in the Introduction, de Vries claimed that the greater freedom enjoyed by women in northern Europe, particularly within the nuclear family system, allowed for greater female participation rates in the labour market. There is little evidence, however, to suggest that particular family forms were more restrictive of female labour allocation than others. Richard Wall finds no association between family forms and the allocation of married women's time, while Ogilvie points out that the predominance of the nuclear family and a European marriage pattern in early

---

[30] Ibid., pp. 517–18, 520–21 (Òdena), p. 522 (Vilanova del Camí).

[31] Kriedte, Medick and Schlumbohm, *Industrialization before Industrialization*, pp. 61–2.

[32] Ogilvie, *Bitter Living*, p. 232.

modern Württemberg did little to enhance female labour force participation in the face of severe opposition from guilds and community authorities.[33] It seems more reasonable, in fact, to suggest that the causal relationship was the reverse: late female marriage in northern Europe was sustainable because of a high demand, in certain periods at least, for female labour.[34]

Quantifying female participation in different types of work is next to impossible in the case of Igualada. The response to a particularly leading question from Zamora on women's work describes women as occupied in much the same activities that were considered typically female for other areas of Europe:

> In this region women work in the fields at the tasks suitable for their sex, such as digging, weeding and pruning vines, harvesting grapes and picking mulberry leaves for silk worms, and similar tasks. They also collect and sell wood in Igualada, and food, such as vegetables, fresh and dried fruit, furred and feathered game, hens, chickens, turkeys and pigeons, eggs and mushrooms when in season. They also card cotton and wool, twist yarn, knit stockings, make lace, sew, spin and other womanly tasks.[35]

Women are also occasionally visible as servants and as wet nurses. In the household listing of 1716, there were 65 female domestic servants, of whom 50 were unmarried, with a mean age of 19.4 years, and 13 were widowed, with a mean age of 46.7 years.[36] References to wet nurses appear in 205 burials of foundlings put out to nurse in Igualada by the Barcelona hospital.[37] Otherwise, there are occasional references to women working in retail, food provisioning and as artisans, references which are too scattered to provide a systematic breakdown of women's work patterns, yet which nonetheless confirm the diversity of women's

---

[33]   Richard Wall, 'The Contribution of Married Women to the Family Economy Under Different Family Systems: Some Examples from the Mid-Nineteenth Century from the Work of Frédéric Le Play', in A. Fauve-Chamoux and S. Sogner (eds), *Socio-Economic Consequences of Sex-Ratios in Historical Perspective, 1500–1900* (Milan, 1994), pp. 139–48; Ogilvie, *Bitter Living*, pp. 40–9.

[34]   Richard M. Smith, 'Women's Work and Marriage in Pre-Industrial England: Some Speculations', in S. Cavaciocchi (ed.), *La donna nell'economia secc. XIII–XVIII* (Prato, 1990), pp. 31–55; id., 'Relative Prices, Forms of Agrarian Labour and Female Marriage Patterns in England, 1350–1800', in Devos and Kennedy (eds), *Marriage and Rural Economy*, pp. 19–48; Moor and van Zanden, 'Girl Power', pp. 11–16.

[35]   Torras Ribé, *La comarca de l'Anoia*, p. 352 (response to q. 115). Rather than simply asking what work women do, the question asks if women work at the tasks listed in the answer. For similar replies from elsewhere in Catalonia, see Barba i Roca, *El corregiment i partit de Vilafranca del Penedès*, p. 67; R. Serra and L. Ferrer, 'Un questionari de Francisco de Zamora (1789)', *Estudis d'història agrària*, 5 (1985), pp. 190–91; Navarro-Mas, 'Respuesta al interrogatorio del sr. D. Francisco de Zamora', p. 446.

[36]   API, *caixa* 4, 'Respostas a Patiño'; two with marital status unknown.

[37]   See Marfany, 'Proto-Industrialisation and Demographic Change', pp. 216–20.

work. The sector in which women are most visible and for which some figures are occasionally given, is the textile industry. As discussed in Chapter 3, in 1820 the cotton industry in Igualada employed 1,886 women and 60 children. The majority (75 per cent) of the women were spinners, the remainder worked in auxiliary tasks alongside male weavers.

The reasons for and significance of such a strong female presence in proto-industry, here as elsewhere in Europe, are difficult to assess. Arguments about the relative ease of entry due to the lack of formal training required should not be taken at face value. It is true that there were no formal barriers to women spinning, but this does not mean that spinning was any less skilled than weaving.[38] It is also clear that women could acquire skills without formal training. In response to a royal declaration that schools to teach spinning be set up wherever seemed appropriate, the Junta de Comerç carried out a survey in 1786 of various locations to see if the idea would be welcome.[39] The reply from Igualada is the longest of those preserved in the documents. As in most places, a school was considered unnecessary, expensive and unworkable, given how dispersed spinning was.[40] Skill was not considered an issue: the authorities were explicit that most spinners were extremely able and that skills were easily transmitted to young girls by experienced spinners. Similarly, the Real Companyia de Filats was happy to employ women among its agents (filadors) when attempting to put cotton spinning out to rural areas in the 1780s.[41] More importantly, despite guild restrictions, women could also learn to weave to at least the same standards as men. According to Zamora, some women in Sant Joan de les Abadesses and Centelles worked as woollen weavers, in the latter place earning the same wages as men and sometimes even double, since 'they break fewer threads and weave them with more care and evenness'.[42]

On closer examination, arguments about skill are usually masking arguments about control. Just as clothiers and weavers used perceptions of skill as a weapon in their struggles for control over production, so male textile workers used perceptions of skill when arguing for and against the exclusion of women from their activities. In 1758, for example, the woollen weavers of Igualada complained that clothiers were allowing women to weave, despite their lack of skill. In response, the clothiers argued that they employed women only under the supervision of male weavers, in the same way that the wives of weavers had always worked.[43]

---

[38]   Ogilvie, *Bitter Living*, pp. 297–8.

[39]   AHCB, FJC, vol. 80, fos 38–65; the response from Igualada is at fos 46–7.

[40]   Zamora records that existing schools in Olot were poorly attended because 'here every house is a school' (*Diario de los viajes hechos por Cataluña*, p. 77).

[41]   See the lists of *filadors* in BC, FEG, 56/7, 56/8, 56/9, 57/1, 57/2, 57/3.

[42]   Zamora, *Diario de los viajes hechos por Cataluña*, pp. 56 (Centelles), 85 (Sant Joan de les Abadesses). For female weavers elsewhere, see Gullickson, *Spinners and Weavers*, pp. 104–10.

[43]   Torras, 'Gremio, familia y cambio económico', p. 27 n. 45. Similar disputes are described for the Lyon silk industry in D. Hafter, 'Women who Wove in the Eighteenth-

Supervision of female work also lies behind contemporary emphasis on the domestic nature of proto-industrial work. While the *bergadana* received praise for the ease with which any mother could operate it in the midst of her domestic chores, what actually mattered was the confinement of women to the domestic sphere. Carmen Sarasúa has drawn attention to attempts by the Spanish state to control women's work by pushing them out of areas such as peddling and retailing.[44] Significantly, when contemporaries describe women spinning in groups and in public spaces outdoors, they voice suspicion as to how productive women could be under such circumstances.[45] More importantly, it should not be assumed that married women could only participate in domestic work. Numerous examples show that, when necessary, married women worked outside the home, in proto-industry as well as in other sectors.[46]

The most important question, however, regarding the household economy, is whether proto-industry offered higher wages than other tasks and whether these higher wages enhanced women's status. In the Catalan case, while it is impossible to say how textiles compared overall with other sectors, wages for carding and spinning cotton were two to three times higher than for wool, for both sexes. In 1784 the authorities of Monistrol de Montserrat sent a declaration to this effect to the Junta de Comerç.[47] Attached to it were a series of statements by various household heads, some in their own handwriting, stating what wages their families earned. Joseph Jané, his mother and sister had earned 13 *rals* carding and spinning wool; now, carding and spinning cotton, they earned 42 *rals*. Similar testimonies were provided by other households, in which female wages in spinning dominated. In promoting cotton, manufacturers made much of the earning potential of spinning for women of all ages, from 'ten-year old girls, pregnant women, lame and crippled women, and those of advanced age, provided they still had their sight and the use of their hands'.[48] Moreover, they argued, such earnings facilitated marriage,

---

Century Silk Industry of Lyon', in id. (ed.), *European Women and Pre-Industrial Craft* (Bloomington, 1995), pp. 42–64.

[44]   C. Sarasúa, 'The Role of the State in Shaping Women's and Men's Entrance into the Labour Market: Spain in the Eighteenth and Nineteenth Centuries', *Continuity and Change*, 12 (1997), pp. 341–71. For similar attempts to crack down on women peddlers in England, see Beverly Lemire, *Dress, Culture and Commerce: The English Clothing Trade Before the Factory, 1660–1800* (Basingstoke, 1997), pp. 99–104.

[45]   Zamora, *Diario de los viajes hechos por Cataluña* p. 77.

[46]   For Catalonia, see Vicente 'Artisans and Work'; for elsewhere, see Domínguez, *El campesino adaptativo*, pp. 81–92 (including work done not just outside the home, but as seasonal migrants); Chapman and Chassagne, *European Textile Printers*, pp. 171–82; Hafter, 'Women who Wove'; Caspard, 'The Calico Painters of Estavayer', p. 112. A quantitative analysis of the spatial patterns of women's work by Ogilvie shows that less than half of the work done by all women was domestic and only 51% of that done by married women (*Bitter Living*, pp. 146–9, 323).

[47]   AHCB, JC, 79, fos 161–2.

[48]   BC, FEG, 44/4 IV.

since women 'could now be partners in meeting the needs of their families'. For single women, spinning may well have been an alternative to domestic service, the other sector most open to them.[49] Certainly by the nineteenth century, there were comments in Igualada that, 'since this is a manufacturing town, maidservants are scarce and hard to find when needed'.[50] Spinning does not, unlike elsewhere in Europe, appear to have been sufficient to enable single women to live alone. The handful of independent spinsters that can be identified in Igualada had sources of income other than spinning. It is difficult to gauge whether wages from spinning enabled women to save a dowry more easily than before. The small number of marriage contracts that state women had earned dowries through work never specify the nature of the work, nor how many years the women had worked prior to marriage. In a couple of cases, however, women were given spinning machines as part of their dowries, suggesting these were seen as a worthwhile investment.

As shown in the previous chapter, ages at marriage in Igualada were early for women, compared with elsewhere in Europe, and thus most women spent most of their working lives as married women or widows, unlike elsewhere. What matters, therefore, is whether proto-industry offered better opportunities than other sectors for women to earn a living alongside the demands of running a household and reproduction. Although the contemporary comments reproduced here suggest that women could contribute more to the household through spinning, caution is required. Female earnings were clearly essential to keeping the household economy going and may have made it easier for households to survive with smaller landholdings, but as several historians rightly remind us, the value of women's earnings to the household should not blind us to how low such wages were and to how exploited such women were.[51] In Hufton's words, the 'married woman was the lowest cipher on the labour market, the least able to defend her own interests'.[52] Berg is sceptical that married women's labour productivity could ever have been high, suggesting that it was simply the sheer numbers of women and children available to work and the lowness of their wages that made them such an attractive labour force for proto-industry. It seems that if married women's labour was productive, this could only be at the expense of households and children. The most obvious example of this is Lyons, where Hafter has calculated that married women accounted for a third of production in silk-weaving, but only because they put their children out to nurse.[53] Igualada women were not doing so, but the previous chapter has shown they were spending less time on average breastfeeding their children.

---

[49]   For similar examples, see Ogilvie, *Bitter Living*, pp. 58–60.

[50]   AT, Isidro Torelló to Albert Combelles (10 Feb. 1820).

[51]   Maxine Berg, 'Women's Work, Mechanisation and the Early Phases of Industrialisation in England', in P. Joyce (ed.), *The Historical Meanings of Work* (Cambridge, 1987), pp. 64–98; Veyrassat, *Négociants et fabricants*, p. 44.

[52]   Hufton, *The Poor of Eighteenth-Century France*, p. 26.

[53]   Hafter, *European Women and Preindustrial Craft*, pp. 52–4.

Indeed, what evidence there is for allocation of time by women, in Igualada and elsewhere, points to increased time pressures and greater exploitation. One calculation for England suggests women might spend as much as 13 hours a day just doing domestic chores.[54] The discussion of food production above reveals no tendency for households to abandon bread-making: a task that is likely to have been women's work. Similarly, as mentioned in Chapter 2, keeping poultry and rabbits continued to be a feature of many household economies throughout the period. A municipal ban on collecting water before five in the morning reveals that women were queuing at the fountain at four o'clock in the morning.[55] In the responses to Zamora's questionnaire, Gálvez noted that local shepherds rarely combined watching flocks with other tasks, but shepherdesses were usually to be found spinning.[56] Francesc Papiol describes the women in Cañellas making brooms and ropes from palm leaves while walking behind donkeys laden with wood.[57] For him, it was 'a delight to see the most hard-working women and girls, who barely eat or who cook only the lightest of meals so as not to leave their work [lace-making], and even when breast-feeding, their fingers are still working'.[58] The Baró de Maldà describes his children's former wet-nurse cooking a meal for her visitors at the same time as breastfeeding her infant and giving instructions to the girls to whom she taught embroidery.[59] Zamora makes a special note on how industrious the women in the Vall d'Aran are, going so far as to describe them as 'slaves'.[60] In northern Spain, rare accounts show women working longer hours already than men at paid work and then presumably doing other unpaid chores on top.[61] Similar findings are reported for Japan.[62] There are numerous examples across Europe of the kind of female sociability described above, where women got together not to drink, play cards or gamble as their husbands did, but to share light and warmth while spinning, weaving or sewing, often well into the night.[63]

---

[54]   Weatherill, *Consumer Behaviour*, table 7.1 (p. 143); see also R. Sarti, *Europe at Home: Family and Material Culture 1500–1800* (New Haven, 2002), pp. 189–91.

[55]   AMI 114, *Registre municipal*, 1783, fos 74v–75r.

[56]   Torras Ribé, *La comarca de l'Anoia*, p. 347 (response to q. 86); Zamora himself notes shepherdesses spinning on more than one occasion (*Diario de los viajes hechos por Cataluña*, pp. 63, 67, 268).

[57]   F. Papiol, *Resposta de Francesc Papiol al qüestionari Zamora: Vilanova i la Geltrú, 1790* (Vilanova i la Geltrú, 1990), p. 42.

[58]   Ibid., p. 66.

[59]   Amat, *Calaix de sastre*, vol. 1, pp. 143–4.

[60]   Zamora, *Diario de los viajes hechos por Cataluña*, p. 194.

[61]   Domínguez, *El campesino adaptativo*, p. 40.

[62]   Osamu Saito, 'Gender, Workload and Agricultural Progress: Japan's Historical Experience in Perspective', in R. Leboutte (ed.), *Proto-industrialisation: Recherches récentes et nouvelles perspectives* (Geneva, 1996), pp. 129–51.

[63]   See Veyrassat, *Négociants et fabricants*, p. 47; Gullickson, *Spinners and Weavers* p. 152; Ogilvie, *Bitter Living*, pp. 284–5.

Proletarianisation in the family economy

Assessing the reality of production for most household economies but particularly for poorer ones is hampered not just by the absence of systematic information on women's work but also by the difficulty of capturing wage labour. Inventories only tend to record goods that were owned, not those that were rented or borrowed. In other words, the absence of goods relating to a particular activity cannot be taken as definitive proof that the activity was not practised in that household. It is thus impossible to gauge the full extent to which production may have become more specialised. Rather than abandoning some activities in order to concentrate on others, households may have increasingly been practising some or all activities from a position of wage dependency. Chapters 2 and 3 have already addressed the question of proletarianisation in the case of proto-industry and also on the land. One way in which proletarianisation can be assessed to a certain extent is by examining first, those inventories where no or only one productive activity could be seen and second, those that show no evidence of goods relating to the occupation mentioned in the inventory. In other words, how many individuals continue to describe themselves as smallholders (*pagesos*) without owning land or as artisans without owning tools?

There were 16 inventories of households labelled by Overton et al. as 'unproductive households', that is, households with no evidence of any kind of production. As with the English evidence, inventories of 'part households', that is, lodgers and the elderly living with kin, and of women dominate: 10 out of the 16 were inventories of goods owned by women, Seven were widows, one was a spinster, one was married and one was of uncertain marital status. The remaining six inventories show no clear pattern: one or two suggest poverty and proletarianisation, but the priest and doctor of law who appear in this category are more likely to represent 'part households' of the type described above.

The 56 households with only one productive activity recorded also lack any clear pattern. Again, 15 were of women's goods. In terms of occupations, the distribution matched that for the sample population as a whole: 16 or 28 per cent were textile occupations, 9 or 16 per cent in agriculture with very small percentages for other occupational groups. Merchants and shopkeepers were underrepresented with only two inventories, while professionals were overrepresented with 9 or 16 per cent, mostly due to the inventories of priests. Again, there was no clear correlation between single-activity households and poverty.

Better evidence of proletarianisation comes from comparing the occupation given in the inventory with the actual productive activities found in the inventory. This exercise of course assumes that all productive goods are equally likely to have been recorded, regardless of value. Such an assumption does not appear unreasonable in practice, with inventories recording even such things as needles in the case of tailors. In some areas, there is no sign of proletarianisation. All households headed by merchants and shopkeepers and by those in the food trades had evidence of commercial activity or food production of some kind. Similarly, all metalworkers owned tools. In other cases, the absence of evidence of goods relating to occupation reflects the particular nature of that occupation, as with the 17 inventories of priests, minor nobility and professionals. An absence of the means of production could also reflect a preference for other activities, such as land or commercial investment. In other cases, however, it was clearly combined with poverty, particularly among those who made clothing and footwear, especially hatters, among the four muleteers with no mules and in textiles. Thirty-two (26 per cent) of the textile households had no equipment for spinning, weaving or carding at all, but with the proportion being higher still for weavers (33 per cent). By contrast, it was relatively rare to describe oneself as a *pagès* without owning some land and the tools with which to cultivate it. Only in four inventories did this occupation appear without any evidence of agricultural production, and two of these were of women and another of a couple whose inventory was taken because they had left their lodgings without giving notice. In six more cases, inventories recorded no land but did include tools, so the individuals in question presumably worked entirely as agricultural labourers. For these households, the only other productive activity recorded, and not in all cases, was bread-making. Whatever other activities might have kept these households afloat were not captured by inventories.

Other evidence of proletarianisation is provided by a different source, the *cadastres* or tax listings already described in previous chapters. In this instance, the evidence is in the form of the different payments made by adult males for the poll tax or *personal*. The amount paid depended partly on status within the household, household heads paid a higher rate of tax than their sons, journeymen and apprentices, but also on status as an artisan, independent masters paid more than journeymen employed by others. It is not clear how the different categories were determined among smallholders. The only exemptions apart from women were those aged over 60, those unable to work, paupers, those with large families (12 children and grandchildren) and the clergy, nobility and employees of the crown.

Table 5.4 shows the numbers of male household heads paying the different rates of tax for each of the three years for which *cadastres* survive. The higher rates of 45 and 35 *rals* were paid by household heads with independent artisan status, the lower rates by sons, apprentices and those of journeymen status.[64] Sons and apprentices have, however, been excluded from the table, since the lower rates they paid reflect dependency as a life-cycle stage, not necessarily a permanent condition. The greater percentage of males who were exempt in 1765 may reflect the particularly harsh circumstances of the previous year, but also the greater care taken to record those who were exempt than in the other years. Far more detail is given as to why individuals are exempt, and there are more priests recorded. Exemptions aside, however, what is clear is the sharp decline over time of adult

---

[64] I have not been able to find any explanation for the appearance of the new rates of 35 and 15 *rals* in 1824, but it is clear from marginal notes that they frequently represent concessions to those formerly on the higher rates of tax.

Table 5.4   The *personal* contributions paid by male household heads

Amount (rals)	1724		1765		1824	
	N	%	N	%	N	%
0	21	8.3	142	23.7	183	11.8
15	—	—	—	—	719	46.3
25	119	47.0	333	55.7	527	33.9
35	—	—	—	—	41	2.6
45	113	44.7	123	20.6	82	5.3
Total	253		598		1,552	

males paying the higher rates of 45 and 35 *rals* consistent with independent status and the concomitant rise in men paying the lower rates of 25 and 15 *rals*. Leaving aside those who were exempt, since not all cases of exemption were based on poverty, 80 per cent of male household heads by 1824 were paying lower rates. Alongside this trend is a severe fall in the proportion of households with apprentices and resident journeymen, from 8.1 per cent in 1724 to 4 per cent in 1765 to only 0.7 per cent in 1824. In other words, wage dependency was becoming a condition of entire households, not just a life-cycle stage for young artisans, and a condition that was not restricted just to the proto-industrial sector.

As with the question of ownership of the means of production, what such dependent status meant for households varied from occupation to occupation. In the leather industry, for example, journeyman status for a household head and the lack of his own tannery did not necessarily have to signal poverty given the ability of many tanners to find places for their younger sons in the family tannery. For the textile industry, as described in Chapter 3, however, it meant an increasing subordination of production to the control of a handful of manufacturers and vulnerability to poverty. To an extent, the clothing and footwear trades were following suit.

While the forms of production in which households were engaged were becoming more specialised, such as commercial viticulture and proto-industry, the household economy itself was not. Households continued to practise a narrow range of those activities which can be revealed by inventories, although women in particular are likely to have been more flexible in the tasks they performed. Households, though, were becoming more industrious in terms of the intensification of their labour, again, particularly that of women, and more engaged with markets for labour and foodstuffs. The questions that remain to be answered, however, are whether such engagement with markets could be the result of choice and whether the new opportunities to earn a living provided by proto-industry and viticulture were enabling households to acquire more material goods. The attempt to answer these questions forms the subject of the next chapter.

Chapter 6
Consumption in the Household Economy

Introduction

The final question for this study is whether the industriousness identified in the previous chapter was associated with new forms of consumer behaviour, as suggested by de Vries. As noted in the Introduction, de Vries did not believe that households in southern Europe were capable of a consumer revolution. It would be more accurate, however, to say that too little work has been done on consumption and material culture, in Spain at least, for definite statements to be made. Those historians who have begun to work on these topics have identified changes, including the introduction of new goods, especially textiles, and an increase in ownership of luxury goods such as paintings and clocks.[1] Such changes did not, however, become evident until the nineteenth century in many areas, with sharp rural/urban and regional differences.[2] For Catalonia, Belén Moreno's work on the Penedès district, the most complete study of inventories carried out to date, does point to a rising consumption of certain material goods during the eighteenth century, but a rise accompanied by increased social stratification.[3] Lídia Torra's work on textile consumption in towns, discussed below, shows some change, but questions how widely diffused the demand for new textiles was.[4] Ramona Huguet's study of artisans in Lleida, in the poorer western area, reveals more static and traditional patterns of consumption.[5]

This chapter therefore seeks to identify new forms of consumer behaviour in Igualada during the long eighteenth century. The first question is simply what goods were being consumed? What interests us is both which new goods appeared during this period, such as colonial groceries or new fabrics, but also whether ownership of traditional goods, such as linen, increased or fell. The second

---

[1]   For an overview of current research, see Jaume Torras and Bartolomé Yun (eds), *Consumo, condiciones de vida y comercialización: Cataluña y Castilla, siglos XVII–XIX* (Valladolid, 1999); *Revista de história económica* 21 (2003) (special issue dedicated to consumption).

[2]   Bartolomé Yun, 'Peasant Material Culture in Castille (1750–1900): Some Proposals', in A. Schuurman and L. Walsh (eds), *Material Culture: Consumption, Life-Style, Standard of Living, 1500–1900* (Milan, 1994), pp. 125–36.

[3]   Moreno, *Consum i condicions de vida*.

[4]   Lídia Torra, 'Pautas de consumo textil en la Cataluña del siglo XVIII: Una visión a partir de los inventarios post-mortem', in Torras and Yun (eds), *Consumo, condiciones de vida y comercialización*, pp. 89–105.

[5]   Ramona Huguet, *Els artesans de Lleida: 1680–1808* (Lleida, 1990).

question is how such goods were acquired: what were the forms of distribution and access to markets? The third and perhaps most important question is by whom were such goods consumed. As noted, de Vries's industrious revolution places great weight on the freedom of women as consumers and the penetration of new forms of consumer behaviour far down the social scale. This chapter therefore considers what role women played as consumers in Catalonia, compared with elsewhere in Europe, and whether extended family forms could be said to have restricted consumption choices. It also addresses the extent to which more plebeian households participated in new consumption patterns.

This final aspect leads naturally into considering the other major question for this chapter, namely, what were the effects of new consumer behaviour? Of particular interest given Moreno's findings is the extent to which consumer behaviour reflected or contributed to increased social differentiation in Igualada. More important, however, is the relationship between consumption and the industriousness identified in the previous chapter. If the scale of consumption were limited, then what else motivated people to work harder in Igualada? The final section of the chapter addresses this question by looking at the evidence for forced commercialisation in the form of debts, taxes, rent and interlocking markets and at the extent of poverty in eighteenth-century Igualada.

Methodological issues

Identifying and interpreting new forms of consumer behaviour are not straightforward. The reasons why individuals and households might choose to invest in certain goods or combinations of goods are more complex than a simple matter of having more disposable income. If the prices of goods are falling, or an old good is replaced with one that is cheaper, changes in consumption habits will not reflect greater purchasing power. Equally important is an understanding of the meanings ascribed to objects, and to the process of consumption.[6] Gold and silver objects, for example, can be signs of ostentation and are decorative, but can also have practical functions as forms of investment or, in the case of religious objects such as christening gifts, spiritual functions. Comfort may be a better term than luxury to describe much new consumption over the period, exemplified by new fabrics such as cotton, the substitution of upholstered for wooden furniture and new ways of heating and lighting homes.[7] In this regard, consumption lower down the

---

[6] Still useful amongst a huge literature is Mary Douglas and Baron Isherwood, *The World of Goods: Towards an Anthropology of Consumption* (2nd edn, London, 1996); see also Lorna Weatherill, 'The Meaning of Consumer Behaviour in Late Seventeenth- and Early Eighteenth-Century England', in Brewer and Porter, *Consumption and the World of Goods*, pp. 206–27.

[7] De Vries, *Industrious Revolution*, pp. 126–9; D. Roche, *Histoire des choses banales: Naissance de la consommation dans les societies traditionnelles (xviiie–xixe siècles)* (Paris,

social scale was dependent to some extent on the ability to produce cheap imitations of certain goods, on the relative cheapness of new goods, such as cotton fabrics, or on access to second-hand markets.[8] Nowhere are supply-side considerations more important perhaps than in textiles. It is impossible to ignore the role played here by technological changes, such as the development of techniques for printing rather than weaving coloured calicoes. Similarly, the question of availability through retail and transport networks was an essential connection between supply and demand.

A more specific set of problems stems from the nature of the inventories as a source.[9] These problems are common to many European settings and need only be rehearsed briefly here. Inventories represent a snapshot of the household economy at a particular point in the life-cycle, usually the death of the household head in middle or old age. Average age of the inventory sample for Igualada was 53.8 years. As such, they may not represent the height of productive activities or of consumption, depending on the composition of the household at that point in time. As a snapshot, they also record 'stocks' rather than 'flows' of goods, that is, they are biased towards capturing durables rather than perishables and do not allow us to control for rates of acquisition of goods, nor whether such goods were purchased or inherited. The level of detail varies considerably, not just from case study to case study, but from notary to notary or appraiser to appraiser within the same society. We also have no idea how many items may have gone unrecorded because they were considered of little value by the appraisers. Moreover, inventories are a poor source for assessing the meanings attached to objects.[10]

Finally, an important question is that of social representativeness. As already mentioned, historians differ on how far down the social scale inventories can be found in different contexts and thus how far we can be confident of capturing middling-sort or plebeian consumption patterns alongside those of the elite. Inventories were not cheap to draw up. According to Moreno, the cost of drawing up an inventory in the Penedès in 1684 was 10 *lliures*, which represented approximately a month's wages for a skilled artisan.[11] Chapter 5 has already shown that not all occupations are equally represented in the Igualada inventory sample.

1997), pp. 121–49.

  [8] B. Lemire, *Fashion's Favourite: The Cotton Trade and the Consumer in Britain, 1660–1800* (Oxford, 1991).

  [9] See A.J. Schuurman, 'Probate Inventory Research: Opportunities and Drawbacks', in M. Baulant, A.J. Schuurman and P. Servais (eds), *Inventaires après-décès et ventes de meubles* (Louvain, 1988), pp. 19–28; for a discussion of the problems specific to Catalan inventories, see Moreno, 'Pautas de consumo y diferenciación social', pp. 51–63.

  [10] T.H. Breen, 'The Meaning of Things: Interpreting the Consumer Economy in the Eighteenth Century', in Brewer and Porter (eds), *Consumption and the World of Goods*, pp. 249–60; Amanda Vickery, 'Women and the World of Goods: A Lancashire Consumer and her Possessions', in Brewer and Porter (eds), *Consumption and the World of Goods*, pp. 274–301.

  [11] Moreno, 'Pautas de consumo y diferenciación social', p. 63; estimated from data in G. Feliu, *Precios y salaries en la Cataluña moderna* (2 vols, Madrid, 1991), vol. 2, pp. 104–8.

A further issue with regard to representativeness concerns gender. Catalan women retained their own property after marriage. There are, however, few inventories *post mortem* of women's possessions, nor can we be sure if their goods are included in the inventories left by their husbands unless the inventory makes this explicit. A rare example is the inventory of Isidro Domingo, which includes a detailed list of all the goods his wife Elisabeth had brought to the marriage.[12] Far more typical is the inventory of Josep Mata, which simply includes 'a chest containing the clothing of Maria [his widow] and her daughters'.[13] There are only 43 inventories left by women (8 per cent of the total) and 19 (4 per cent) left by married couples, that is, inventories where it is clearly stated that the goods of both spouses were included and these are listed in detail.[14] In some cases, the goods are listed separately for each spouse, in other cases, no distinction is made. The proportion here of inventories including detailed lists of female possessions (12 per cent) matches that found by Moreno for the Penedès, but is a little lower than the proportions of 15–17 per cent found for England.[15]

Perhaps the main drawback of the Catalan inventories, however, is that they rarely have valuations of most of the items recorded. The prevailing custom of impartible inheritance meant there was no need for valuations, since the estate would not be divided. In most cases, therefore, Catalan inventories cannot be used to estimate wealth in any satisfactory way. By contrast, they have the advantage that all property was recorded, including real property. Land, buildings and livestock appear, along with moveable goods. While some goods may still have been omitted, it is nonetheless possible to build up a fairly complete picture of the type of activities engaged in by the household and the sources of income available to it. The one significant exception is debt. Debts owing to the deceased are recorded more frequently (24 per cent of cases) than debts owed by the deceased (12 per cent), but both are clearly under-recorded.

Material goods in Igualada

Overall patterns

The sheer wealth of detail in the inventories prevents an exhaustive analysis of all types of good. Table 6.1 therefore gives the percentages of inventories recording certain goods over time, some of which are then analysed in further detail below. The goods chosen here were selected mainly for comparative

---

[12]   ACA, NI 780, fos 137–8.

[13]   ANI 409, fos 75r–78r.

[14]   Many other inventories left by men include female clothing, but without indicating whether this belonged to a wife, mother, sister or other female relative.

[15]   Moreno, *Consum i condicions de vida*, p. 193; Overton et al., *Production and Consumption*, p. 27; Weatherill, *Consumer Behaviour*, pp. 209–11.

Table 6.1 Inventories recording certain goods

	1680–1754		1755–1829	
	N	%	N	%
Clocks and watches	1	*1*	36	*10*
Pictures	100	*58*	194	*55*
Mirrors	47	*27*	114	*32*
Books	20	*12*	60	*17*
Gold items	61	*36*	59	*17*
Silver items	102	*60*	158	*45*
Hot-drink utensils	21	*12*	155	*44*
Tobacco	6	*4*	17	*5*
Sheets	159	*93*	337	*96*
Shirts	132	*77*	287	*82*
Forks	36	*21*	185	*53*
Spoons	99	*58*	278	*79*

purposes with other studies, but also as representing goods indicative of a desire for greater comfort, luxury or ostentation, such as pictures, mirrors, gold or silver, or as being new consumption goods, such as utensils for hot drinks and tobacco.

Table 6.1 suggests new consumption patterns were relatively slow to develop. Some goods show a rise in ownership over time, slight in the case of books, more striking in the case of hot-drink utensils, clocks and cutlery, but were still only owned by a small proportion of households in the second half of the period. The proportions of inventories recording other goods, such as pictures (including all kinds of paintings and prints), mirrors and tobacco, remained virtually static. Perhaps most strikingly, ownership of gold and silver objects, including even small objects such as buttons, fell dramatically. The figures for Igualada are similar to those for the Penedès.[16] For most goods, rates of ownership in the period 1755–1829 in Catalonia are equivalent to or lower than the levels recorded for England half a century earlier, though comparisons are not straightforward.[17]

Clocks and watches

The ownership of timepieces is regarded as significant for many reasons.[18] Clocks and watches could be expensive status items, the latter often in silver

[16] Moreno, 'Pautas de consumo y diferenciación social', pp. 213–18, 220, 223, 227, 247.

[17] See Weatherill, *Consumer Behaviour*, table 2.1 (p. 26).

[18] See the discussion and references in de Vries, *Industrious Revolution*, pp. 1–3.

or gold, but cheaper versions also proliferated.[19] At the same time, they were easily pawned.[20] Moreover, their increased ownership is taken as indicating a growing concern with the kind of accurate time-keeping associated with the work-discipline essential for the rise of industrial capitalism.[21] They diffused rapidly through the upper and middling ranks of society in England, France and the Netherlands during the eighteenth century. In Paris, 70 per cent of servants and 32 per cent of wage earners in Roche's sample owned watches.[22] Watch production rose from an estimate in the tens of thousands to around 400, 000 by the end of the eighteenth century.[23] Catalonia was therefore behind in this diffusion process. How far behind is hard to assess. The figures for Igualada show a tenfold increase during the eighteenth century, but still only 10 per cent of inventories had either a clock or a watch in the period 1755–1829. The first inventory in the Igualada sample to record a clock, owned by a priest, dates from 1740.[24] The majority of inventories with clocks and watches, just under two-thirds, are concentrated in the period after 1800. Figures for a small sample of Barcelona inventories show that 17 per cent of households owned watches or clocks in 1770–90, higher than elsewhere in Catalonia, but behind the levels recorded for Paris, for example, despite the Baró de Maldà's claim that 'even tailors, cobblers and other artisans have silver watches or the like'.[25]

The anecdotal evidence, however, suggests that both clocks and watches, particularly the latter, were significant new items of consumption by the end of the eighteenth century. Watches appear to have been betrothal gifts and, as now, rewards for loyal service.[26] They were also a common purchase for sudden windfall earnings, as in the case of a Barcelona servant who bought one with his lottery winnings in 1783.[27] With regard to time-keeping and industriousness, Dutch and English evidence suggests farmers were often more likely to own clocks than those in other occupations and that such clocks were located in kitchens or

---

[19]   See the range of prices recorded for watches in eighteenth-century Paris by Laurence Fontaine ('The Circulation of Luxury Goods in Eighteenth-Century Paris: Social Redistribution and an Alternative Currency', in M. Berg and E. Eger (eds), *Luxury in the Eighteenth Century* (Basingstoke, 2003), pp. 89–102 (p. 92)).

[20]   Ibid., pp. 99.

[21]   Thompson, 'Time, Work-Discipline and Industrial Capitalism'.

[22]   D. Roche, *The People of Paris* (Leamington Spa, 1987), p. 222.

[23]   De Vries, *Industrious Revolution*, p. 2.

[24]   ANI 344, fos 17–20.

[25]   Comparative figures for 127 Barcelona inventories of smallholders, artisans and professionals in Moreno, 'Pautas de consumo y diferenciación social', pp. 460–66; R. d'Amat i de Cortada, *Vïles i ciutats de Catalunya*, ed. M. Aritzeta (Barcelona, 1994), p. 87.

[26]   Amat, *Calaix de sastre*, vol. 2, pp. 7, 10 (betrothal gifts); vol. 1, p. 148 (gifts to servants).

[27]   Ibid., vol. 1, p. 100; cf. Thompson, 'Time, Work-Discipline and Industrial Capitalism', pp. 361–70.

other work-related spaces, thus serving primarily practical functions.[28] Only in one instance does a clock appear in a workspace in Igualada, significantly in the workshop of a calico manufacturer.[29] All other clocks are located in main rooms, the equivalents of parlours or dining rooms, or on landings or in passageways. In two inventories, rooms are actually referred to as the 'clock corridor' and the 'clock room', indicating the primacy of this particular item of furniture.[30] Placing clocks in corridors or on landings may have permitted the entire household to be aware more easily of the time but is less obviously related to work discipline than placement in a workshop or kitchen.

The absence of clocks or watches in households does not, however, preclude a concern with accurate time-keeping. The greater prevalence of clocks in rural farmhouses in England and the Netherlands may reflect a greater distance from public clocks in the form of church or town-hall clocks and bells. An important addition to the numerous church clocks and bells of Barcelona and emblematic of the new desire for accurate time-keeping among industrialists was the clock tower of the Gònima factory, built in 1798.[31] It is not known when Igualada acquired a church clock, but a new one was made in 1753, interestingly, at the expense in part of the clothiers' and tanners' guilds.[32] Night watchmen, one of whose duties was to call out the time on the hour, were employed by the town from 1798.[33] Watches could only ever be second in importance as timepieces to such public clocks, given that the latter, then as now, were used to set the former. Nonetheless, even if relatively slow to diffuse through Catalonia, they were clearly taking on the status of desirable consumer items by the late eighteenth century.

Books

The rise in book ownership for Igualada was only slight during the eighteenth century, as for elsewhere in Catalonia, despite some indication of rising literacy rates for men at least. In Igualada, 349 grooms out of 796 (44 per cent) signed their marriage contracts over the period 1730–79, compared with 796 out of 1,135 (70 per cent) for the period 1780–1829. By contrast, only 38 (21 per cent) of the 796 brides could sign their names in 1730–79 and still fewer (155 or 14 per cent) could sign in 1780–1829. Marriage contracts are not an ideal source for literacy rates, given their increasing bias towards the upper ends of the social hierarchy during the eighteenth century. Nevertheless, they suggest that

28   J. de Vries, 'Peasant Demand Patterns and Economic Development, Friesland, 1550–1700', in W. Parker and E. Jones (eds), *European Peasants and their Markets* (Princeton, 1975), pp. 221–2; Overton et al., *Production and Consumption*.
29   ANI 607, fos 228r–231r.
30   ANI 373, fos 150r–172r; ANI 632, fos 112–24.
31   Amat, *Calaix de sastre*, vol. 4, p. 27.
32   AMI, 1104, *Registre municipal*, fo. 22v.
33   Segura, *Història d'Igualada*, vol. 2, p. 150.

male literacy rates, at least, were on a par with those of other Catalan towns.[34] In Igualada, the rise in male literacy may be attributed to the founding of the Escola Pia (Piarist school) in 1732.[35] As elsewhere, female education remained neglected until well into the nineteenth century, despite a legacy left in 1802 by one of Igualada's few wealthy spinsters, Felicia Mateu i Padró, to found a free school for girls.[36] Among the Torelló family letters, a rare example of a letter written by an Igualada girl, Maria Torelló, daughter of a lawyer, displays extremely poor spelling and handwriting.[37]

Some ability to read and write among men at least did not, however, translate into the acquisition of books in Catalonia. While Catalan towns show higher rates, with books appearing in 35 per cent of Girona inventories between 1747 and 1807 and a third of Barcelona inventories over the eighteenth century, these rates are low for Europe.[38] In Paris, 30–5 per cent of wage earners and servants had books by 1780.[39] German towns had even higher rates of ownership, at around 80 per cent.[40]

The low presence of books in Catalan inventories was not a function of cost either. Prices of secondhand books varied from 1 *sou* to 3 *lliures* at auctions in Igualada, the Penedès and Tossa de Mar.[41] At the cheaper end of the range, therefore, they were within the reach of an artisan's purchasing power, albeit as an occasional rather than a regular purchase.[42] Their ownership, however, tended to be associated with devotional or professional purposes: after books of a religious nature, the most likely subject areas were law and medicine, and the most likely owners were priests, lawyers and doctors.[43] Works of fiction, history and philosophy were rare,

---

[34]   J. Antón, *La herencia cultural: Alfabetización y lectura en la ciudad de Girona (1747–1807)* (Bellaterra, 1998), table 12 (pp. 148–50); M. Ventura, *Lletrats i illetrats a una ciutat de la Catalunya moderna: Mataró, 1750–1800* (Mataró, 1991), pp. 85–8.

[35]   There had been a grammar school before then, but the Piarist schools were less elitist (see Segura, *Història d'Igualada*, vol. 2, pp. 64–85).

[36]   ANI 632, fos 95–104.

[37]   AT, *lligall* 1460, Maria Torelló to Albert Combelles (7 Mar. 1812); she was 14.

[38]   Antón, *La herencia cultural*, p. 325 (Girona); J. Burgos, 'Imprenta y cultura del libro en la Barcelona del Setecientos (1680–1808)' (Ph.D thesis, Universitat Autònoma de Barcelona, 1993), pp. 600–67 (Barcelona).

[39]   Roche, *The People of Paris*, pp. 211–14.

[40]   James Van Horn Melton, *The Rise of the Public in Enlightenment Europe* (Cambridge, 2001), p. 83.

[41]   Moreno, 'Pautas de consumo y diferenciación social', pp. 215–6; N. Figueras, J.M. Grau and R. Puig, 'La possessió dels llibres a través dels inventaris *post mortem*: Un mostreig (s.XVIII)', *Annals de l'Institut d'Estudis Gironins*, 34 (1994), pp. 129–60 (pp. 152–3).

[42]   For much of the eighteenth century, daily wages in construction ranged from 10 to 15 *sous* for skilled artisans and 7 to 8 *sous* for unskilled labourers and apprentices (see Feliu, *Precios y salarios*, pp. 69–129).

[43]   Antón, *La herencia cultural*, pp. 328–9; Enric Moreu-Rey, 'Sociologia del llibre a Barcelona al segle XVIII', *Estudis històrics i documents dels Arxius de Protocols*, 7 (1980), pp. 275–303; Figueras, Grau and Puig, 'La possessió dels llibres'.

although some studies suggest their presence was becoming more notable during the eighteenth century.[44]

In Igualada, 61 out of 80 inventories mentioning books quantify at least some of them. The mean number of books per household owning them was 36. As will be discussed below, those in the liberal professions and commerce accounted for half of all inventories with books. The four who owned over 100 books were Narcís Mateu, a lawyer (407), Joan Padró Serrals, a minor noble (212), Josep Riera, a merchant (143) and Jaume Bergadà, a physician (140).[45] Only two artisans other than surgeons and apothecaries owned books: a haberdasher and a carpenter.[46] Only two smallholders in Igualada owned books.[47] This is in contrast to the Penedès, where 23 per cent of book owners were peasants and reflects the greater presence of substantial landholders in the latter region.[48]

Of the 2,210 books in Igualada inventories, subject matter could be identified for only 1,291. As elsewhere, religious subjects dominated, if canon law is included, accounting for 31.7 per cent, followed by law (25.9 per cent) and medicine (16.9 per cent). The emphasis was therefore, as noted above, on ownership of books for professional use. Even within the religious category, though the 200 devotional works made up the largest sub-category, there was a notable presence of more technical and practical works, such as canon-law texts, manuals for parish priests and liturgical works. Subjects other than religion, law or medicine tended to be confined to only a few inventories. Only five individuals owned history books and nine literature, for example. The most varied book collections and those showing some signs of reading for pleasure or interests other than professional or devotional were the large collections described above. Such individuals stand out, however, against a background where book ownership was restricted and mostly for professional use.

Pictures

If all types of paintings, engravings and the like are taken together, levels of ownership actually fell slightly in Igualada. Not only did the percentage of

---

[44]   J. Fontana, *La fi de l'Antic Règim i la industrialització*, Història de Catalunya, 5 (Barcelona, 1989), pp. 106–9.

[45]   ANI 373, fos 150r–172r (Narcís Mateu); Torras Ribé, *Evolució social i econòmica d'una família catalana*, pp. 243–53 (Joan Padró Serrals); ANI 678, fos 15–20 (Josep Riera); ANI 207, fos 255r–259r (Jaume Bergadà).

[46]   ANI 454, fos 61r–72r; ANI 633, fos 239–41; see also Huguet, *Els artesans de Lleida*, pp. 204–8

[47]   Joan Roig (23 Aug. 1782), ANI 492, unfol.; Rafel Matoses (3 Jan. 1710), ACA, NI 791, unfol.

[48]   Moreno, 'Pautas de consumo y diferenciación social', p. 216. The four *pagesos* in the sample of bookowners from the Selva region studied by Figueras, Grau and Puig were also wealthy ('La possessió dels llibres').

households owning them decline slightly, as shown in Table 6.1, but the mean number of pictures per household also fell from 13.0 in 1680–1754 to 12.4 in 1755–1829. Pictures were not necessarily valuable: like books, their value depended upon subject, age, condition (e.g. whether framed or not) and type (e.g. print, water colour, oil painting). Two oil paintings were sold together in 1687 for 2 *lliures*, 15 *sous*, but six pictures described as 'on paper' and 'poor' went for only 4 *sous*.[49] It is therefore no surprise that we find them even in modest households. Only the wealthy had really large collections of pictures, however, with only four having over 50. The largest collection was that of Gaspar Rovira, a priest, who had 163.[50]

As with books, an important distinction can be drawn between pictures with a religious and non-religious theme. The former were at least in part devotional aids, the latter solely for decoration, interest and ostentation. Contemporary comments underline this distinction: pictures which catch the attention of observers are often of non-religious subjects. Zamora comments on the 'curious' pictures owned by Josep Rovira of Igualada, including one of a dog nursing her puppies.[51] When the Baró de Maldà showed off his Barcelona house to visitors, it was his paintings of Barcelona street scenes that received the most praise.[52] By contrast, in his country house, the family prayed the rosary before the least tattered print of Our Lady of Carmen.[53]

Of the 3,702 pictures in Igualada inventories, the subject matter was described for only 1,134. Of these, 764 (67 per cent) were of religious subjects, followed by landscapes (18 per cent), still lifes (7 per cent), maps (2 per cent) and historical scenes (1 per cent). The non-religious pictures were concentrated in 39 inventories (13 per cent of those with pictures). These were mostly the inventories of those in the professions or commerce, but also included three cloth manufacturers and the widow of another, one calico manufacturer and one clothier. Among these were Josep Torelló and Josep Anton Lladó. As with books, there was a clear association between owning non-religious works and wealth and status. Even then, this new trend towards owning art for purposes other than devotion was limited. If anything, it is in the traditional area of devotion that some increase in consumption can be seen. *Estampes*, which were cheap, usually religious, prints accounted for 15 per cent of all pictures in 1680–1754 but 26 per cent in 1755–1829. Those households that acquired pictures, therefore, displayed a continued preference for traditional items of consumption.

---

[49]   ACA, NI 780, fos 96–9.

[50]   ANI 344, fos 17–20.

[51]   Zamora, *Diario de los viajes hechos por Cataluña*, p. 265. Unfortunately, no inventory survives.

[52]   Amat, *Calaix de sastre*, vol. 1, p. 63.

[53]   Ibid., vol. 2, pp. 125–6.

Colonial groceries

Perhaps the most significant form of new consumer behaviour in Catalonia as elsewhere in eighteenth-century Europe was the demand for new colonial goods, in particular caffeinated beverages.[54] Such demand was responsible not just for the expansion of colonial trade and slave plantations, it also went hand-in-hand with changes in European mealtimes and new forms of sociability. Demand varied across Europe for tea, coffee or chocolate, depending on access to markets and relative prices, in turn influenced by fiscal policies.[55] Britain led the way in terms of per capita consumption of both tea and sugar, followed by Antwerp, Amsterdam and areas of colonial America by the end of the eighteenth century, though in France it remained a drink for the rich.[56] Coffee appears to have been an urban drink or for social elites outside of England and the Netherlands.[57] Chocolate is less frequently discussed, but appears to have also been an elite good in Antwerp, Amsterdam and France.[58]

In Catalonia, by contrast, chocolate was the common drink, captured in inventories mainly by *xocolateres*, chocolate-pots. Chocolate was sold in tablet form, to be broken up, grated and dissolved in water to make a hot drink, rather than eaten. Coffee was also consumed, but in cafés rather than at home.[59] Again, urban consumption was ahead of rural consumption. The first mill for producing chocolate appears to have been established in Barcelona in 1664 by the guild of sugar and colonial merchants (*adroguers*), but gradually the separate profession

---

[54]   De Vries, *Industrious Revolution*, pp. 151–64; Sarti, *Europe at Home*, pp. 183–4.

[55]   S.D. Smith, 'Accounting for Taste: British Coffee Consumption in Historical Perspective', *Journal of Interdisciplinary History*, 27 (1996), pp. 183–214.

[56]   McCants, 'Poor Consumers as Global Consumers'; Roche, *Histoire des choses banales*, p. 265; P. Servais, 'Ustensiles de cuisine et vaisselle dans les campagnes du Pays de Herve aux XVIIe et XVIIIe siècles', in Baulant, Schuurman and Servais, *Inventaires après-décès*, pp. 333–46 (tables 1, 2).

[57]   D. Hiler and L. Wiedmer, 'Le rat de ville et le rat des champs: Une approche comparative des interieurs ruraux et urbains à Genève dans la seconde partie du XVIIIe siècle', in Baulant, Schuurman and Servais, *Inventaires après-décès*, pp. 131–51 (p. 141); A. Pardailhé-Galabrun, *The Birth of Intimacy: Privacy and Domestic Life in Early Modern Paris* (Oxford, 1991), pp. 93–4; B. Garnot, *La culture matérielle en France aux XVIe– XVIIe–XVIIIe siècles* (Paris, 1995), p. 26; Cailly, 'Structure sociale', p. 755; R. Lick, 'Les intérieures domestiques dans la seconde moitié du XVIIIe siècle d'après les inventaires après-décès de Coutances', *Annales de Normandie*, 20 (1970), pp. 293–316.

[58]   De Vries, *Industrious Revolution*, pp. 152–3; Roche, *Histoire des choses banales*, pp. 264–5; Garnot, *La culture matérielle*, p. 26; McCants, 'Poor Consumers as Global Consumers', p. 184.

[59]   Only four inventories in Igualada record coffee or coffee pots, one the inventory of a French immigrant (ANI 419, fos 82–7; ANI 385, fos 59r–64r; ANI 663, fos 57–68; ANI 678, fos 15–20), but by 1816 there was a café, also run by a French immigrant (AMI 18.6.1, 'Relación de las tiendas que se hayan en esta villa …' (20 Sept. 1816)).

of chocolate-maker (*xocolater*) emerged, with a guild founded in 1722.[60] The first reference to chocolate in an Igualada inventory is in that of a doctor in 1705.[61] Thereafter, the rise was fairly rapid, especially from 1740 onwards. The 44 per cent of households with chocolate-pots in the latter half of the eighteenth century is higher than for the Penedès, where only a third of inventories included them.[62] Seven individuals, mostly immigrants from Barcelona, are described in the parish registers as *xocolaters*, with the first appearing in 1791, although chocolate was usually sold by *adroguers*. Chocolate had therefore attained a relatively high presence in Igualada by the end of the eighteenth century, representing a significant shift in the diet and consumption of households even below the elite, if perhaps not the poorest.

The importance of chocolate, as with tea and coffee elsewhere in Europe, lay in its properties as a stimulant, its association with new forms of sociability, exemplified by the term *xocolatada* to refer to a social gathering for the purpose of drinking chocolate, along the lines of a tea-party, and also its significance as a new form of breakfast. It was also considered beneficial to health. References to drinking chocolate are ubiquitous in the diary of the Baró de Maldà, suggesting that the aristocracy were consuming chocolate daily at breakfast and mid-afternoon. It is less likely that those lower down the social scale could afford to consume it every day, but it was certainly a feature of celebrations and social gatherings among artisans at least.[63] By the end of the eighteenth century, chocolate even appeared as a bequest in wills.[64]

The other important new colonial grocery on the European scene in the eighteenth century was tobacco. Patterns of consumption are harder to assess, since an apparent decline in per capita consumption may simply reflect the changing preference for ingesting snuff tobacco rather than for smoking. Contemporary accounts suggest that tobacco was relatively unknown in Catalonia at the start of the eighteenth century, but had become more widespread by the end. For the elites and middling sort, the fashion was for snuff, as elsewhere, but Barcelona factory workers in particular smoked. Attitudes towards it changed over the period: from being regarded as 'a very ugly habit', to quote one contemporary, taking snuff (but not smoking) came to be accepted as a pleasurable activity, and one with possible medicinal benefits.[65] It does not, however, seem to have been associated with sociability. The Baró de Maldà usually only mentions taking snuff as a

---

[60]   Pere Molas, *Economia i societat al segle XVIII* (Barcelona, 1975), p. 67.

[61]   ANI 207, fos 255–9.

[62]   Moreno, 'Pautas de consumo y diferenciación social', pp. 251–4; id., *Consum i condicions de vida*, pp. 40–1.

[63]   For chocolate at the wedding of an artisan in 1793, see Amat, *Calaix de sastre*, vol. 2, p. 89.

[64]   Moreno, *Consum i condicions de vida*, p. 40; Amat, *Calaix de sastre*, vol. 3, pp. 174–5.

[65]   Cited in Moreno, *Consum i condicions de vida*, p. 41.

solitary activity, often in an attempt to get to sleep or before starting to write.[66] Smoking, on the other hand, was a sociable activity, but a distinctly plebeian form of sociability, as will be discussed below.

Snuff tobacco first appears in Igualada in 1695, but the first inventories to record this are of shopkeepers, listing tobacco among the goods in the shop, not in the household proper.[67] Clearly, someone locally must have been purchasing tobacco for the shopkeepers to bother stocking it, but the first instance of tobacco clearly for domestic consumption is a snuffbox in the 1723 inventory of a lawyer.[68] As Table 6.1 shows, such consumption was restricted to just 4–5 per cent of inventoried households, rather less than elsewhere. Seventeen per cent of inventories for the Penedès region recorded tobacco between 1770 and 1790.[69]

Cutlery

Perhaps the area where a rise in consumption is most noticeable in the Igualada inventories is in the ownership of forks and spoons, rising from 21 and 53 per cent respectively in 1680–1754 to 58 and 79 per cent in 1755–1829. Moreover, the mean number also rose from 5.8 to 9 forks and 7.0 to 12.5 spoons per inventoried household. Igualada seems to be a little ahead of the Penedès: Moreno notes a rise in spoons from appearances in 30 per cent to 70 per cent of inventories over a hundred-year period, while forks went from having 'a negligible presence' to being present in 40 per cent of inventories.[70] In the Baix Llobregat, appearances of spoons rose from around 33 per cent of inventories in the 1740s to 70 per cent in the 1750s and up to 80 per cent by the 1790s.[71] The spread of cutlery has been noted for other areas of Europe over the eighteenth century, associated with greater refinement in table manners and domestic hygiene.[72]

The above figures mask a more important shift, however, in the nature of the cutlery used. Initially, the only type of cutlery found in inventories was silver. Often these were christening or wedding gifts, as well as having investment value.[73] It is therefore unlikely silver cutlery would have been used except on special

[66] See e.g. *Calaix de sastre*, vol. 1, pp. 104, 116, 122, 266.

[67] Josep Jorba (18 July 1695), ANI 207, fos 20r–30r.

[68] Josep Padró Bas (Torras Ribé, *Evolució social i econòmica d'una família catalana*, pp. 237–42).

[69] Moreno, *Consum i condicions de vida*, p. 41.

[70] Ibid., p. 39.

[71] J. Codina, *El gir de 1750: Origen i creixement modern de la població* (Lleida, 1998), pp. 51–2.

[72] Sarti, *Europe at Home*, pp. 150–53; for comparative figures, see Overton et al., *Production and Consumption*, table 5.2 (p. 99), p. 106; Weatherill, *Consumer Behaviour*, p. 26; Roche, *Histoire des choses banales*, p. 259; B. Garnot, *Un déclin: Chartres au XVIIIe siècle* (Paris, 1991), pp. 208–9; Cailly, 'Structure sociale', pp. 758–9.

[73] Amat, *Calaix de sastre*, vol. 3, p. 258.

occasions. By contrast, tin or wooden cutlery would have been for everyday use, and it is this that starts to appear in inventories with increasing frequency over the eighteenth century. Wooden and tin spoons are recorded right from the start of the inventoried period, though they are rare, appearing in only three inventories before 1730. The paucity of inventories for the 1720s and 1730s compared with other decades, however, makes the precise dating of this shift difficult. Non-silver forks are rarer still, with the first one making its appearance, strikingly, in the inventory of Josep Torelló in 1745. Between 1680–1754, only 13 per cent of inventories with cutlery had only non-silver cutlery, while a further 21 per cent combined both silver and non-silver. By 1755–1829 only 8 per cent of inventories with cutlery had just silver cutlery, and 58 per cent had only tin and wooden spoons and forks. It is this latter figure that is the most significant, showing ownership of cutlery as a practical item for everyday use, rather than as a form of investment. While tin cutlery could still be pawned or sold, its value was low.[74] Moreover, the rise in the mean number of spoons and forks overall was driven almost entirely by a rise in the numbers of tin and wooden spoons and forks, with silver cutlery remaining fairly static.

Clothing and textiles

Perhaps the key area highlighted by contemporaries and by historians as the one in which new forms of consumer behaviour can be identified over the early modern period is clothing and textiles.[75] Here is where the dictates of fashion and novelty are perceived to have had most sway. Clothing and household linen were essential goods, but also a key area for social differentiation. Contemporaries believed the social differentiation imposed initially by sumptuary laws was increasingly being challenged by new fashions and cheaper fabrics, although not all historians agree.[76] Where historians do agree is on the changes in dress taking place during the eighteenth century in the form of new garments, an increase in the number of garments owned, changes in the fabrics from which these were made and an expansion in the range of colours.[77]

---

[74]   Tin cutlery sold at auctions of second-hand goods for around 1 *sou*, wooden cutlery for a few *diners*.

[75]   Lemire, *Fashion's Favourite*; id., *Dress, Culture and Commerce*; Roche, *La culture des apparences* (Paris, 1989).

[76]   On the complicated history of sumptuary laws, see A. Hunt, *Governance of the Consuming Passions: A History of Sumptuary Law* (Basingstoke, 1996). Belfanti and Giusberti have suggested that fashion replaced sumptuary laws as the determinant of class over the early modern period, rather than eroding social differences (C.M. Belfanti and F. Giusberti, 'Clothing and Social Inequality in Early Modern Europe: Introductory Remarks', *Continuity and Change*, 15 (2000), pp. 359–65).

[77]   See Roche, *La culture des apparences*, ch. 6; Garnot, *Un déclin*, pp. 216–26.

Contemporary observers make similar comments on changing fashions in eighteenth-century Catalonia as are found elsewhere in Europe: bemoaning the expansion of luxury and pretensions of the lower sorts in seeking to ape their betters, particularly in urban areas.[78] The Baró de Maldà gives a sketch of the social hierarchy in 1784 that is based mainly on dress, and describes well the prevalent fashions.[79] He also frequently describes the clothing worn by people he met, particularly that of boys and young men, in whom he took a special interest. More elite forms of dressing included, as elsewhere, wigs, swords and walking canes (often silver-topped). Equally important was the presence in male wardrobes of the *casaca*, a garment similar to a frock coat, as a replacement for the *gambeto* or cloak. The Baró describes himself as 'looking the part with my *casaca*, wig, sword and cane', items which ensured him a good seat at mass.[80] The *casaca*, however, was worn right down the social scale in towns, at least as best clothing. Colour was also important. Ramon Ferrer, the son of a muleteer, caught the Baró's eye in his holiday best of blue breeches and jacket, with silver buttons and buckles on his shoes.[81]

A more systematic study of inventories and marriage contracts confirms for Igualada the changes noted by contemporaries and by historians of other areas of Europe. The study of clothing and textiles on the basis of inventories is particularly complicated, since clothing was frequently sold, pawned or given away to kin or to the poor.[82] In Catalonia, there is the additional problem, as mentioned already, that some inventories record the clothing of all household members, some only that of the deceased, excluding women's clothing in particular. Nonetheless, two basic items of clothing were quantified for all inventories: shirts and sheets, selected for comparative purposes, but also because some historians have identified them as the most essential items of clothing and household linen.[83] In Igualada, however, as shown in Table 6.1, the proportion of inventories recording shirts and sheets rose only very slightly during the eighteenth century. The rise in the mean number per household owning such items was also slight: from 8.4 to 9.7 for shirts and

---

[78]   Navarro-Mas, 'Respuesta al interrogatorio del sr. D. Francisco de Zamora', p. 463; Juan Sempere Guariños, *Historia del luxo y de las leyes suntuarias de España* (2 vols, Madrid, 1788; facs. edn, 1973), vol. 1, pp. 178–9.

[79]   Amat, *Viles i ciutats*, pp. 255–62. While the text starts from the idea that clothes marked the social hierarchy, what becomes evident is that fashions were no longer clearly associated with rank. Instead, certain occupations such as muleteers, sailors and fishermen had distinctive forms of dress.

[80]   Amat, *Calaix de sastre*, vol. 2, p. 32

[81]   Ibid., vol. 1, p. 220.

[82]   See e.g. ANI 471, fos 223–8. For similar problems elsewhere, see Roche, *La culture des apparences*, pp. 88–91.

[83]   Ibid., p. 253; Garnot, *La culture matérielle*, p. 101; P. Malanima, *Il lusso dei contadini: Consumi e industrie nelle campagne toscane del sei e settecento* (Bologna, 1990), pp. 17–19.

17.5 to 17.8 for sheets. A similarly slight rise in shirts is described by Moreno for the Penedès, from a mean of 7.9 to 9.3, but the patterns for sheets are strikingly different, with the Penedès seeing a noticeable rise from 12.5 to 19.2 over the eighteenth century, a difference that is hard to explain.

A more useful analysis is that undertaken by Lídia Torra and others, examining the full range of clothing and household linen appearing in inventories and marriage contracts. Torra has analysed patterns of textile consumption in 258 inventories for Igualada, alongside samples for two other Catalan towns, Figueres and Mataró.[84] In conjunction with others, she has carried out a similar analysis of the trousseaux described in 222 marriage contracts, just from Igualada.[85] The trousseaux are by definition limited to female clothing but, as the authors point out, they are in many ways a better guide to changing patterns of textile consumption than inventories, since they represent an expenditure at a given point in the life-cycle, one subject to certain cultural norms and for which families could prepare over many years.[86]

The mean number and range of articles of household linen found in both inventories and trousseaux do not vary greatly over the period 1600 to 1800. The number and type of goods considered essential seems to have been fixed: tablecloths, napkins, towels, sheets and pillow cases were the usual items. By contrast, the range of clothing in inventories rose over the period for all three towns studied by Torra and for all social groups but less dramatically than in trousseaux, where the range of items more than doubled from 11 in 1600–1650 to 24 in 1751–1800, and the mean number of items tripled from 8 to 24.5. The new items of clothing were those described above for Barcelona: the frock coat for men, calico skirts and petticoats for women, along with accessories such as handkerchiefs, neckerchiefs, stockings, gloves and cravats.

The relative importance of different fabrics in inventories did not change during the eighteenth century. Linen dominated, accounting for around 70 per cent of all items. Cotton and wool both accounted for around 12 per cent, while only 3 per cent of items were made of silk. Among cotton, printed calicoes (*indianes*) dominated. Around 20 per cent of all items of clothing made from cotton were calico. Cotton and silk were important in terms of novelty, a fact reflected in their more significant presence in trousseaux.[87] The cotton and silk industries were the ones offering greatest variety and innovation in terms of products. A third of the 31 different types of silk mentioned in inventories appeared for the first time in the

---

[84]   Torra 'Pautas de consumo textil'.

[85]   Jaume Torras, Montserrat Duran and Lídia Torra, 'El ajuar de la novia: El consumo de tejidos en los contratos matrimoniales de una localidad catalana, 1600–1800', in Torras and Yun (eds), *Consumo, condiciones de vida y comercialización*, pp. 61–9.

[86]   Similar arguments are made for southern France by Agnès Fine, 'A Consideration of the Trousseau: A Feminine Culture?', in M. Perrot (ed.), *Writing Women's History* (Oxford, 1992), pp. 118–45.

[87]   Torras, Duran and Torra do not give any figures for types of fabric ('El ajuar de la novia').

second half of the eighteenth century. Similarly, many new cottons appear during the same period. Their uses also tend to be for new products: handkerchiefs, neck scarves and cravats.[88] Silk, while being a minority item of consumption, was used not just for small items, but also for dresses, skirts, capes and hoods, which Torra attributes to a desire for display among those who could afford it. What also stands out in terms of novelty is the range of colours, as noted above for clothing in Barcelona.[89] Whereas linen, even for clothing, tended to be in dark or muted colours, calicoes and silks, especially the former, were brightly coloured and patterned. The colours of fabrics were partly a question of technology, as new dyes and methods of fixing colours were invented during the eighteenth century, but demand was equally significant in determining choice, as discussed in Chapter 3.[90] The changes in the consumption of clothing and textiles put Catalan consumption not quite on a par with that of northern Europe (although a study of Barcelona inventories might redress the balance to some extent), yet well ahead of the rest of Spain. Consumption of new textiles was slow to diffuse in Castile, only becoming marked in the nineteenth century, when prices fell dramatically.[91]

A final important development is the extent to which households were purchasing ready-made clothing, as opposed to making their own. Here cotton and silk were important indicators of purchased goods. Linen and wool were more likely to be spun at home, then taken to a weaver. The sale of ready-made garments began with smaller items such as hats and stockings, but eventually spread to dresses, cloaks and the like. As Beverley Lemire points out, the trade in ready-made clothing allowed people to be fashionable, but the garments could also be utilitarian and quickly produced.[92] It also employed women in significant numbers. The same developments can be identified for Igualada as those for England. Rather

[88] On a similar use of cotton for accessories in England 1750s onwards, see Lemire, *Fashion's Favourite*, pp. 87–9.

[89] A similar increase in the range of colours available has been noted for women's clothing in Meaux and for male and female clothing in Laichingen (M. Baulant, 'Niveaux de vie paysans autour de Meaux en 1700 et 1750', in id., *Meaux et ses campagnes: Vivre et survivre dans le monde rural sous l'Ancien Régime* (Rennes, 2006), pp. 271–85 (pp. 282–4); Medick, 'Une culture de la considération', pp. 764–70).

[90] Blue had a noticeable rise in popularity in many areas (see Pardailhé-Galabrun, *The Birth of Intimacy*, pp. 170–3; Roche, *La culture des apparences*, pp. 126–9, 134–40; Garnot, *Un déclin*, pp. 221–2; Medick, 'Une culture de la considération', pp. 764–70). Thomson has shown that Catalan calico-printers were able to introduce indigo printing very rapidly ('Technological Transfer', pp. 256–8).

[91] Jaume Torras and Bartolomé Yun, 'Historia del consumo e historia del crecimiento: El consumo de tejidos en España, 1700–1850', *Revista de historia económica*, 21, special issue (2003), pp. 17–41; Fernando Ramos, 'La demanda de textiles de las familias castellanas a finales del antiguo régimen, 1750–1850: ¿Aumento del consumo sin industrialización?', *Revista de Historia Económica*, 21, special issue (2003), pp. 141–78.

[92] Lemire, *Fashion's Favourite*, pp. 176–97; ead. *Dress, Culture and Commerce*, pp. 43–74.

than ready-made clothing taking over entirely from textiles, the two co-existed. In 1816 there was only one shop selling exclusively ready-made clothes (although three makers and dealers in ready-made clothing, *roperos*, are recorded in the 1824 *cadastre*), but 26 shops stocked a mixture of ready-made garments and lengths of different fabrics.[93] Co-existence was not always harmonious, however; the same hostility and resistance from tailors and the like as described by Lemire was also present in Igualada.[94]

Marketing and distribution of goods

The differences in patterns of consumption of clothing, like those for other goods, were in part determined by retail networks. One of the crucial aspects of the industrious revolution is precisely the greater weight within household consumption of purchased, as opposed to domestically produced, goods. Ideally, the historian would work with household budgets in order to examine this question, but such budgets are rarely forthcoming for the early modern period. Some indirect indicators, however, are provided by the widening of market networks, particularly the rise of the retail shop. De Vries describes a retailing revolution for the period 1650–1750, which according to him, took the form of a shift from markets, fairs and guild-controlled distribution to retail shops and pedlars. The rise of the shop can certainly be documented for England, France and the Netherlands, but Laurence Fontaine has shown that networks of pedlars were already well established in Europe by the fifteenth and sixteenth centuries.[95]

Fairs and markets may, however, have remained important for longer than de Vries allows. While few Catalan fairs were on the scale of Beaucaire or the fair at Valdemoro that was so important to the Torelló family, with most being primarily for the exchange of agricultural products, particularly tools and livestock, they nonetheless could still be important occasions for consumption, associated with particular feast days as described in Chapter 5.[96] Much depended upon location. The replies to Zamora's questionnaire suggest that smaller fairs were losing their importance during the eighteenth century, but those in Barcelona, by contrast, were clearly still major occasions. The fair associated with the feast of St Thomas on 21 December, although supposedly for the sale of poultry in preparation for Christmas, was taken advantage of by all shopkeepers and artisans to display their

---

[93]   AMI 18.6.1, 'Relación de las tiendas que se hayan en esta villa ... (20 Sept. 1816)'; for similar patterns in the inventories of English traders, see Lemire, *Dress, Culture and Commerce*, pp. 57–63.

[94]   Ibid., pp. 44–59; for a scathing attack on *roperos*, not least in its view of the trade as 'feminine', see AMI 1116, *Registre municipal*, fos 11r–12r.

[95]   L. Fontaine, *Histoire du colportage en Europe: Xve–XIXe siècles* (Paris, 1993).

[96]   Roche, *Histoire des choses banales*, pp. 59–61. Three-quarters of the 4,264 fairs documented for France were associated with parishes of fewer than 2,000 inhabitants.

wares in doorways.[97] In Igualada, the principal fair was celebrated on and around 24 August, the feast day of the patron saint, St Bartholomew.

Markets were perhaps becoming more, not less, important in Catalonia by the eighteenth century. Although traditionally for the sale of foodstuffs and livestock, other goods were also bought and sold, making markets in certain locations crucial nodes in a network of extended commerce. Papiol describes how the market at Vilanova i la Geltrú, though centred on the sale of poultry brought from the surrounding villages, served increasingly to distribute goods from overseas to these same villages.[98] According to Zamora, Figueres had the busiest market in all of Catalonia, attracting buyers and vendors from France.[99] Igualada had an important fortnightly market. The Baró de Maldà, visiting on market day in 1794, was struck by the crowds and the range of goods for sale: besides wheat, vegetables and fruit, there were stalls selling earthenware, pots and pans, clothes and many more goods.[100]

Nevertheless, even if markets continued to thrive in Catalonia during the eighteenth century, shops were becoming more important.[101] Quantifying them along the lines of other studies is difficult, but contemporary comments testify to their increased presence and their novelty. The Baró de Maldà was impressed by a shop in Mataró, the only one of its kind in the town: 'a treasure trove, selling chocolate, sugar, starch, powder for wigs and hair, all types of sweet things, noodles, white paper and innumerable other goods'.[102] Shops such as these, though, represent a type of general village shop that had always existed, albeit with a narrower range of goods. The innovation of the eighteenth century was the increasingly specialised shop, particularly in clothing and textiles, with textile or merchant companies setting up or investing in shops in particular locations, as described in Chapter 3. Igualada had a surprisingly high number of specialised shops by 1816, five of which appear to be outlets for companies. There was one shop selling liquors, one pots and pans, one ready-made clothing, two salted fish, three glassware and five ironmongers, two apothecaries, a café, 18 inns and taverns, 37 selling foodstuffs and another 37 selling clothing and textiles. Clothing and textiles often included imported goods. Zamora comments on a shop in Manlleu 'in which all the clothes were of this country', the implication being that this was rare.[103] In 1778 a survey found four Igualada shops stocking foreign cloths, though since the survey was for tax purposes, this may be an underestimate.[104]

---

[97]   Amat, *Calaix de sastre*, vol. 1, pp. 73–4, 98, 155; Navarro-Mas, 'Respuesta al interrogatorio del sr. D. Francisco de Zamora', pp. 454–5.

[98]   Papiol, *Reposta de Francesc Papiol*, p. 57.

[99]   Zamora, *Diario de los viajes hechos por Cataluña* p. 355.

[100]   Amat, *Calaix de sastre*, vol. 2, pp. 207–8; see also Torras Ribé, *La comarca de l'Anoia*, pp. 359–60.

[101]   Vilar, *La Catalogne*, vol. 3, pp. 144–87.

[102]   Amat, *Calaix de sastre*, vol. 1, p. 267.

[103]   Zamora, *Diario de los viajes hechos por Cataluña*, p. 67.

[104]   Vilar, *La Catalogne*, vol. 3, pp. 171–6.

Shops were only part of the story, though. One of Torra's most interesting findings is that household inventories in Igualada show a wider range of clothing and textiles than the inventories of shops selling those goods. Part of the access to goods in general and to foreign goods in particular was provided by pedlars, part by larger urban markets, particularly Barcelona.[105] To the longstanding networks of pedlars from France were added during the eighteenth century networks of muleteers, trading across the peninsula, connecting shops established by Catalans as discussed in Chapter 3. Some places, such as Calaf, Copons and Prats del Rei took advantage of their favourable location on the routes to Castille by dedicating themselves to transport as muleteers. Smuggling, particularly of English and French goods, also played an important though unquantifiable part of this trade. While most noticeable in the Pyrenees and along the coast, smuggled goods were to be found across Catalonia according to Zamora, who was particularly vexed by the issue.[106]

That demand for new goods could not always be met locally is clearly illustrated by the correspondence of the Torelló family and others with Albert Combelles, whose sister Teresa was married to Isidro Torelló. The majority of the letters mention the purchase of goods in Barcelona. The pursuit of fashion is evident: on one occasion, Isidro had requested a hat for his son to be made 'in the latest fashion'.[107] Printed handkerchiefs feature twice as items for Teresa.[108] However, the requests encompassed a wide range of goods, from crosses for rosaries to oranges to glass for a new skylight to serum for smallpox vaccination.[109] The absence of accounts makes it impossible to know what the volume of these purchases was within household expenditure, but the frequency of these purchases testifies to their importance. This kind of access to the better-supplied Barcelona markets was more likely for elite households with connections to the city, though pedlars undoubtedly supplied some goods to other households. Crucially, however, all exchanges with Barcelona relied upon the existence of a network of pedlars and muleteers.

A focus on the retailing and distribution of new goods, however, ignores the greater importance in this period of second-hand goods, gifts and bequests. As Lemire points out with reference to the clothing trade, the needs of the whole population could not be satisfied by the existing structures of production.[110]

---

[105]   Torras Ribé, *La comarca de l'Anoia*, pp. 359, 498.

[106]   Zamora, *Diario de los viajes hechos por Cataluña* pp. 73, 92, 283, 323.

[107]   Isidro Torelló, letter (27 Apr. 1822), AT, *lligall* 1480.

[108]   Isidro Torelló, letters (21 Dec. 1822), AT, *lligall* 1480; (17 May 1800). AT, *lligall* 1460.

[109]   Isidro Torelló, letters (10 Apr. 1822), AT, *lligall* 1480 (crosses for rosaries); (13 Apr. 1822), ibid. (smallpox serum); (13 Oct. 1814), AT, *lligall* 1455 (glass); (23 June 1817), ibid. (oranges).

[110]   Lemire, *Fashion's Favourite*, pp. 61–7; ead., 'Peddling Fashion: Salesmen, Pawnbrokers, Tailors, Thieves and the Second-Hand Clothes Trade in England', *Textile History*, 22 (1991), pp. 67–82.

The second-hand-clothes trade was thus 'a flexible, adaptable, intermediary phenomenon'. Poor households in eighteenth-century France had an estimated 18 *livres* to spend on clothing per person per year, but with a new shirt costing 10 *livres*, new shoes 4 to 6 *livres* and a dress or suit between 30 and 40 *livres*, this budget would not get them far if clothing were purchased new.[111] Second-hand clothing allowed the poor in Paris to follow fashions, but at a distance and within limits. More importantly, even better-off households still purchased goods second-hand or recycled existing goods in various ways.[112] The Torelló family, for all their desire to be fashionable, were no exception. Isidro Torelló sent a calico dressing-gown of his to Albert Combelles with the request that he have it used to make 'a little dress of fine calico, that should be well-made and look smart' for Isidro's daughter, but with the request that the seamstress use enough material for the seams to be let out at a later date.[113]

The importance of gifts can be ascertained only through scattered references. Second-hand markets, by contrast, are more visible, in the form of *vendes a l'encant* or sales at auction of moveable goods. Given the Catalan system of inheritance, these were fairly rare, occurring only when goods needed to be sold to satisfy creditors or if the deceased had specifically ordered such a sale in order to raise a cash bequest for the heir or heirs. Nonetheless, the records of such sales are extremely valuable, since they record the names of purchasers, as well as the goods purchased and the amounts paid. It is therefore possible to see who participated in the markets for such goods and which goods were the most significant in terms of number and value of purchases.

I have collected a sample of nine such sales for Igualada, two of which are from 1686, the remainder from 1754–84. Though few and unevenly distributed chronologically, they still yield 701 purchases for analysis. What stands out is the importance of the second-hand-clothes trade. Clothes account for 29.4 per cent of all items sold and 34.9 per cent of the total value of these goods. Behind clothing came kitchen equipment, 21.1 per cent of goods sold and 14.4 per cent of the value; linen, 16 per cent of purchases and 16.9 per cent of the total value; and furniture, 8.8 per cent of purchases and 10.6 per cent of the total value. No other type of good sold accounted for more than 5 per cent of goods sold or their value, except for gold items, which were only 1 per cent of items sold but 5.1 per cent of the total value. Assessing individual prices is trickier, since the nature of a public auction may have inflated the price of more popular items and much depends on quality and state of wear. There was a considerable range of prices, from a salt cellar, saucepan and pieces of cloth that sold for as little as 4 *diners* each, up to the 12 *lliures* paid for two chests. The most expensive goods sold, at 5 *lliures* or more,

---

[111] Roche, *La culture des apparences*, pp. 206–10, 327–45.

[112] For examples, see Vickery, 'Women and the World of Goods', pp. 282–3; S. Nenadic, 'Middle-Rank Consumers and Domestic Culture in Edinburgh and Glasgow, 1720–1840', *Past and Present*, 145 (1994), pp. 122–56.

[113] Isidro Torelló, letter (20 Mar. 1806), AT, *lligall* 1455.

were items such as a silk dress, gold and silver, a bed and carding equipment. Most goods sold (74 per cent), however, were for under 1 *lliura*, with the average price being 18.4 *sous*, testifying to the importance of such second-hand markets for the acquisition of everyday goods.

Who were the consumers?

Gender and life-cycle

As already discussed, the role of women as consumers has been considered of paramount importance. Much has been written since the eighteenth century about the propensity of women to follow fashion and spend money, particularly on clothing, a discourse that has often carried negative associations with vanity and frivolity.[114] A more positive view points to greater female consumption of basic household goods, and a greater allocation of female earnings to household resources, rather than to their own gratification.[115] One of the effects of the greater labour market participation by women discussed in the previous chapter was supposedly the greater freedom wages gave them to consume.[116] De Vries takes the argument a step further by suggesting that such freedom to make individual consumer choices derived from the nuclear family structure prevalent in north-western Europe and contributed to an industrious revolution in a way that was impossible in other areas where women's workforce participation and consumer choices were much more restricted. In making this argument, de Vries draws only upon examples quoted by Raffaella Sarti of decision-making processes in different Italian households for the nineteenth and early twentieth centuries. In larger sharecropper families, new wives were less likely to have made purchasing decisions than their parents-in-law.[117]

In fact, evidence on female expenditure is mixed. Some historians have found equal or greater levels of expenditure on clothing by women than men for certain periods, but no constant trend or geographical pattern.[118] Inventory

---

[114]   Victoria de Grazia, 'Changing Consumption Regimes', in V. de Grazia and E. Furlough (eds), *The Sex of Things: Gender and Consumption in Historical Perspective* (Berkeley, 1996), pp. 11–21

[115]   Joan Thirsk, *Economic Policy and Projects: The Development of a Consumer Society in Early Modern England* (Oxford, 1978), esp. pp. 22–3.

[116]   Roche, *La culture des apparences*, p. 206; Lemire, *Fashion's Favourite*, pp. 54–5.

[117]   De Vries, *Industrious Revolution*, pp. 17–19 n. 47; Sarti, *Europe at Home*, p. 218. Sarti's examples and her discussion suggest seniority within the household, rather than gender, was the more important factor.

[118]   Roche, *La culture des apparences*, p. 111; J.M. Jones, '*Coquettes* and *Grisettes*: Women Buying and Selling in Ancien Régime Paris', in de Grazia and Furlough (eds), *The Sex of Things*, pp. 25–53; J. Cruz, 'Elites, Merchants and Consumption in Madrid at the End

studies show few differences in the number and type of possessions owned by men and women.[119] As regards bargaining power within the household, Sandra Cavallo has argued that women in Turin increasingly lost control over their property during the early modern period.[120] Although Catalan law gave women the right to keep their own property after marriage and gave widows the usufruct of their husbands' property, Moreno is similarly sceptical that women had much freedom as consumers, believing that the husband's right to administer his wife's dowry effectively removed it from her control.[121] In her study, women are far less significant than men as consumers. It is not clear, however, that such restrictions were only a feature of southern European societies and particular family systems. Sheilagh Ogilvie has provided compelling evidence of how little power over their income and expenditure sumptuary law and family power structures allowed women in early modern Württemburg, despite this region having all the hallmarks of Hajnal's European marriage pattern.[122] Even for England a cautious note has been sounded by Richard Wall, who suggests that management of household resources did not necessarily equate to control over them: married women might be granted the former, but were far less likely to enjoy the latter.[123] Bengtsson, Campbell and Lee have suggested nuclear European households were no more egalitarian than more complex Asian ones when it came to allocation of scarce resources, resulting in pervasive gender biases in mortality.[124]

As Sarti points out, however, the real difficulty is that we know far too little about how consumption was organised within families and have perhaps been too ready to associate consumption with women.[125] Female account books and discussions of expenditure in diaries are rare and do not shed much light on how

of the Old Regime', in Schuurman and Walsh, *Material Culture*, pp. 137–46 (pp. 142–3); Ogilvie, *Bitter Living*, p. 204; Richard Wall, 'Some Implications of the Earnings, Income and Expenditure Patterns of Married Women in Populations in the Past', in J. Henderson and R. Wall (eds), *Poor Women and Children in the European Past* (London, 1994), pp. 312–35 (pp. 328–30).

[119] L. Weatherill, 'A Possession of One's Own: Women and Consumer Behavior in England, 1660–1740', *Journal of British Studies*, 25 (1986), pp. 131–56; C. Fairchild, 'Determinants of Consumption Patterns in Eighteenth-Century France', in Schuurman and Walsh (eds), *Material Culture*, pp. 55–67.

[120] S. Cavallo, 'What did Women Transmit? Ownership and Control of Household Goods and Personal Effects in Early Modern Italy', in M. Donald and L. Hurcombe (eds), *Gender and Material Culture in Historical Perspective* (Basingstoke, 2000), pp. 38–53.

[121] Moreno, *Consum i condicions de vida*, pp. 189–217.

[122] Ogilvie, *Bitter Living*, pp. 136–8, 200–4; ead., 'Consumption, Social Capital and the Industrious Revolution in Early Modern Germany', *Journal of Economic History*, 70 (2010), pp. 287–325.

[123] Wall, 'Some Implications of the Earnings, Income and Expenditure Patterns of Married Women', p. 318.

[124] Bengtsson, Campbell and Lee, *Life under Pressure*, chs 4, 5, pp. 434–5.

[125] Sarti, *Europe at Home*, pp. 214–9.

the allocation of income and expenditure took place within the household.[126] Moreover, male diaries show an equal involvement by men in the purchasing of food, clothing and other items for the home and a strong emotional investment by men in such goods.[127] A single set of Catalan accounts kept by a widow, Francisca Nin, show much higher levels of expenditure on her son and heir, a university student, than on herself or her daughter.[128]

As this last example suggests, age and status within the household may also have had an impact on the relative positions of men and women. Those who view the nuclear family as permitting higher levels of consumption by promoting greater independence are not always clear as to whether it is consumption by women or by young adults that matters most.[129] More importantly, young men and women saved up for marriage within all family forms, and marriage was always a point in the life-cycle that was closely associated with consumption. In extended family systems, more of the goods consumed in relation to marriage may have come from kin than from saved earnings, but there is no a priori reason to assume that demand for goods would necessarily vary. The only sense in which the nuclear family would have generated more or different consumer demand is that the formation of an entirely separate household on marriage would require greater investment in furniture and kitchen equipment than a marriage followed by co-residence with parents.

What evidence there is for Igualada indicates that questions of gender are difficult to separate from age and status. Women's inventories, as elsewhere, show no significant differences in patterns of ownership from men's inventories. As mentioned above, however, few survive, and they are often atypical in being the inventories of heiresses. Moreover, it is often unclear whether inventories left by women simply cover the goods brought to the marriage as part of a dowry or include goods purchased since or inherited from a spouse. Less equivocal lists of female possessions are provided by the descriptions of dowries and trousseaux within marriage contracts, which have been discussed above in the context of textile consumption. A comparison between the marriage contracts of spinsters and widows gives some idea of what goods women might have accumulated during marriage as well as before.[130] Another comparison can be made between

---

[126]   For one example, which highlights how complex the division of purchasing could be, see Vickery, 'Women and the World of Goods', pp. 279–81.

[127]   Margot Finn, 'Men's Things: Masculine Possession in the Consumer Revolution', *Social History*, 25 (2000), pp. 133–55.

[128]   Moreno, *Consum i condicions de vida*, p. 217.

[129]   e.g. Hajnal sees the accumulation of household goods by young men and women in service as crucial to generating consumer demand, but does not make clear if it is gender or life-cycle stage that matters most ('European Marriage Patterns', p. 132; 'Two Kinds of Pre-Industrial Household Formation System', pp. 474–5).

[130]   Excluding heiresses, there are 1,810 contracts of spinsters and 168 of widows.

the goods given to women on marriage and those given to younger sons in order to see if there were differences according to gender when it came to setting up home.

As discussed above, clothing and household linen, usually in a chest or chests, made up the bulk of trousseaux, but other household goods did feature from time to time. The most common goods were mattresses and beds, other furniture such as tables, chairs, benches and stools and kitchen equipment, including bread-making implements and barrels. In a few cases, as already mentioned, women brought spinning wheels or spinning jennies with them on marriage. Unsurprisingly, such goods were relatively more common in the marriage contracts of widows than of spinsters, either because women purchased such items while married or because they had inherited them from their previous husbands or could claim them as repayment of a dowry or the future property of their children. While only 1 per cent of first-time brides brought furniture and 2 per cent brought beds or kitchen equipment to their husbands, 8 per cent of widows brought furniture or beds and 13 per cent brought kitchen equipment. In fact, if the type of goods given to men on marriage are compared with those of women, the patterns suggest that age rank and life-cycle stage mattered more than gender.[131] Men were more likely to be given land and houses or tools or a workspace than women. When it came to moveable household goods, however, clothes, linen, mattresses and beds were the main goods for both sexes at first marriage. More importantly, men were just as likely as single women to bring kitchen equipment to a marriage. The choice of goods was determined more by future residence. Where the couple would continue to reside with one set of parents after marriage, then clothes, linen, a bed and a mattress were more important than other furniture and kitchen equipment, which would be shared with the older couple. The latter items were much more likely to be given to couples setting up houses on their own, as were the few instances of wine and grain.

How far consumer choices were constrained by gender, age or status within the family is difficult to assess. Dowries were constrained by the desire for equality among sisters, a desire borne out by the remarkably close similarities in the numbers of items of clothing and linen provided for sisters, although colours and styles may still have been a matter of individual preference. In 80 cases, marriage contracts record sums of money to be spent on clothing and household goods or quantities of material, rather than finished items, perhaps allowing the bride a greater say in the final purchases. It seems that clothing was an area reserved to some extent for feminine decision-making, as evidenced by a handful of marriage contracts where, rather than listing all the items of clothing and linen, the notary

---

[131]   The comparison is not straightforward since women always have some kind of a dowry specified, whereas only 374 of 1,428 contracts of younger sons specify what goods they were bringing to the marriage. Moreover, the marriage contracts can only tell us what types of goods were included, not what their relative value was within the overall marriage portions of men and women.

restricted himself to the single phrase *roba a coneguda de sa mare* (clothing as determined by her mother).[132]

Expenditure on goods during marriage is far harder to assess. Although no household accounts survive for Igualada that would shed any light on this matter, in the Torelló family correspondence, Teresa's voice can occasionally be heard behind various different requests for purchases from Barcelona, usually to do with clothing or food, as when Isidro wrote that 'for the marmalade Teresa says to buy juicy oranges'.[133] The only source in which women can be seen making actual purchases on a more extensive basis is the sales at auction described above. Here, the findings corroborate Moreno's to a certain extent.[134] Women made up only 32 per cent of the purchasers and accounted for only 26.5 per cent of the number of purchases and 25.7 per cent of the total expenditure at such sales. The difference between the average price of items purchased by women (19.0 *sous*) and by men (21.8 *sous*) is, however, far less marked than in the Penedès, where Moreno finds a difference of over 3 *lliures*. This may reflect the larger size of her sample (20 sales) or possibly the type of goods sold (men in her sample purchased agricultural tools, which may have been more expensive). As with dowries and inventories, however, in neither my sample nor hers does the type of goods purchased vary much according to gender. Men accounted for all ten instances of book-buying, the two instances in which foodstuffs were bought and the one purchase of a firearm (which women were not allowed to own). Otherwise, men and women purchased the same goods with a similar order of priorities.[135] Clothing was top for both, accounting for 31 per cent of female and 29 per cent of male purchases and 40 and 33 per cent of the total expenditure by each sex respectively. Kitchen equipment followed, significantly, at 18 per cent and 22 per cent of female and male purchases and 12 and 15 per cent of expenditure; linen came in third at 16 per cent of purchases made by both sexes, but accounting for 22 per cent of female expenditure and 15 per cent of male. Marital status is rarely given, so we cannot compare the purchasing patterns of single, married and widowed women.

Sarti would therefore seem to be right that gendered aspects of consumption should not be overemphasised, at least in the absence of solid evidence. There is some suggestion in the Catalan evidence that age and status may have counted for more than gender. Young adults may perhaps have been less free in this area to make their own consumption choices than they were elsewhere in Europe, but the rituals of consumption surrounding marriage and the formation of a new

---

[132]   Fine has also found that, in south-western France, trousseaux were usually left to mothers and daughters ('A Consideration of the Trousseau', pp. 128–33).

[133]   Isidro Torelló to Albert Combelles (30 Apr. 1823), AT, *lligall* 1480.

[134]   Moreno, *Consum i condicions de vida*, p. 200.

[135]   In Moreno's sample, the order of importance for women was linen, clothes, kitchen equipment and religious prints; for men, linen, clothes, agricultural tools and kitchen equipment.

household still provided opportunities for the acquisition of new goods and the following of fashion.

Elite or plebeian consumption?

In the absence of any sharp distinctions in consumption within households, the final question to address is that of distinctions across households. In assessing the role of wealth and status in consumer behaviour, de Vries has two main arguments: first, that many consumer durables, as revealed by inventories, can be found further down the social scale in England and the Netherlands than is often acknowledged by historians; second, that plebeian households also developed a distinctive consumer culture, focusing more on the increased purchase of ready-made food and drink and on forms of leisure and sociability than on domestic comforts.[136] Both claims rest on fairly shaky empirical foundations: the first is weakened by the social bias of inventories, the second depends on the indirect evidence of taxation of certain forms of food and drink and on anecdotal evidence of plebeian habits.[137]

The preceding discussion has already shown that certain goods were more widely consumed than others among Igualada households. The following section attempts to investigate the issue in more depth. Addressing the first of de Vries's claims is difficult given the lack of valuations in Catalan inventories. Two different proxies for wealth and status are used here: occupation and amount of land held. A better proxy might have been credit, but too few inventories contained information on this. Tables 6.2 and 6.3 thus give the breakdown according to occupational sector and to how much land households held.

The most widely diffused new goods were chocolate, forks and spoons, though even here there were limits. Otherwise, Table 6.2 shows that certain types of consumer behaviour were associated with particular groups for reasons to do with culture and professional needs as well as wealth. Books were far more likely to be found in the inventories of those in the liberal professions and in commerce. The same is true of clocks and watches and most strikingly of snuff-boxes and other items related to tobacco. Even among such professional and commercial households, these items were not widely distributed. Professionals such as priests, often living as lodgers in other households, are responsible for the relatively high levels of consumption shown by landless households in Table 6.3. Otherwise, there is a steady rise in the presence of most goods the more land households possessed, with often a sharp

---

[136]   De Vries, *Industrious Revolution*, pp. 149–80; for the second claim, see also Braun, *Industrialization and Everyday Life*, ch.3.

[137]   De Vries acknowledges the social bias of inventory samples as used by Weatherill, for example, basing his claims on the evidence of the more exceptional inventories studied by Peter King and Anne McCants (see ch. 1 n. 43). Both authors are far more cautious in their assessments than de Vries is in his use of their work. Anecdotal evidence, as in Braun's work, is often derived from hostile observations made by elite observers.

Table 6.2 Rates of ownership of goods across occupations

		Agriculture	Professions and commerce	Leather	Textiles	Goods and services	Artisans	Others and unknown
Clocks	N	0	16	2	9	7	3	0
	%	0	17	4	7	7	5	0
Pictures	N	24	71	29	69	49	43	9
	%	32	75	52	56	52	65	9
Mirrors	N	8	51	16	30	22	29	75
	%	11	54	29	24	23	44	5
Books	N	2	40	2	11	7	15	42
	%	3	42	4	9	7	23	3
Gold	N	11	31	8	31	23	15	25
	%	15	33	14	25	24	23	1
Silver	N	24	61	23	63	46	39	8
	%	32	64	41	51	48	59	6
Chocolate	N	9	55	17	31	28	33	50
	%	12	58	30	25	29	50	6
Tobacco	N	0	19	0	0	3	0	50
	%	0	20	0	0	3	0	1
Shirts	N	53	74	48	98	81	56	8
	%	71	78	86	80	85	85	9
Sheets	N	71	87	55	114	92	65	75
	%	95	92	98	93	97	98	12
Forks	N	13	65	20	47	36	34	100
	%	17	68	36	38	38	52	6
Spoons	N	51	73	40	79	73	53	50
	%	68	77	71	64	77	80	8
								67

Table 6.3 Rates of ownership of goods according to extent of landholdings

	Clocks	Pictures	Mirrors	Books	Chocolate	Tobacco	Gold	Silver	Shirts	Sheets	Forks	Spoons
Landless	9	63	31	24	44	6	27	58	120	135	56	90
	6	*43*	*21*	*17*	*30*	*4*	*19*	*40*	*83*	*90*	*39*	*62*
<2	0	11	4	8	6	0	2	10	23	26	7	17
	0	*38*	*14*	*7*	*21*	*0*	*7*	*34*	*79*	*90*	*24*	*59*
2–4.9	5	71	32	8	39	4	28	60	121	138	44	102
	3	*49*	*22*	*5*	*27*	*3*	*19*	*41*	*83*	*95*	*30*	*70*
5–9.9	10	60	27	15	35	2	20	52	71	94	44	77
	10	*63*	*28*	*16*	*36*	*2*	*21*	*54*	*74*	*98*	*46*	*80*
10–49.9	6	69	49	20	38	5	33	66	69	83	52	72
	7	*80*	*57*	*23*	*44*	*5*	*38*	*77*	*80*	*97*	*60*	*84*
50–99.9	4	12	11		10	2	6	9	9	12	11	12
	33	*100*	*92*	*42*	*83*	*17*	*50*	*75*	*75*	*100*	*92*	*100*
>100	3	8	7	6	7	4	4	7	6	8	7	7
	38	*100*	*88*	*75*	*88*	*50*	*50*	*88*	*75*	*100*	*88*	*88*

jump in levels of ownership above 50 *jornals*. If land is acceptable as a proxy for wealth, then the extent to which households participated in older and newer forms of consumption depended very much upon their position in the social hierarchy.

Assessing the second issue of greater plebeian expenditure on prepared foodstuffs, alcoholic beverages and forms of commercialised sociability is much more difficult. Admittedly, the widespread diffusion of chocolate is significant: this is one of the few areas where plebeian households can be seen as participating in the same changes as the elite. It has already been shown, however, that inventoried households in Igualada were not abandoning domestic production and preparation of food. As mentioned above, there is some anecdotal evidence of a new form of plebeian consumer culture emerging in Barcelona in association with the new class of factory workers, described as given to smoking tobacco.[138] The discussion of retailing above gives some indication of the presence of cafes and taverns in Igualada by the early nineteenth century, but comparisons with earlier dates are lacking, as is evidence of the clientele these establishments served. To speak of a distinct plebeian culture of consumption may be a step too far. It is just as likely that elite households consumed durables and perishables, whereas poorer households consumed only those perishables they could afford and which provided the stimulants necessary to endure long working hours. Insofar as households may have purchased more prepared foods, the limited evidence from elsewhere in Europe suggests this was often at the expense of the quality of diets.

While conceding that there were negative features of plebeian participation in the industrious revolution in north-western Europe, de Vries still highlights what he considers 'the positive achievement: the exercise of choice across a widened array of available goods to construct consumption clusters'.[139] The exercise of consumer choice in Igualada, as elsewhere in Catalonia, was not absent, but outside of elite households it was restricted and served only to mark further differences between these and plebeian households. Moreno's work shows clearly how the acquisition of new goods in the Penedès was used by an elite of wealthy peasants and urban households of doctors, lawyers and a few others to set themselves apart from the rest. In Igualada, the elite consisted of merchants, manufacturers and professionals rather than peasants, but otherwise the same picture holds true. Examples of this new elite include Pau Anton Lladó, son of the clothier described in Chapter 3, who died in 1794, aged 49.[140] His house had three cellars for wine, two for grain, wood and coal, stables and rooms on a further two floors, including a chapel. His is the only inventory to mention a carriage. The rooms were wallpapered, and lavishly decorated. They were clearly designed for entertaining: the parlour had 30 chairs. Other luxury items included a violin, a set of playing cards, a set of pistols, silver snuff-boxes, a silver watch, a clock, some 20 volumes of books, satin curtains and a bathtub. Another wealthy household, inventoried in 1818, was that of Anton

---

[138] Amat, *Calaix de sastre*, vol. 3, p. 173; vol. 4, p. 165.

[139] De Vries, *Industrious Revolution*, p. 180.

[140] ANI 546, fos 279–90.

Amigó, a hat manufacturer who owned five houses, around 64 *jornals* of land, a paper mill, a tannery and a calico-spinning workshop.[141] In his residence, work and living space were clearly separate, with the workrooms on the ground floor along with cellars and stables. The rooms above occupied by the family included a dining room, a parlour (again, clearly for entertaining, with 26 upholstered chairs), a study, a kitchen with separate larder and rooms for making bread and curing meat, and bedrooms including those of the servants. Even the latter were decorated, albeit with prints rather than the paintings and mirrors that adorned other rooms. Luxury items included a dozen silver spoons and forks (with two dozen in tin for everyday use), a silver watch, a clock, an organ, a nativity scene with little figures (a fashion recently imported from Naples), seven chocolate pots, two coffeepots and two dozen coffee cups, a library including fiction as well as devotional works and 98 sheets among the linen belonging to Anton Amigó alone (the clothes and linen of his wife and daughters-in-law were not inventoried). The family kept chickens and pigeons in the loft, as well as storing wood there, but also had a roof garden, with flower pots and benches.

Although the overall sample is biased towards better-off households, the handful of inventories from poor households throw the differences in material culture into stark relief. Francisco Piquer, a shepherd or goatherd, left at his death in 1781 a pine chest, a bench, two stools, a small frying-pan, a basket, a lamp, two tin and six wooden spoons, six plates and six dishes, two sacks, two cloaks, a pair of breeches, two nightshirts, a pair of espadrilles, a pair of clogs, three shirts, a tablecloth, a straw mattress, a sackcloth and a pillow. His only fixed property was 2 *jornals* of vines on a *rabassa morta* contract.[142] Jaume Aguilera, a carter, died in the hospital in 1820, leaving a bed, a straw mattress, a sheet, two shirts and a set of bread-making equipment and 2 *jornals* of vines.[143]

While these examples represent the poorest end of the spectrum covered by the inventory sample, they are by no means extreme. More importantly, these households were not the poorest of the poor: however scanty their possessions, they usually had some tiny claim to property in the form of a *rabassa morta* contract or similar that made the expense of an inventory worthwhile. As will be seen below, others were poorer still.

Choices or constraints?

Forced commercialisation

As has been argued throughout this work, freedom to respond to changing market opportunities is central to the concept of an 'industrious revolution' as defined

---

141   ANI 663, fos 57–68.
142   ANI 380, fos 174r–175r.
143   ANI 606, unfol.

by de Vries. As discussed in Chapter 1, de Vries has moved away from the initial recognition that households might be forced into market participation by increased taxation or rising prices, factors long stressed by historians of peasant societies.[144] In Catalonia, however, such forces were very much evident. In various ways, households were increasingly enmeshed in a web of obligations that frequently had to be met in cash. Previous chapters have already shown that households were increasingly caught in the trap of interlocking markets when it came to accessing livestock and credit and were also increasingly dependent on markets for basic foodstuffs, especially grain. In addition, many more households were paying rent by the early nineteenth century. The *cadastres* record which households owned one or more houses, since these were liable for tax. By 1824 the percentage of Igualada households who owned a house was down to 40 from 62 in 1765. Figures for rent are not available for Igualada, but it is likely that they were rising, as they were in Barcelona.[145]

Particularly acute was the burden of taxation, which increased during the eighteenth and early nineteenth centuries. The *cadastre* was a new tax for Catalonia, imposed in 1716 as part of the Bourbon reforms. The Napoleonic wars brought various extra contributions, with the result that all regions of Spain were paying more taxes per capita in 1813 than they had been in 1791.[146] In Catalonia, the burden had increased from 16.8 *reales* per head to 43.5. Chapter 2 has already described the extent to which feudal dues were increasingly transferred down the landowning hierarchy to the smallholder. The same was true of the *cadastre*, which was levied as a fixed sum for each locality, the raising of which sum from the inhabitants was then left to the discretion of local authorities. This allowed for considerable abuse and inequality in the distribution of the tax. Tello has estimated that for many localities, the *cadastre* represented double the amount paid in other dues, such as tithe.[147] Most importantly, it had to be paid in cash, not kind, forcing communities to sell grain or other produce. In Tello's examples from the Segarra, communities that might otherwise have been self-sufficient in grain often ended up with a deficit as the result of meeting *cadastre* payments.

Poverty

Living in an increasingly commercialised society thus benefited some, but imposed new obligations on others. It also represented a considerable degree of uncertainty. In the short-term, waged work was plentiful, as during the initial expansion of the

---

[144] Aymard, 'Autoconsommation et marchés'; Thoen, '"Commercial Survival Economy"'.

[145] E. Badosa, 'Els lloguers de cases a la ciutat de Barcelona (1780–1834)', *Recerques*, 10 (1980), pp. 139–56.

[146] Domínguez, *El campesino adaptativo*, pp. 121–39, esp. table 37 (p. 128).

[147] E. Tello, 'Vendre per pagar. La comercialització forçada a l'Urgell i a la Segarra al final del segle XVIII', *Recerques*, 23 (1990), pp. 141–90 (here pp. 144–8).

cotton industry. In the long run, however, rising nominal wages in both agriculture and in the Barcelona textile and construction industries were offset by rising prices and periodic unemployment.[148] Agricultural wages took 6 years to adjust to grain prices in coastal regions and 8 years in the interior, with all wage series showing sharp fluctuations from year to year. Waged work in proto-industry, while better-paid than agricultural labour, was particularly sensitive to fluctuations in demand. This sensitivity was evident in crisis years such as 1764, when Barcelona cotton manufacturers and other leading figures organised the first of many soup kitchens for the out-of-work cotton operatives, and the Igualada parish priest reported a deficit of 238 inhabitants in the Easter duty listing because so many textile families had temporarily left to seek work elsewhere.[149] At the turn of the century, war and economic blockade exacerbated the effects of poor harvests. In 1808 the parish priest appealed to the town council to find work for the poor left destitute by the collapse of manufacturing.[150] There are references to soup kitchens in 1812, and as late as 1817 measures were still being devised to raise funds for the hospital.[151]

It would be a mistake, however, to view poverty as simply a feature of extraordinarily difficult years. Evidence of deeper, structural poverty is not hard to find. In addition to the inventories of poor households described above, another source is the surviving listings of applicants chosen to participate in an annual lottery fund for Igualada's most significant charitable dowry fund or *causa pia*.[152] Fifty women were selected out of those that applied, and the name of one would be drawn out of a sack to receive a dowry of 100 *lliures*. For 1766 and 1767 we have details of all those who applied, 80 in the first year, 78 in the next, with brief notes on the family situation. What stand out are the degrees of poverty here: those with smallholdings of some kind, however burdened with debt, are distinguished from those who simply warrant the curt phrase: 'has nothing' (*no te res*), judged to be the situation of the majority. That of the others, however, testifies to how little

---

[148] On agricultural wage series (based on very limited evidence for the eighteenth century), see Garrabou, Tello and Roca 'Preus del blat'; Garrabou and Tello, 'Salario come costo, salario come reditto'; on textile wages in Barcelona, see Mora-Sitjà, 'Labour Supply and Wage Differentials', pp. 60–76; for building wages and various series of grain prices, see Feliu, *Precios y salarios*.

[149] On the situation in Barcelona, see Vilar, *La Catalogne*, vol. 2, pp. 410–18; Antoni Simon, 'Barcelona i Catalunya durant la crisi de subsistències de 1763–1764', in id., *La població catalana a l'edat moderna: Deu estudis* (Bellaterra, 1996), pp. 193–210. The Igualada Easter duty listing is in API, *caixa* 164, 'Llibretes de precepte Pascual'.

[150] AMI 1132, *Registre municipal*, fos 32r–33r (1802); AMI 1135, *Registre municipal*, fols 7r–10r (1808).

[151] AMI 1137, *Registre municipal*, fols 7v–9r (1812); AMI 1139, *Registre, municipal*, fols 33r–34r (1817).

[152] API, *caixes* 13, 15, 'Causa pia Geroni Cornet', discussed in Marfany, 'Choices and Constraints', pp. 98–9. For 1765 and 1783 we have the listing of just the 50 chosen; for 1766 we have the listing of the applicants and the final 50; for 1767 just the list of applicants, but 50 of these have crosses by their names.

security and possibility for paying dowries a smallholding provided, particularly for large families or where fathers had died. Isabel and Maria Olivellas were two of seven siblings in a household with a mortgage of 180 *lliures* on their house and other debts. Teresa Gual's family was described as having a 'smallholding on a *rabassa morta* contract, subject to a mortgage, but I believe they are very poor'.

Becoming trapped in a spiral of debt frequently forced many households into commercial activity. Elsewhere, I have examined the extent to which land-market activity in Igualada was the result not of a more commodified view of land but of increasing debt and necessity among families.[153] Similar accounts of forced sales as the only remaining option left to indebted and impoverished households have been presented by Llorenç Ferrer and Enric Tello.[154] Similarly, Chapter 2 provided examples of households being forced to relinquish *rabassa morta* holdings. Inventories, while not systematically recording debts, provide some examples of petty loans and sales of possessions that allowed households to 'make shift'. Josepa Biosca had sold her deceased husband's clothes to buy coal.[155] Margarida Cendra had sold a cloak to pay for her husband's funeral.[156] Josep Castelltort had a barrel out at pawn for 18 *sous*.[157] Anton Valls had accepted a towel as surety for a pair of espadrilles.[158] Joan Riera had accepted a cauldron from Magí Ortines as surety for 3 *quartans* of grain.[159] The paltriness of such debts is eloquent testimony to the poverty of many households.

In the final analysis, it is clear that Hufton's 'economy of makeshifts', with its emphasis upon survival, reflects more accurately the situation of most Igualada households than does any notion of industrious, willing consumers. Many did seek to make modest improvements in their standards of comfort, increasing the range of their clothing and linen, eating with forks and spoons and drinking chocolate on occasion, but more significant changes in lifestyle were reserved for a small elite. Increased market orientation was indeed a feature of most household economies, but as much out of necessity as choice.

---

[153] J. Marfany, 'Proto-Industrialisation, Property Rights and the Land Market in Catalonia, 18th and Early 19th Centuries', in Phillipp Schofield and Gérard Béaur (eds), *Property Rights, the Land Market and Economic Change* (Brussels, forthcoming).

[154] L. Ferrer, 'Censals, vendes a carta de gràcia i endeutament pagès al Bages', *Estudis d'història agrària*, 4 (1983), pp. 101–28; Tello, 'Vendre per pagar'.

[155] ANI 344, fos 103r–104r.

[156] ANI 477, fos 22r–23r.

[157] ANI 430, unfol.

[158] ANI 424, fos 66r–69r.

[159] ACA, NI 791, unfol.

Conclusion

In 1736 Joan Padró, lawyer and priest, member of the newly ennobled family mentioned in Chapter 2, published an account of the Holy Christ of Igualada, a statue purported to have sweated and wept blood in the sixteenth century and henceforth ascribed with miraculous powers.[1] Padró dedicated the sixth chapter of his work to a lengthy description of the geography, history and noteworthy features of Igualada. Padró's was a celebratory account. He was able to cite with pride many recent additions to the town, including the Piarist school he himself had helped to found, the barracks for royal troops built at the town's expense and, above all, the 'large, costly and wealthy woollen and cloth manufactures', the source of the town's 'good credit' and commerce and the 'decency' in which the inhabitants lived.[2]

Over a century later, Padró's work was republished, with an updated account of the town's history and current state by its then parish priest, Jaume Gomis.[3] Gomis took a more mixed view of Igualada's fortunes in the mid-nineteenth century. He was able to praise 'the enthusiasm and ardour' with which the Igualada militia had helped defeat the Napoleonic troops at the battle of Bruc in 1808 and to note the rapid growth promoted by the cotton industry in the years following the war.[4] He was forced to confess, however, that the town's fortunes were in decline as the 'great revolution' of steam power left Igualada unable to compete with other locations. There were other troubling signs. Population pressure left the town still struggling with inadequate water supplies.[5] While there had been additions that could still stir civic pride, such as wide, tree-lined streets, the longest and finest of these had been built in 1834 as a public-works initiative in order to provide relief to unemployed cotton workers.[6] Economic change had also brought social divisions. Whereas Padró's only distinction was between 'men of distinction' and the rest, Gomis described three groups: the labouring class, supposedly 'peaceful', 'hardworking' and 'submissive to authority'; the manufacturers and owners of manufactures, who

[1]   Juan Padró Serrals, *La sagrada y prodigiosa imagen del S. Christo de la villa de Igualada ...* (Cervera, 1736).

[2]   Ibid., p. 111.

[3]   Juan Padró Serrals, *La sagrada y prodigiosa imagen del S. Christo ... Segunda edición, mejorada considerablemente y con una estensa descripción de aquella villa por Don Jaime Gomis y Galtés, presbítero* (Igualada, 1852).

[4]   Ibid., pp. 67–8.

[5]   Ibid., pp. 80–1.

[6]   Ibid., p. 82.

were also hardworking but distinguished as well by their 'good judgement and discretion' and a group consisting of a few rich landowners, along with lawyers, doctors and other professionals, distinguished above all by 'the fineness of their manners'.[7] Social divisions, here as elsewhere in Catalonia, could and frequently did, translate into social tension and conflict. One of the few attempts at building a modern factory in Igualada by four manufacturers in 1847 was burned down two years later, despite all Gomis's claims about regard for authority.[8]

Conflict was not new, as we have seen in the struggles between clothiers and weavers for control of production during the eighteenth century and by sharecroppers against attempts to erode the property rights granted by *rabassa morta* contracts, conflicts which again were not unique to Igualada. Nor should the existence of conflict be surprising, given the economic and social upheaval through which Catalans were living over the long eighteenth century. This work has been concerned not just with trying to describe and understand different aspects of such upheaval, but also with trying to relate the Catalan experience to that of Europe more widely. Was this an alternative transition to capitalism, to be set against that described for north-western Europe, especially England? Or were contemporaries right to see Catalonia as 'a little England'? Either way, there is much that needs to be explained. In the second case, what requires explanation is what features made Catalonia distinct from other areas of southern Europe and enabled the region to follow the 'English' transition to capitalism. The first case to some extent encompasses the second: historians still need to understand why it occurred in Catalonia and not in other areas of the 'periphery' but also in what ways the Catalan route was not that of north-western Europe.

It has been a major contention of this work that more needs to be known about the experience of southern and eastern Europe, to set against the dominant paradigm of the north-west. 'Divergence' is now a buzz word among economic historians, but as well as discussion of divergence between Europe and Asia, we need more focus on divergence within Europe. If north-western Europe did follow a unique trajectory from feudalism to capitalism, then such uniqueness can only be appreciated through comparison with other areas. Identifying what made north-western Europe unique requires knowing what features of the economy and society were different from elsewhere. As Ogilvie has already pointed out, claims for Hajnal's European marriage pattern as a key distinguishing feature are rather weakened by the recognition that other areas of Europe with this marriage pattern did not experience the same kinds of engagement with markets and economic growth as England and the Netherlands.

The introductory chapter set out much of the current scholarship on the transition to capitalism in Europe and particularly the different ways in which

---

[7]   Serrals, *La sagrada y prodigiosa imagen del S. Christo* (1736), p. 111; (1852), p. 87.

[8]   Ibid. (1852), p. 94. The Bonaplata mill, the first successful steam-powered mill in Barcelona, was also burned down in 1835 (Thomson, *Distinctive Industrialization*, pp. 307–10).

households increasingly engaged with different markets over the early modern period. As well as older theories concerning changes on the land and proto-industrialisation, considerable space was given to more recent work focusing on markets for consumer goods and Jan de Vries's idea of an 'industrious revolution'. The remainder of the work was concerned with analysing the Catalan experience in the light of such scholarship, through the case study of Igualada. Part I analysed the growth of markets in Catalonia over the eighteenth century, first through the expansion of commercial viticulture, second through proto-industrial production of wool and cotton. Part II was concerned with the ways in which households engaged with such markets in terms of specialisation or diversification of economic activities, intensification of labour, the extent to which goods were purchased rather than domestically produced and the association or otherwise of more industrious forms of behaviour with changing patterns of consumption.

Chapter 2 showed that changes on the land in Catalonia were similar in many ways to those of many areas of France and to inland Flanders, in that the commercialisation of agriculture, in this case viticulture, was achieved through the medium of continued family farming of small plots, with a significant degree of involvement by sharecroppers. Where Catalonia did differ from other areas of Europe, north and south, was in its distinctive set of property rights. Emphyteusis, as has been shown, conferred quasi-property rights upon cultivators, with the *rabassa morta* contract as an important form of emphyteutic transfer where vines were concerned. While these rights should not be idealised as they often were by contemporaries, they nonetheless provided incentives for landowners and cultivators alike that facilitated the important expansion of viticulture over the eighteenth century. In Igualada, as elsewhere, however, most households had well below the 5 hectares considered the minimum for self-sufficiency, and many appear to have been landless, despite the view that a rural proletariat was not a feature of Catalan agrarian society at this stage. The implication of small-scale landholding, further discussed in Chapter 5, was that households needed both great self-discipline and other economic activities in order to make ends meet.

Among other economic activities open to households, the most important, as discussed in Chapter 3, was proto-industry. Despite the difficulties involved, some Catalan woollen manufacturers in Igualada, Terrassa and Sabadell were able to capture a niche in Castilian markets by producing higher quality cloths and responding quickly to changes in demand for fashions and colours. Initial success remains hard to explain, but was consolidated by the establishment of commercial networks across the country, trading with Catalan contacts and maintaining first-hand knowledge of markets. Flexibility in responding to demand for higher quality products, however, also required the ability to control production to a greater extent than previously. Such control was achieved, as with other areas of Catalonia and Europe where proto-industry was commercially successful, through the subordination of other producers, especially weavers, to a few dominant merchant manufacturers within a particularly hierarchical form of putting-out or *Verlagssystem*. Subordination of other producers was in turn accomplished by the ability to ignore or side-step guild regulations that had previously protected to a certain extent the independence of both smaller clothiers and weavers. The latter resisted the erosion of their independent artisan status, but to no avail: by the 1780s, the three main manufacturing families controlled large networks of dependent weavers, often to the extent that these no longer owned the means of production.

As discussed in the introductory chapter, the role of proto-industrialisation as a contributory factor to factory-based capitalist industrialisation has been questioned for many regions of Europe. In Catalonia, however, it retains its explanatory force. The rural origins of industry are now well established. As discussed here, there are important continuities between the eighteenth-century woollen industry and the early stages of the cotton industry that largely displaced it, including in Igualada. The first was the transfer of skilled labour from one fibre to the other. Not only did the putting-out networks of wool spinners and weavers provide a source of cheap labour for the expansion of the cotton industry, but many clothiers took on the role of cotton manufacturers. The second was the importance of domestic production. Even the workshops of the cotton manufacturers remained small-scale, centred on the labour of an extended family. The persistence of small-scale production until the advent of steam from the 1830s is a notable feature of Catalan industrialisation, though not unique to it. This persistence is unsurprising: family-based production was more resilient through downturns, more flexible, better able to impose discipline upon a workforce and often cheaper.

The family unit was thus central to the two great transformations taking place in the Catalan economy. The expansion of viticulture and of proto-industry were both achieved through the multiplication of family concerns: the taking on of small plots under emphyteutic land transfers such as the *rabassa morta* and the participation of some or all family members in textile production. In turn, however, these transformations changed the basis of family formation and, in doing so, had implications for population growth and living standards. *Pace* de Vries, family ties, though especially strong in Catalonia, were not incompatible here with a dynamic response to changing economic circumstances. In Igualada, this response took the form identified by early studies of proto-industrial regions, namely, a fall in the age at first marriage as new opportunities for household formation presented themselves. In particular, it was younger sons, traditionally disadvantaged by inheritance customs, who benefited, but average first age at marriage fell for all men and for women, though less dramatically. Marital fertility also increased, though conscious choice is less evident here than is the impact of decreased breastfeeding. Earlier marriage and higher marital fertility, in combination with a likely decline in migration out of the parish, were responsible for rapid population growth over the eighteenth and early nineteenth centuries.

Growth, however, brought penalties. Catalonia was not entirely free of Malthusian constraints, manifested through continued episodes of crisis mortality and, in Igualada but probably also in other rapidly growing areas, increasing rates of infant and child mortality. If the north-western European marriage pattern could operate so effectively as a preventive check in areas such as England, this may have been in part attributable to the relative weakness of the positive check.

The family was thus capable of both the dynamism and the discipline necessary to engage with growing markets in Catalonia. How it did so and what the incentives were were the subjects of Part II. Chapter 5 investigated the evidence for 'industrious' behaviour on the basis mainly of probate inventories and found little evidence of the specialisation and reduction in the number of productive activities and self-provisioning hypothesised by de Vries. Households in Igualada did respond to market changes, as described in Chapters 2 and 3, but the household economy in Catalonia remained essentially a dual economy, combining landholding with some form of artisan activity. Increasingly during the eighteenth century, this artisan activity was proto-industrial textile production. Aside from a handful of wealthier households, however, most combined small-scale landholding with modest artisan production or trade. If viticulture and proto-industry proved compatible in Catalonia, compared with the experience of other regions, it was because of the small size of plots ceded on *rabassa morta* contracts and other emphyteutic transfers. The two were not so much compatible as mutually essential: as Chapter 2 showed, most households had holdings well below the minimum required for self-sufficiency and to absorb all available family labour. Some other activity was thus essential for survival, but land in turn offered some protection against the uncertainties of production for distant markets.

Where male household heads were not themselves textile producers, however, proto-industrial production was likely to be restricted to spinning and thus undertaken by women. A key aspect of industrious behaviour in Catalonia was indeed the intensification of female labour, as evidenced not just by anecdotal evidence but more powerfully by the decline in time spent breastfeeding. While quantification remains impossible, the available evidence suggests that such intensification was not limited to women: the length of the working year and probably also the working day were increasing for all.

Industrious behaviour thus existed, yet the motives for such behaviour do not fit with de Vries's vision of active consumer preferences. Chapter 6 examined the consumption patterns revealed by inventories *post mortem* and other sources and compared them with elsewhere in Catalonia and Europe. Signs of increased consumption were not entirely absent: the luxury items identified as new elsewhere in Europe, such as clocks, watches and mirrors had started to make an appearance in Catalonia by the second half of the eighteenth century. Luxury and goods associated with extended leisure and the pursuit of culture such as books and musical instruments were, however, very much the preserve of a minority. The association was not entirely, though mainly, with wealth: education and professional occupations also played a role. Only in a few areas were there indications of more widespread diffusion down the social scale, again, in ways similar to elsewhere: new textiles, particularly cotton, were making their mark, as was the consumption of new stimulating beverages, in this case, chocolate, and forks and spoons were becoming more commonplace. All in all, however, even if de Vries's claims for plebeian consumption can be upheld for north-western Europe, the same was not true of Catalonia. Rather, the evidence points to new consumption patterns as associated primarily with greater social differentiation: setting apart a small elite from the rest.

If most households were working harder, it was through necessity, not choice. Not only did the small size of most landholdings or workshops require intense labour, but other factors were at work to compel households in this direction. Insofar as specialisation of production was taking place, in the form of an increasing focus upon viticulture rather than other types of farming, it left households increasingly reliant upon markets for the purchase of basic foodstuffs, especially grain, at a time when prices of such commodities were rising faster than wages. As we have seen, households remained self-provisioning to a greater extent than de Vries's model hypothesises: there was no decline in the proportion of households engaged in bread-making, keeping poultry or rabbits, curing meat or distilling wine and spirits. Nonetheless, the majority still had to purchase their grain and any meat consumed from the market. Moreover, the clauses of *rabassa morta* and *subestabliment* contracts increased market dependence by enforcing payments in grain or cash most heavily when prices were highest. In addition, the weight of taxation increased during the eighteenth century with the introduction of the *cadastre*. Payment of taxes and other debts forced households into buying and selling, if only to raise cash.

To return to the earlier question of whether Catalonia followed an 'English' path to capitalism or a different route, it should be clear that the answer is the second. For all the similarities that can be drawn and were drawn by contemporaries between Catalonia and north-western Europe, the differences are greater and appear so most clearly if the north-western path is taken to be an industrious revolution in the manner described by de Vries. The key distinction is that drawn by Robert Brenner between market involvement and market dependence. In de Vries's paradigm, households became involved with markets freely, out of a desire to consume more goods, and thus made active choices as to how their labour was to be allocated. As we have seen, however, the relationship in Catalonia tended much more towards dependence: households did become more involved with markets in a variety of ways and did change the allocation of their labour, but for most such involvement was dictated by the need to survive.

The argument here could be taken at one level as merely confirming de Vries's view that an industrious revolution driven by consumption could only be a feature of north-western Europe. One answer might be that an industrious revolution remains to be established for England at least: the small number of historians who have so far addressed the question remain unconvinced. Certainly, the particular institutional features de Vries credits with creating the right context, particularly Hajnal's marriage pattern, were not unique to England and the Netherlands. Setting this issue aside, however, I would contend that a return to the original concept of an industrious revolution, as developed by Japanese scholars, is more useful here: not just for describing the Catalan experience, but for broadening our understanding more generally. It would seem that a labour-intensive path towards capitalism and industrialisation was more common, globally, than the capital-intensive path taken by England. Industrious behaviour was therefore not lacking, but the motives for it and the ways in which it was manifested varied considerably.

To be useful, historical concepts need to be flexible. It has been recognised that agrarian capitalism could take many forms. Similarly, the particular forms and the impact of proto-industrialisation have been shown to be very much determined by context. Context is equally relevant to consumer and industrious behaviour. The Catalan case demonstrates this amply. This was a transition to capitalism, a growth of markets, participation in global networks, eventually an industrial revolution. It came about in very specific ways, however. Some institutional features facilitated the process, namely, specific property rights and, despite claims to the contrary, strong family forms and ties. Factor endowments conditioned the process in various ways: land and climate determined the particular regional specialisation that occurred and ensured that a heavy penalty had to be paid for growth in the form of higher mortality, freedom from which constraint is perhaps insufficiently acknowledged in work on north-western Europe. Labour was abundant, capital was not, thus making production based on small units and the capacity for self-exploitation of family labour the most viable option for both viticulture and industry. Proto-industrialisation was indeed the first phase of industrialisation in Catalonia. New consumer goods were not absent, and some changes in lifestyle can be observed, but on a more modest scale than elsewhere in Europe. For most households, industrious behaviour was a response to pressure. This was an alternative transition to capitalism, perhaps more Asian than European, possessing features in common with both, yet ultimately very different. Understanding difference, however, is what historical inquiry is all about.

Bibliography

Ackerberg, D., and M. Botticini, 'The Choice of Agrarian Contracts in Early Renaissance Tuscany: Risk Sharing, Moral Hazard or Capital Market Imperfections?', *Explorations in Economic History*, 37 (2000), pp. 241–57.

Amat i de Cortada, R. de (Baró de Maldà), *Calaix de sastre*, ed. R. Boixareu (11 vols, Barcelona: Curial, 1987–2005).

—— *Viles i ciutats de Catalunya*, ed. M. Aritzeta (Barcelona: Barcino, 1994).

Antón, J., *La herencia cultural: Alfabetización y lectura en la ciudad de Girona (1747–1807)* (Bellaterra: Universitat Autònoma de Barcelona, 1998).

Arnabat, R., 'Notes sobre la conflictivitat senyorial al Penedès (1759–1800)', *Estudis d'història agrària*, 8 (1990), pp. 101–22.

—— *Vins, aiguardents, draps i papers* (Vilafranca del Penedès: Museu de Vilafranca, 1996).

Aymard, M., 'Autoconsommation et marchés: Chayanov, Labrousse ou Le Roy Ladurie', *Annales ESC*, 38 (1983), pp. 1392–410.

Badosa, E., 'Els lloguers de cases a la ciutat de Barcelona (1780–1834)', *Recerques*, 10 (1980), pp. 139–56.

—— *Explotació agrícola i contractes de conreu, 1670-1840: Les finques del clergat de Barcelona* (Barcelona: Collegi Notarial, 1985).

Barba i Roca, M., *El corregiment i partit de Vilafranca del Penedès a l'últim terç del segle XVIII* (Vilafranca del Penedès: Museu de Vilafranca, 1991).

Bardhan, P.K., *Land, Labor and Rural Poverty: Essays in Development Economics* (Delhi: Oxford University Press, 1984).

Barrera, A., *Casa, herencia y familia en la Cataluña rural* (Madrid: Alianza, 1990).

Baulant, M., 'Niveaux de vie des paysans autour de Meaux en 1700 et 1750', in id., *Meaux et ses campagnes: Vivre et survivre dans le monde rural sous l'Ancien Régime* (Rennes: Presses Universitaires de Rennes, 2006), pp. 271–85.

——, A.J. Schuurman and P. Servais (eds), *Inventaires après-décès et ventes de meubles* (Louvain: Academia, 1988).

Bavel, B.J.P. van, 'Early Proto-Industrialization? The Importance and Nature of Market-Oriented Non-Agricultural Activities in the Countryside in Flanders and Holland, c.1250–1570', *Revue Belge de philologie et d'histoire*, 81 (2003), pp. 1109–65.

Belfanti, C.M., and F. Giusberti, 'Clothing and Social Inequality in Early Modern Europe: Introductory Remarks', *Continuity and Change*, 15/3 (2000), pp. 359–65.

Benaul, J.M., 'La comercialització dels teixits de llana en la cruïlla dels segles XVIII i XIX: L'exemple de la fàbrica de Terrassa Anton y Joaquín Sagrera 1792–1807', *Arraona*, 2 (1988), pp. 35–47.

—— 'Los orígenes de la empresa textil lanera en Sabadell y Terrassa en el siglo XVIII', *Revista de historia industrial*, 1 (1992), pp. 39–61.

—— 'Cambio tecnológico y estructura industrial en los inicios del sistema de fábrica en la industria pañera catalana, 1815–1835', *Revista de historia económica*, 13 (1995), pp. 199–226.

—— and E. Deu, 'The Spanish Wool Industry, 1750–1935: Import Substitution and Regional Relocation', in G.L. Fontana and G. Gayot (eds), *Wool: Products and Markets (13th–20th Century)* (Padua: CLEUP, 2004), pp. 845–84.

Bengtsson, T., C. Campbell and J.Z. Lee (eds), *Life under Pressure: Mortality and Living Standards in Europe and Asia, 1700–1900* (Cambridge, MA: MIT Press, 2004).

Berg, M., 'Women's Work, Mechanisation and the Early Phase of Industrialisation in England', in P. Joyce (ed.), *The Historical Meanings of Work* (Cambridge: Cambridge University Press, 1987), pp. 64–98.

Bernstein, H., 'Agrarian Classes in Capitalist Development', in L. Sklair (ed.), *Capitalism and Development* (London: Routledge, 1994), pp. 40–71.

Braun, R., *Industrialisation and Everyday Life* (Cambridge: Cambridge University Press, 1990).

Breen, T.H., 'The Meaning of Things: Interpreting the Consumer Economy in the Eighteenth Century', in J. Brewer and R. Porter (eds), *Consumption and the World of Goods* (London: Routledge, 1993), pp. 249–60.

Brenner, R., 'Agrarian Class Structure and Economic Development in Pre-Industrial Europe', in T.H. Aston and C.H.E. Philpin (eds), *The Brenner Debate: Agarian Class Structure and Economic Development in Pre-Industrial Europe* (Cambridge: Cambridge University Press, 1985), pp. 10–63.

—— 'The Agrarian Roots of European Capitalism', in T.H. Aston and C.H.E. Philpin (eds), *The Brenner Debate: Agarian Class Structure and Economic Development in Pre-Industrial Europe* (Cambridge: Cambridge University Press, 1985), pp. 213–327.

Breschi, M., R. Derosas and M. Manfredini, 'Mortality and Environment in Three Emilian, Tuscan and Venetian Communities, 1800–1883', in T. Bengtsson, C. Campbell and J.Z. Lee (eds), *Life under Pressure: Mortality and Living Standards in Europe and Asia, 1700–1900* (Cambridge, MA: MIT Press, 2004), pp. 209–51.

Brewer, J., and R. Porter (eds), *Consumption and the World of Goods* (London: Routledge, 1993).

Burgos, J., 'Imprenta y cultura del libro en la Barcelona del Setecientos (1680–1808)' (PhD thesis, Universitat Autònoma de Barcelona, 1993).

Cadalso, J. de, *Cartas marruecas*, ed. E. Martínez and N. Glendinning (Barcelona: Crítica, 2000).

Cailly, C., 'Structure sociale et consommation dans le monde proto-industriel rural textile: Le cas du Perche Ornais au XVIIIe siècle', *Revue d'histoire moderne et contemporaine*, 45 (1998), pp. 746–74.

Caminal, M., et al., 'Moviment de l'ingrés senyorial a Catalunya (1770–1835)', *Recerques*, 8 (1978), pp. 51–72.

Camps, E., *La formación del mercado de trabajo industrial en la Cataluña del siglo XIX* (Madrid: Ministerio de Trabajo y Seguridad Social, 1995).

Carmona, J., and J. Simpson, 'The "Rabassa Morta" in Catalan Viticulture: The Rise and Decline of a Long-Term Sharecropping Contract, 1670s–1920s', *Journal of Economic History*, 59 (1999), 290–315.

—— and —— 'Why Sharecropping? Explaining its Presence and Absence in Europe's Vineyards, 1750–1950', Universidad Carlos III, Departamento de Historia Económica e Instituciones Working Papers in Economic History, 11 (2007), available at <www.uc3m.es/dpto/HISEC/working_papers/working_papers_general.html>.

Caspard, P., 'The Calico Painters of Estavayer: Employers' Strategies toward the Market for Women's Labor', in D.M. Hafter (ed.), *European Women and Preindustrial Craft* (Bloomington: Indiana University Press, 1995), pp. 108–36.

Cavallo, S., 'What did Women Transmit? Ownership and Control of Household Goods and Personal Effects in Early Modern Italy', in M. Donald and L. Hurcombe (eds), *Gender and Material Culture in Historical Perspective* (Basingstoke: Macmillan, 2000).

Chapman, S.D., and S. Chassagne, *European Textile Printers in the Eighteenth Century: A Study of Peel and Oberkampf* (London: Heinemann, 1981).

Cobos, J.M., *Pagesos, paraires i teixidors al Llobregat monserratí, 1550–1850* (Barcelona: Abadia de Montserrat, 2006).

Codina, J., *Contractes de matrimoni al delta del Llobregat (segles XIV a XIX)* (Barcelona: Fundació Noguera, 1997).

—— *El gir de 1750: Orígen i creixement modern de la població* (Lleida: Pagès, 1998).

Cohen, J.S., and F.L. Galassi, 'Sharecropping and Productivity: "Feudal Residues" in Italian Agriculture, 1911', *Economic History Review*, 43 (1990), pp. 646–56.

Coleman, D.C., 'Proto-Industrialization: A Concept too Many', *Economic History Review*, 36 (1983), pp. 435–48.

Colomé, J., 'Pequeña explotación agrícola, reproducción de las unidades familiares campesinas y mercado de trabajo en la viticultura mediterránea del siglo XIX: El caso catalán', *Revista de historia económica*, (2000), pp. 281–307.

Congost, R., 'Derechos señoriales, análisis histórico y estrategias de información: El ejemplo catalán', in *Tierra, leyes, historia* (Barcelona: Crítica, 2007), pp. 159–90.

—— *Notes de societat (La Selva, 1768–1862)* (Santa Coloma de Farnés: Centre d'Estudis Selvatans, 1992).

—— *Els propietaris i els altres: La regió de Girona 1768–1862* (Vic: Eumo, 1990).

——, L. Ferrer and J. Marfany, 'The Formation of New Households and Social Change in a Single Heir System: The Catalan Case, 17th to 19th Centuries', in P. Pozsgai and A-L. Head-König (eds), *Inheritance Practices, Marriage Strategies and Household Formation in European Rural Societies* (Brussels: Brepols, 2012).

Cots, A., 'Aproximació a l'estudi dels conflictes senyorials a Catalunya (1751–1808)', *Estudis d'història agrària*, 6 (1986), pp. 241–68.

Cruz, J., 'Elites, Merchants and Consumption in Madrid at the End of the Old Regime', in A.J. Schuurman and L. Walsh (eds), *Material Culture: Consumption, Life-Style, Standard of Living, 1500–1900* (Milan: Bocconi, 1994), pp. 137–46.

—— and J. Sola-Corbacho, 'El mercado madrileño y la industrialización en España durante los siglos XVIII y XIX', in J. Torras and B. Yun (eds), *Consumo, condiciones de vida y comercialización: Cataluña y Castilla, siglos XVII–XIX* (Valladolid: Junta de Castilla y León, 1999), pp. 335–54.

De Vries, J., 'Between Purchasing Power and the World of Goods: Understanding the Household Economy in Early Modern Europe', in J. Brewer and R. Porter (eds), *Consumption and the World of Goods* (London: Routledge, 1993), pp. 85–132.

—— *European Urbanization, 1500–1800* (London: Methuen, 1984).

—— 'The Industrial Revolution and the Industrious Revolution', *Journal of Economic History*, 54 (1994), pp. 249–70.

—— *The Industrious Revolution: Consumer Behavior and the Household Economy, 1650 to the Present* (Cambridge: Cambridge University Press, 2008).

—— 'Peasant Demand Patterns and Economic Development, Friesland, 1550–1700', in W.N. Parker and E.L. Jones (eds), *European Peasants and their Markets* (Princeton: Princeton University Press, 1975), pp. 205–66.

—— 'The Transition to Capitalism in a Land without Feudalism', in P. Hoppenbrouwers and J.L. van Zanden (eds), *Peasants into Farmers? The Transformation of the Rural Economy and Society in the Low Countries (Middle Ages–19th Century) in Light of the Brenner Debate* (Turnhout: Brepols, 2001), pp. 67–84.

Devos, I., 'Marriage and Economic Conditions since 1700: The Belgian Case', in I. Devos and L. Kennedy (eds), *Marriage and Rural Economy* (Turnhout: Brepols, 2005), pp. 101–32.

—— and L. Kennedy (eds), *Marriage and Rural Economy: Western Europe since 1400* (Turnhout: Brepols, 1999).

Deyá, M.J., 'La industria rural textil en la Mallorca moderna: Producción y formas de comercialización interior', *Estudis d'història econòmica*, 2 (1988), pp. 15–41.

Deyon, P., 'Proto-Industrialization in France', in S.C. Ogilvie and M. Cerman (eds), *European Proto-Industrialization* (Cambridge: Cambridge University Press, 1996), pp. 38–48.

Domínguez, R., *El campesino adaptativo: Campesinos y mercado en el norte de España, 1750–1850* (Santander: Universidad de Cantabria, 1996).

Douglas, M., and B. Isherwood, *The World of Goods: Towards an Anthropology of Consumption* (2nd edn, London: Routledge, 1996).

Duplessis, R., *Transitions to Capitalism in Early Modern Europe* (Cambridge: Cambridge University Press, 1997).

Ellis, F., *Peasant Economics: Farm Households and Agrarian Development* (2nd edn, Cambridge: Cambridge University Press, 1993).

Elvin, M. *The Pattern of the Chinese Past* (Stanford: Stanford University Press, 1973).

Epstein, S.R., *Freedom and Growth: The Rise of States and Markets in Europe, 1300–1750* (London: Routledge, 2006).

Fabré, A., *Aproximació a l'estudi de la immigració i de l'occupació a Igualada, Manlleu i Centelles, segles XVII i primera meitat del XVIII* (Postgraduate thesis, Universidad Autònoma de Barcelona, 1991).

Fairchild, C., 'Determinants of Consumption Patterns in Eighteenth-Century France', in A.J. Schuurman and L. Walsh (eds), *Material Culture: Consumption, Life-Style, Standard of Living, 1500–1900* (Milan: Bocconi, 1994), pp. 55–70.

Farnie, D., and D. Jeremy (eds), *The Fibre that Changed the World: The Cotton Industry in International Perspective, 1600–1990s* (Oxford: Oxford University Press, 2004).

Feliu, G., *El funcionament del règim senyorial a l'Edat Moderna: L'exemple del Pla d'Urgell* (Lleida: Institut d'Estudis Ilerdencs, 1990).

—— *Precios y salarios en la Cataluña moderna* (2 vols, Madrid: Banco de España, 1991).

Ferrer, L., 'Bergadanas, continuas y mules: Tres geografías de la hilatura del algodón en Cataluña (1790–1830)', *Revista de historia económica*, 22 (2004), pp. 337–86.

—— 'Censals, vendes a carta de gràcia i endeutament pagès al Bages', *Estudis d'història agrària*, 4 (1983), pp. 101–28.

—— 'El Moianès en els segles XVIII i XIX: De l'especialització llanera a la decadència per manca d'aigua', *Modilianum*, 22 (2000), pp. 64–92.

—— *Pagesos, rabassaires i industrials a la Catalunya central* (Barcelona: Abadia de Montserrat, 1987).

—— 'Les primeres fàbriques i els primers fabricants a la Catalunya central', in M. Gutiérrez (ed.), *La industrialització i el desenvolupament economic d'Espanya: Homenatge al Dr Jordi Nadal* (2 vols, Barcelona: Universitat de Barcelona, 1999), vol. 2, pp. 1038–56.

—— 'Una revisió del creixement demogràfic de Catalunya en el segle XVIII a partir dels registres parroquials', *Estudis d'història agrària*, 20 (2007), pp. 17–68.

——— et al., 'Edat de casament i celibatiu definitiu a la Catalunya central (1803–1807)', *Manuscrits*, 10 (1992), pp. 259–86.

Figueras, N., J.M. Grau and R. Puig, 'La possessió dels llibres a través dels inventaris *post mortem*: Un mostreig (s.XVIII)', *Annals de l'Institut d'Estudis Gironins*, 34 (1994), pp. 129–60.

Fine, A., 'A Consideration of the Trousseau: A Feminine Culture?', in M. Perrot (ed.), *Writing Women's History* (Oxford: Blackwell, 1992), pp. 118–45.

Finn, M., 'Men's Things: Masculine Possession in the Consumer Revolution', *Social History*, 25 (2000), pp. 133–55.

Fontaine, L., 'The Circulation of Luxury Goods in Eighteenth-Century Paris: Social Redistribution and an Alternative Currency', in M. Berg and E. Eger (eds), *Luxury in the Eighteenth Century: Debates, Desires and Delectable Goods* (Basingstoke: Palgrave, 2003), pp. 89–102.

——— *Histoire du colportage en Europe: Xve–XIXe siècles* (Paris: Albin Michel, 1993).

Fontana, G.L., and G. Gayot (eds), *Wool: Products and Markets (13th–20th Century)* (Padua: CLEUP, 2004).

Fontana, J., *La fi de l'Antic Règim i la industrializació 1787–1868*, Història de Catalunya, 5 (Barcelona: Enciclopedia Catalana, 1989).

Garcia Balaña, A., *La fabricació de la fàbrica: Treball i política a la Catalunya cotonera (1784–1874)* (Barcelona: Abadia de Montserrat, 2004).

Garcia Sanz, A., 'Competitivos en lanas pero no en paños: Lana para la exportación y lana para los telares nacionales en la España del Antiguo Régimen', *Revista de história económica*, 12 (1994), pp. 397–434.

Garnot, B., *La culture matérielle en France aux XVIe, XVIIe et XVIIIe siècles* (Paris: Ophrys, 1995).

——— *Un déclin: Chartres au XVIIIe siècle* (Paris: CTHS, 1991).

Garrabou, R., and E. Tello, 'Salario come costo, salario come reditto: Il prezzo delle giornate agricole nella Catalogna contemporanea (1727–1930)', *Meridiana*, 24 (1995), pp. 173–203.

———, ——— and A. Roca, 'Preus del blat i salaris agrícoles a Catalunya (1720–1936)', in M. Gutiérrez (ed.), *La industrialització i el desenvolupament econòmic d'Espanya: Homenatge al Dr Jordi Nadal* (2 vols, Barcelona: Universitat de Barcelona, 1999), vol. 2, pp. 422–60.

———, J. Planas and E. Saguer, *Un capitalisme impossible? La gestió de la gran propietat agrària a la Catalunya contemporània* (Vic: Eumo, 2000).

Garrett, E.M., 'The Trials of Labour: Motherhood versus Employment in a Nineteenth-Century Textile Centre', *Continuity and Change*, 5 (1990), pp. 121–54.

Giralt, E., 'El conflicto *rabassaire* y la cuestión agraria en Cataluña hasta 1936', in id., *Empresaris, nobles i vinyaters* (Valencia: Universitat de Valencia, 2002), pp. 115–39.

Grazia, V. de, 'Changing Consumption Regimes', in V. de Grazia and E. Furlough (eds), *The Sex of Things: Gender and Consumption in Historical Perspective* (Berkeley: University of California Press, 1996).

—— and E. Furlough (eds), *The Sex of Things: Gender and Consumption in Historical Perspective* (Berkeley: University of California Press, 1996).

Gullickson, G.L., *Spinners and Weavers of Auffay: Rural Industry and the Sexual Division of Labour in a French Village, 1750–1850* (Cambridge: Cambridge University Press, 1986).

Hafter, D.M., 'Women who Wove in the Eighteenth-Century Silk Industry of Lyon', in id. (ed.), *European Women and Preindustrial Craft* (Bloomington: University of Indiana Press, 1995), pp. 42–64.

Hajnal, J., 'European Marriage Patterns in Perspective', in D.V. Glass and D.E.C. Eversley (eds), *Population in History: Essays in Historical Demography* (London: Edward Arnold, 1965), pp. 101–47.

—— 'Two Kinds of Pre-Industrial Household Formation System', *Population and Development Review*, 8/3 (1982), pp. 449–94.

Hareven, T., 'The History of the Family and the Complexity of Social Change', *American Historical Review*, 96/1 (1991), pp. 95–124.

Hendrickx, F.M.M., *In Order not to Fall into Poverty: Production and Reproduction in the Transition from Proto-Industry to Factory Industry in Borne and Wierden (The Netherlands), 1800–1900* (Amsterdam: IISG, 1997).

Hiler, D., and L. Wiedmer, 'Le rat de ville et le rat des champs: Une approche comparative des interieurs ruraux et urbains à Genève dans la seconde partie du XVIIIe siècle', in M. Baulant, A.J. Schuurman and P. Servais (eds), *Inventaires après-décès et ventes de meubles* (Louvain: Academia, 1988), pp. 131–51.

Hoffman, P.T., 'The Economic Theory of Sharecropping in Early Modern France', *Journal of Economic History*, 44 (1984), pp. 309–19.

—— *Growth in a Traditional Society: The French Countryside 1450–1815* (Princeton: Princeton University Press, 1996).

Hoppenbrouwers, P., 'Mapping an Unexplored Field: The Brenner Debate and the Case of Holland', in P. Hoppenbrouwers and J.L. van Zanden (eds), *Peasants into Farmers? The Transformation of the Rural Economy and Society in the Low Countries (Middle Ages–19th Century) in Light of the Brenner Debate* (Turnhout: Brepols, 2001), pp. 41–66.

—— and J.L. van Zanden, *Peasants into Farmers? The Transformation of the Rural Economy and Society in the Low Countries (Middle Ages–19th Century) in Light of the Brenner Debate* (Turnhout: Brepols, 2001).

—— and —— 'Restyling the Transition from Feudalism to Capitalism: Some Critical Reflections on the Brenner Thesis' in eid. (eds), *Peasants into Farmers? The Transformation of the Rural Economy and Society in the Low Countries (Middle Ages–19th Century) in Light of the Brenner Debate* (Turnhout: Brepols, 2001), pp. 19–40.

Hudson, P., *The Genesis of Industrial Capital: A Study of the West Riding Wool Textile Industry c.1750–1850* (Cambridge: Cambridge University Press, 1986).

—— and S. King, 'Two Textile Townships, c.1660–1820: A Comparative Demographic Analysis', *Economic History Review*, 53/4 (2000), pp. 706–41.

Hufton, O., *The Poor of Eighteenth-Century France, 1750–1789* (Oxford: Clarendon, 1974).

Huguet, R., *Els artesans de Lleida: 1680–1808* (Lleida: Pagès, 1990).

Hunt, A., *Governance of the Consuming Passions: A History of Sumptuary Law* (Basingstoke: Macmillan, 1996).

Iglésies, J., *Evolució demogràfica de la comarca d'Igualada* (Igualada: CECI, 1972).

Johnson, C.H., 'Capitalism and the State: Capital Accumulation and Proletarianization in the Languedocian Woolens Industry, 1700–1789', in T.M. Safley and L.N. Rosenband (eds), *The Workplace before the Factory: Artisans and Proletarians, 1500–1800* (Ithaca: Cornell University Press, 1993), pp. 37–62.

Jones, E., *The European Miracle: Environments, Economies and Geopolitics in the History of Europe and Asia* (3rd edn, Cambridge: Cambridge University Press, 2003).

Jones, J.M., '*Coquettes* and *Grisettes*: Women Buying and Selling in Ancien Régime Paris', in V. de Grazia and E. Furlough (eds), *The Sex of Things: Gender and Consumption in Historical Perspective* (Berkeley: University of California Press, 1996), pp 25–53.

Junta de Comerç de Barcelona, *Discurso sobre la agricultura, comercio e industria del Principado de Cataluña (1780)*, ed. E. Lluch (Barcelona: Altafulla, 1997).

King, P., 'Pauper Inventories and the Material Lives of the Poor in the Eighteenth and Early Nineteenth Centuries', in T. Hitchcock, P. King and P. Sharpe (eds), *Chronicling Poverty: The Voices and Strategies of the English Poor, 1640–1840* (Basingstoke: Macmillan, 1997), pp. 155–91.

Kitson, P.M., 'Family Formation, Male Occupation and the Nature of Parochial Registration in England, c.1538–1837' (PhD thesis, University of Cambridge, 2004).

Knotter, A., 'Problems of the "Family Economy": Peasant Economy, Domestic Production and Labour Markets in Pre-Industrial Europe', in M. Prak (ed.), *Early Modern Capitalism* (London: Routledge, 2001), pp. 135–60.

Kriedte, P., H. Medick and J. Schlumbohm, *Industrialization before Industrialization* (Cambridge: Cambridge University Press, 1981).

——, —— and —— 'Protoindustrialization Revisited: Demography, Social Structure and Modern Domestic Industry', *Continuity and Change*, 8 (1993), pp. 217–52.

Landers, J., 'Fertility Decline and Birth Spacing among London Quakers', in J. Landers and V. Reynolds (eds), *Fertility and Resources* (Cambridge: Cambridge University Press, 1990), pp. 92–117.

—— *The Field and the Forge: Population, Production and Power in the Pre-Industrial West* (Oxford: Oxford University Press, 2003).

Larruga, E., *Memorias políticas y económicas* (15 vols, Saragossa: Institución Fernándo el Católico, 1995–6).

Laslett, P., 'Characteristics of the Western Family Considered over Time' in id., *Family Life and Illicit Love in Earlier Generations* (Cambridge: Cambridge University Press, 1977), pp. 12–49.

—— 'Family, Kinship and Collectivity as Systems of Support in Pre-Industrial Europe: A Consideration of the "Nuclear-Hardship" hypothesis', *Continuity and Change*, 3 (1988), pp. 153–73.

Lee, J.Z., and W. Feng, *One Quarter of Humanity: Malthusian Mythology and Chinese Realities, 1700–2000* (Cambridge, MA: MIT Press, 1999).

Lemire, B., *Dress, Culture and Commerce: The English Clothing Trade before the Factory, 1660–1800* (Basingstoke: Macmillan, 1997).

—— *Fashion's Favourite: The Cotton Trade and the Consumer in Britain, 1660– 1800* (Oxford: Oxford University Press, 1991).

—— 'Peddling Fashion: Salesmen, Pawnbrokers, Tailors, Thieves and the Second-Hand Clothes Trade in England, c.1700–1800', *Textile History*, 22 (1991), pp. 67–82.

Le Roy Ladurie, E., *Les payans de Languedoc* (2nd edn, Paris: SEVPEN, 1985).

Levine, D., *Family Formation in an Age of Nascent Capitalism* (New York: Academic, 1977).

Lewis, G., 'Proto-Industrialization in France', *Economic History Review*, 47 (1994), pp. 150–64.

Lick, R., 'Les interieurs domestiques dans la seconde moitié du XVIIIe siècle d'après les inventaires après-décès de Coutances', *Annales de Normandie*, 20 (1970), pp. 293–316.

Liu, T., *The Weaver's Knot: The Contradictions of Class Struggle and Family Solidarity in Western France, 1750–1914* (Ithaca: Cornell University Press, 1994).

Livi-Bacci, M., 'Fertility and Nuptiality Changes in Spain from the Late 18th to the Early 20th century', *Population Studies*, 22 (1968), pp. 83–102, 211–34.

McCants, A., 'Poor Consumers as Global Consumers: The Diffusion of Tea and Coffee Drinking in the Eighteenth Century', *Economic History Review*, 61, special issue (2008), pp. 172–200.

Malanima, P., *Il lusso dei contadini: Consumi e industrie nelle campagne toscane del sei e settecento* (Bologna: Il Mulino, 1990).

Mann, S., and J. Dickinson, 'Obstacles to the Development of a Capitalist Agriculture', *Journal of Peasant Studies*, 5 (1978), pp. 466–81.

Marfany, J., '"Casarse en edad apropriada": Edat al matrimoni i estratègies matrimonials a Igualada, 1680–1829', *Miscellanea aqualatensia*, 11 (2004), pp. 13–44.

—— 'Choices and Constraints: Marriage and Inheritance in Eighteenth- and Early Nineteenth-Century Catalonia', *Continuity and Change*, 21/1 (2006), pp. 1–34.

—— 'Las crisis de mortalidad en una comunidad catalana, Igualada, 1680–1829', *Revista de demografía histórica*, 23/3 (2005), pp. 13–41.

—— 'Is it Still Helpful to Talk about Proto-Industrialisation? Some Suggestions from a Catalan Case Study', *Economic History Review*, 63/4 (2010), pp. 942–73.

—— 'Proto-Industrialisation and Demographic Change in Catalonia, c.1680–1829' (PhD thesis, University of Cambridge, 2003).

—— 'Proto-Industrialisation, Property Rights and the Land Market in Catalonia, 18th and Early 19th Centuries', in Phillipp Schofield and Gérard Béaur (eds), *Property Rights, the Land Market and Economic Change* (Brussels: Brepols, forthcoming).

Martínez, M.A., *La població de Vilanova i la Geltrú en el segle XVIII* (Vilanova i la Geltrú: Institut d'Estudis Penedesencs, 1987).

Masdevall, J., *Relación de las epidemias de calenturas putridas y malignas que en estos últimos años se han padecido en el Principado de Cataluña* (Madrid: Imprenta Real, 1786).

Medick, H., 'Une culture de la considération: Les vêtements et leurs couleurs à Laichingen entre 1750 et 1820', *Annales HSS*, 4 (1995), pp. 753–74.

—— 'The Protoindustrial Family Economy: The Structural Function of Household and Family During the Transition from Peasant Society to Industrial Capitalism', *Social History*, 3 (1976), 291–315.

Melton, J. van Horn, *The Rise of the Public in Enlightenment Europe* (Cambridge: Cambridge University Press, 2001).

Mendels, F., 'Proto-Industrialization: The First Stage of the Industrialization Process', *Journal of Economic History*, 32 (1972), pp. 241–61.

Molas, P., *Economia i societat al segle XVIII* (Barcelona: Curial, 1975).

Moor, T. de and van Zanden, J.L., 'Girl Power: The European Marriage Pattern and Labour Markets in the North Sea Region in the Late Medieval and Early Modern Period', *Economic History Review*, 63 (2010), pp. 1–33.

Mora-Sitjà, N., 'Labour Supply and Wage Differentials in an Industrialising Economy: Catalonia in the Long Nineteenth Century' (DPhil thesis, University of Oxford, 2006).

Moreno, A., J. Soler and F. Fuentes, 'Introducción al estudio socio-demográfico de Cataluña mediante el Censo de Floridablanca (1787)', *Actes del primer congrés d'història moderna de Catalunya* (2 vols, Barcelona: Universitat de Barcelona, 1984), vol. 1, pp. 23–38.

Moreno, B., *Consum i condicions de vida a la Catalunya moderna: El Penedès, 1670–1790* (Vilafranca del Penedès, 2007).

—— *La contractació agrària a l'Alt Penedès durant el segle XVIII: El contracte de rabassa morta i l'expansió de la vinya* (Barcelona: Fundació Noguera, 1995).

—— 'Pautas de consumo y diferenciación social en la Catalunya preindustrial. Una sociedad en transformación a partir de los inventarios post-mortem' (PhD thesis, European University Institute, Florence, 2002).

Moreu-Rey, E., 'Sociologia del llibre a Barcelona al segle XVIII', *Estudis històrics i documents dels arxius de protocols*, 7 (1980), pp. 275–301.

Muñoz, F., 'Creixement demogràfic, mortalitat i nupcialitat al Penedès' (PhD thesis, Universitat Autònoma de Barcelona, 1990).
—— 'Fluctuaciones de precios y dinámica demográfica en Cataluña (1600–1850)', *Revista de historia económica*, 15/3 (1997), pp. 507–43.
—— 'Nivells i tendències de la mortalitat a les localitats del Penedès (segles XVII–XIX)', *Estudis d'història agrària*, 9 (1992), pp. 181–202.
Muset, A., *Catalunya i el mercat espanyol al segle XVIII: Els traginers i els negociants de Calaf i Copons* (Barcelona: Abadia de Montserrat, 1997).
—— 'Protoindústria e indústria dispersa en la Cataluña del siglo XVIII: La pañeria de Esparraguera y Olesa de Montserrat', *Revista de história económica*, 7 (1989), pp. 45–67.
Nadal, J., 'Demografía y economía en el origen de la Cataluña moderna: Un ejemplo local: Palamós (1705–1839)', in id., *Bautismos, desposorios y entierros: Estudios de historia demográfica* (Barcelona: Ariel, 1992), pp. 149–73.
—— *La población española (siglos XVI a XX)* (4th revd edn, Barcelona: Ariel, 1991).
Navarro-Mas, J.A., 'Respuesta al interrogatorio del sr. D. Francisco de Zamora por lo concerniente al corregimiento de Barcelona'; repr. in F. de Zamora, *Diario de los viajes hechos por Cataluña*, ed. R. Boixareu (Barcelona: Curial, 1973), pp.
Nenadic, S., 'Middle-Rank Consumers and Domestic Culture in Edinburgh and Glasgow, 1720–1840', *Past and Present*, 145 (1994), pp. 122–56.
Ogilvie, S.C., *A Bitter Living: Women, Markets and Social Capital in Early Modern Germany* (Oxford: Oxford University Press, 2003).
—— 'Consumption, Social Capital and the Industrious Revolution in Early Modern Germany', *Journal of Economic History*, 70 (2010), pp. 287–325.
—— 'Guilds, Efficiency and Social Capital: Evidence from German Proto-Industry', *Economic History Review*, 57 (2004), pp. 286–333.
—— *State Corporatism and Proto-Industry: The Württemberg Black Forest, 1580–1797* (Cambridge: Cambridge University Press, 1997).
—— and M. Cerman, 'The Theories of Proto-Industrialization', in eid. (eds), *European Proto-Industrialization* (Cambridge: Cambridge University Press, 1996), pp. 1–11.
Okuno, Y., 'Entre la llana i el cotó: Una nota sobre l'extensió de la indústria del cotó als pobles de Catalunya el darrer quart del segle XVIII', *Recerques*, 38 (1999), pp. 47–76.
Overton, M., et al., *Production and Consumption in English Households, 1600–1750* (London: Routledge 2004).
Padró Serrals, J., *La sagrada y prodigiosa imagen del S. Cristo de la villa de Igualada..* (Cervera: Ibarra, 1736).
—— *La sagrada y prodigiosa imagen del S. Christo ... Segunda edición, mejorada considerablemente y con una estensa descripción de aquella villa por Don Jaime Gomis y Galtés, presbitero* (Igualada, 1852).

Papiol, F., *Resposta de Francesc Papiol al qüestionari Zamora. Vilanova i la Geltrú 1790* (Vilanova i la Geltrú: Ajuntament, 1990).

Pardailhé-Galabrun, A., *The Birth of Intimacy: Privacy and Domestic Life in Early Modern Paris*, trans. J. Phelps (Oxford: Polity, 1991).

Pascual, P., *Els Torelló: Una família igualadina d'avocats i propietaris* (Barcelona: Rafael Dalmau, 2000).

Pascual, P., et al., *Macia Vilà i el 'vapor cremat'* (Igualada: CECI, 2004).

Petillon, C., 'S'adapter a la mode et tenir la qualité: La fabrique rurale de Roubaix au XVIIIe siècle', in G.L. Fontana and G. Gayot (eds), *Wool: Products and Markets (13th–20th century* (Padua: CLUEP, 2004), pp. 1103–13.

Pfister, U., 'The Protoindustrial Household Economy: Toward a Formal Analysis', *Journal of Family History*, 17/2 (1992), pp. 201–32.

—— 'Proto-Industrialization and Demographic Change: The Canton of Zürich Revisited', *Journal of European Economic History*, 18 (1989), pp. 629–62.

Pollard, S., *Peaceful Conquest: The Industrialization of Europe 1760–1970* (Oxford: Oxford University Press, 1981).

Pomeranz, K., *The Great Divergence: China, Europe, and the Making of the Modern World Economy* (Princeton: Princeton University Press, 2000).

Poni, C., 'Fashion as Flexible Production: The Strategies of the Lyons Silk Merchants in the Eighteenth Century', in C. Sabel and J. Zeitlin (eds), *World of Possibilities: Flexibility and Mass Production in Western Industrialization* (Cambridge: Cambridge University Press, 1997), pp. 37–74.

Prak, M., 'Early Modern Capitalism: An Introduction', in id. (ed.), *Early Modern Capitalism* (London: Routledge, 2001), pp. 1–21.

Ramos, F.C., 'La demanda de textiles de las familias castellanas a finales del antiguo régimen, 1750–1850: ¿Aumento del consumo sin industrialización?', *Revista de historia económica*, 21, special issue (2003), pp. 141–78.

Reher, D.S., *Familia, población y sociedad en la provincia de Cuenca, 1700–1970* (Madrid: Siglo XXI, 1988).

—— 'Family Ties in Western Europe: Persistent Contrasts', *Population and Development Review*, 24 (1998), pp. 203–34.

—— *Perspectives on the Family in Spain, Past and Present* (Oxford: Clarendon, 1997).

—— *Town and Country in Pre-Industrial Spain: Cuenca 1550–1700* (Cambridge: Cambridge University Press, 1990).

——, V. Pérez Moreda and J. Bernabeu-Mestre, 'Assessing Change in Historical Contexts: Childhood Mortality Patterns in Spain During the Demographic Transition', in C. Corsini and P.P. Viazzo (eds), *The Decline of Infant and Child Mortality: The European Experience: 1750–1990* (UNICEF, 1997), pp. 35–56.

Roche, D., *La culture des apparences* (Paris: Fayard, 1989).

—— *Historie des choses banales: Naissance de la consommation dans les sociétés traditionnelles (xviiie–xixe siècles)* (Paris: Fayard, 1997).

—— *The People of Paris* (Leamington Spa: Berg, 1987).

Romà Rossell, F., *Las señales de la felicidad de España y medios de hacerlas eficaces*, ed. E. Lluch (Barcelona: Altafulla, 1989; 1st edn, Madrid, 1768).

Ros, R., *La industria textil lanera de Béjar (1680–1850)* (Valladolid: Junta de Castilla y León, 1999).

Rosés, J.R., 'Measuring the Contribution of Human Capital to the Development of the Catalan Factory System (1830–61)', *European Review of Economic History*, 2 (1998), pp. 25–48.

Rowland, R., 'Sistemas matrimoniales en la Península Ibérica (siglos XVI–XIX): Una perspectiva regional', in V. Pérez Moreda and D. Reher (eds), *Demografía histórica en España* (Madrid: El Arquero, 1988), pp. 72–137.

Sabel, C.F., and J. Zeitlin, 'Historical Alternatives to Mass Production: Politics, Markets and Technology in Nineteenth-Century Industrialization', *Past and Present*, 108 (1985), pp. 133–76.

—— and —— 'Stories, Strategies, Structures: Rethinking Historical Alternatives to Mass Production', in eid. (eds), *World of Possibilities: Flexibility and Mass Production in Western Industrialization* (Cambridge: Cambridge University Press, 1997), pp. 1–29.

—— and —— (eds), *World of Possibilities: Flexibility and Mass Production in Western Industrialization* (Cambridge: Cambridge University Press, 1997).

Saito, O., 'Gender, Workload and Agricultural Progress: Japan's Historical Experience in Perspective', in R. Leboutte (ed.), *Proto-industrialisation: Recherches récentes et nouvelles perspectives* (Geneva: Droz, 1996), pp. 129–51.

Sánchez, A., 'Crisis económica y respuesta empresarial: Los inicios del sistema fabril en la industria algodonera catalana, 1797–1839', *Revista de historia económica*, 18 (2000), pp. 485–523.

—— 'La empresa algodonera en Cataluña antes de la aplicación del vapor, 1783–1832', in F. Comín and P. Martín Aceña (eds), *La empresa en la historia de España* (Madrid: Espasa, 1996), pp. 155–70.

Sarasúa, C., 'The Role of the State in Shaping Women's and Men's Entrance into the Labour Market: Spain in the Eighteenth and Nineteenth Centuries', *Continuity and Change*, 12 (1997), pp. 341–71.

Sarti, R., *Europe at Home: Family and Material Culture, 1500–1800* (New Haven: Yale University Press, 2002).

Schlumbohm, J., '"Proto-Industrialization" as a Research Strategy and a Historical Period: A Balance Sheet', in S.C. Ogilvie and M. Cerman (eds), *European Proto-Industrialization* (Cambridge: Cambridge University Press, 1996), pp. 12–22.

Schuurman, A.J., 'Probate Inventory Research: Opportunities and Drawbacks', in M. Baulant, A.J. Schuurman and P. Servais (eds), *Inventaires après-décès et ventes de meubles* (Louvain: Academia, 1988), pp. 19–28.

—— and L. Walsh (eds), *Material Culture: Consumption, Life-Style, Standard of Living, 1500–1900* (Milan: Bocconi, 1994).

Segura, A., 'El cadastre: La seva història (1715–1845) i la seva importància com a font documental', *Estudis d'història agrària*, 4 (1983), pp. 129–43.

Segura, J., *Història d'Igualada*, 1st edn, Barcelona, 1907 (facs. edn, 2 vols, Igualada: Ateneu Igualadí, 1978).

Sempere Guarinos, J., *Historia del lujo y de las leyes suntuarias en España*, 2 vols, Madrid: Imprenta Real, 1788 (facs. edn, Madrid: Atlás, 1973).

Serra, R., and L. Ferrer (eds), 'Un questionari de Francisco de Zamora (1789)', *Estudis d'història agrària*, 5 (1985), pp. 159–207.

Servais, P., 'Ustensiles de cuisine et vaisselle dans les campagnes du Pays de Herve aux XVIIe et XVIIIe siècles', in M. Baulant, A.J. Schuurman and P. Servais (eds), *Inventaires après-décès et ventes de meubles* (Louvain: Academia, 1988), pp. 333–46.

Simon, A., 'Barcelona i Catalunya durant la crisi de subsistències de 1763–1764', in id., *La població catalana a l'edat moderna* (Bellaterra: Universitat Autònoma de Barcelona, 1996).

Smith, R.M., 'Relative Prices, Forms of Agrarian Labour and Female Marriage Patterns in England, 1350–1800', in I. Devos and L. Kennedy (eds), *Marriage and Rural Economy: Western Europe since 1400* (Turnhout: Brepols, 1999), pp. 19–48.

—— 'Social Security as a Developmental Institution? Extending the Solar Case for the Relative Efficacy of Poor Relief Provisions under the English Old Poor Law', available at <www.bwpi.manchester.ac.uk/resources/WorkingPapers/bwpi-wp-5608>.

—— 'Women's Work and Marriage in Pre-Industrial England: Some Speculations', in S. Cavaciocchi (ed.), *La donna nell'economia secc. XIII–XVIII* (Prato: Instituto F. Datini, 1990), pp. 31–55.

Smith, S.D., 'Accounting for Taste: British Coffee Consumption in Historical Perspective', *Journal of Interdisciplinary History*, 27 (1996), pp. 183–214.

Solà, A., *Aigua, indústria i fabricants a Manresa (1759–1860)* (Manresa: Centre d'Estudis del Bages, 2004).

—— 'Filar amb berguedanes: Mite i realitat d'una màquina de filar cotó', in *La indústria tèxtil: Actes de les V Jornades d'Arqueologia Industrial de Catalunya, Manresa, 16–28 octubre, 2000* (Barcelona, 2002), pp. 143–68.

—— 'Màquines tèxtils i lexicografia en la història de la llengua catalana', *Miscellània d'estudis Bagencs*, 10 (1997), pp. 153–86.

Solar, P.M., 'Poor Relief and English Economic Development before the Industrial Revolution', *Economic History Review*, 48 (1995), pp. 1–22.

Sugihara, K., 'The East Asian Path of Economic Development: A Long-Term Perspective', in G. Arrighi, T. Hamashita and A. Selden (eds), *The Resurgence of East Asia: 500, 150 and 50 Year Perspectives* (London: Routledge, 2003), pp. 78–123.

Tello, E., *Cervera i la Segarra al segle XVIII: En els orígens d'una Catalunya pobra, 1700-1860* (Lleida: Pagès, 1995).

—— R. Garrabou and A. Roca, 'Preus del blat i salaris agrícoles a Catalunya (1720–1936)', in M. Gutiérrez (ed.), *La industrialització i el desenvolupament econòmic d'Espanya. Homenatge al Dr. Jordi Nadal* (2 vols, Barcelona: Universitat de Barcelona, 1999), vol. 2, pp. 422–60.

E. Tello, 'Vendre per pagar. La comercialització forçada a l'Urgell i a la Segarra al final del segle XVIII', *Recerques*, 23 (1990), pp. 141–90.

Terrier, D., *Les deux âges de la proto-industrie: Les tisserands du Cambrésis et du Saint-Quentinois, 1730–1880* (Paris: EHESS, 1996).

Thirsk, J., *Economic Policy and Projects: The Development of a Consumer Society in Early Modern England* (Oxford: Clarendon, 1978).

—— 'Industries in the Countryside', in F.J. Fisher (ed.), *Essays in the Economic and Social History of Tudor and Stuart England* (Cambridge: Cambridge University Press, 1961), pp. 70–88.

Thoen, E., 'A "Commercial Survival Economy" in Evolution: The Flemish Countryside and the Transition to Capitalism', in P. Hoppenbrouwers and J.L.van Zanden (eds), *Peasants into Farmers? The Transformation of Rural Economy and Society in the Low Countries (Middle Ages–19th century) in the Light of the Brenner Debate* (Turnhout: Brepols, 2001), pp. 102–57.

Thompson, E.P., 'Time, Work-Discipline and Industrial Capitalism', in id., *Customs in Common* (2nd edn, Harmondsworth: Penguin, 1993), pp. 352–403.

Thomson, J.K.J., *Clermont-de-Lodève 1633–1789: Fluctuations in the Prosperity of a Languedocian Cloth-Making Town* (Cambridge: Cambridge University Press, 1982).

—— *A Distinctive Industrialisation: Cotton in Barcelona 1728–1832* (Cambridge: Cambridge University Press, 1992).

—— 'Explaining the Take-Off in the Catalan Cotton Industry', *Economic History Review*, 58 (2005), pp. 701–35.

—— 'Olot, Barcelona and Ávila and the Introduction of the Arkwright Technology to Catalonia', *Revista de historia económica*, 21 (2003), pp. 297–334.

—— 'Technological Transfer to the Catalan Cotton Industry: From Calico Printing to the Self-Acting Mule', in D. Farnie and D. Jeremy (eds), *The Fibre that Changed the World: The Cotton Industry in International Perspective, 1600–1990s* (Oxford: Oxford University Press, 2004), pp. 249–82.

—— 'Variations in the Industrial Structure of Pre-Industrial Languedoc', in M. Berg, P. Hudson and M. Sonenscher (eds), *Manufacture in Town and Country before the Factory* (Cambridge: Cambridge University Press, 1983), pp. 61–91.

Torra, L., 'Pautas de consumo textil en la Cataluña del siglo XVIII: Una visión a partir de los inventarios *post-mortem*', in J. Torras and B. Yun (eds), *Consumo, condiciones de vida y comercialización: Cataluña y Castilla, siglos XVII–XIX* (Valladolid: Junta de Castilla y León, 1999), pp. 89–105.

Torras, J., 'Class Struggle in Catalonia: A Note on Brenner', *Review*, 4 (1980), pp. 235–65.

—— 'Especialización agrícola e industria rural en Cataluña en el siglo XVIII', *Revista de historia económica*, 2 (1984), pp. 113–27.

—— *Fabricants sense fàbrica: Els Torelló, d'Igualada (1691–1794)* (Vic: Eumo, 2006).

—— 'From Craft to Class: The Changing Organization of Cloth Manufacturing in a Catalan Town', in T.M. Safley and L.N. Rosenband (eds), *The Workplace before the Factory: Artisans and Proletarians, 1500–1800* (Ithaca: Cornell University Press, 1993), pp. 165–79.

—— 'Gremio, familia y cambio economico: Pelaires y tejedores en Igualada, 1695–1765', *Revista de historia industrial*, 2 (1992), pp. 11–30.

—— 'The Old and the New: Marketing Networks and Textile Growth in Eighteenth Century Spain', in M. Berg (ed.), *Markets and Manufactures in Early Modern Europe* (London: Routledge, 1991), pp. 93–113.

—— 'Small Towns, Craft Guilds and Proto-Industry in Spain', *Jahrbuch für Wirtschafts Geschichte* 1998/2 (1998), pp. 79–96.

—— and B. Yun (eds), *Consumo, condiciones de vida y comercialización: Cataluña y Castilla, siglos XVII–XIX* (Valladolid: Junta de Castilla y León, 1999).

—— and —— 'Historia del consumo e historia del crecimiento: El consumo de tejidos en España, 1700–1850', *Revista de historia económica*, 21, special issue (2003), pp. 17–41.

——, M. Duran and L. Torra, 'El ajuar de la novia: El consumo de tejidos en los contratos matrimoniales de una localidad catalana', in J. Torras and B. Yun (eds), *Consumo, condiciones de vida y comercialización: Cataluña y Castilla, siglos XVII–XIX* (Valladolid: Junta de Castilla y León, 1999), pp. 61–9.

Torras Ribé, J.M., *La comarca de l'Anoia a finals del segle XVIII. Els 'questionaris' de Francisco de Zamora i altres descripcions (1770–1797)* (Barcelona: Abadia de Montserrat, 1993).

—— *Evolució social i econòmica d'una família catalana de l'Antic Règim: Els Padró d'Igualada (1642–1862)* (Barcelona: Rafael Dalmau, 1976).

—— 'Trajectòria d'un procés d'industrialització frustrat', *Miscellanea aqualatensia*, 2 (1974), pp. 151–97.

Torrents, A., 'Transformacions demogràfiques en un municipi industrial català: Sant Pere de Riudebitlles, 1608–1935' (PhD thesis, University of Barcelona, 1993).

Townsend, J., *A Journey through Spain in the Years 1786 and 1787* (3 vols, London: C. Dilly, 1792).

Valls, F., *La Catalunya atlàntica: Aiguardent i teixits a l'arrencada industrial catalana* (Vic: Eumo, 2003).

—— *La dinàmica del canvi agrari a la Catalunya interior: L'Anoia, 1720–1860* (Igualada: Abadia de Montserrat, 1996).

Vandenbroeke, C., 'Le cas flamand: Évolution sociale et comportements démographiques aux XVIIe–XIXe siècles', *Annales ESC*, 39 (1984), pp. 915–38.

Ventura, M., *Lletrats i illetrats a una ciutat de la Catalunya moderna. Mataró, 1750–1800* (Mataró: Caixa d'Estalvis Laietana, 1991).

Veyrassat, B., *Négociants et fabricants dans l'industrie cotonnière suisse, 1760–1840* (Lausanne: Payot, 1982).

Vicedo, E., *Les terres de Lleida i el desenvolupament català del set-cents: Producció, proprietat i renda* (Barcelona: Crítica, 1991).

Vicens Vives, J., *Notícia de Catalunya* (2nd edn, Barcelona: Destino, 1984).

Vicente, M.V., 'Artisans and Work in a Barcelona Cotton Factory (1770–1816)', *International Review of Social History*, 45 (2000), pp. 1–23.

Vickery, A., 'Women and the World of Goods: A Lancashire Consumer and her Possessions', in J. Brewer and R. Porter (eds), *Consumption and the World of Goods* (London: Routledge, 1993), pp. 274–301.

Vilar, P., *La Catalogne dans l'Espagne moderne: Recherches sur les fondements économiques des structures nationals* (3 vols, Paris: SEVPEN,1962).

—— 'La Catalunya industrial: Reflexions sobre una arrencada i sobre un destí', *Recerques*, 3 (1974), pp. 7–22.

Vives Sabaté, M., *L'arxiu de protocols del districte d'Igualada* (Barcelona, 1997).

Wall, R., 'The Contribution of Married Women to the Family Economy under Different Family Systems: Some Examples from the Mid-Nineteenth Century from the Work of Frédéric Le Play', in A. Fauve-Chamoux and S. Sogner (eds), *Socio-Economic Consequences of Sex-Ratios in Historical Perspective, 1500–1900* (Milan: Bocconi, 1994), pp. 139–48.

—— 'Some Implications of the Earnings, Income and Expenditure Patterns of Married Women in Populations in the Past', in J. Henderson and R. Wall (eds), *Poor Women and Children in the European Past* (London: Routledge, 1994), pp. 312–35.

—— 'Work, Welfare and the Family: An Illustration of the Adaptive Family Economy', in L. Bonfield et al., *The World We have Gained: Essays Presented to Peter Laslett* (Oxford: Blackwell, 1986), pp. 261–94.

Weatherill, L., *Consumer Behaviour and Material Culture in Britain, 1660–1760* (London: Routledge, 1988).

—— 'The Meaning of Consumer Behaviour in Late Seventeenth- and Early Eighteenth-Century England', in J. Brewer and R. Porter (eds), *Consumption and the World of Goods* (London: Routledge, 1993), pp. 85–132.

—— 'A Possession of One's Own: Women and Consumer Behaviour in England, 1660–1749', *Journal of British Studies*, 25 (1986), pp. 131–56.

Werner, M., 'Présentation: Proto-industrialisation et *Alltagsgeschichte*', *Annales HSS*, 4 (1995), pp. 719–23.

Whittle, J., *The Development of Agrarian Capitalism: Land and Labour in Norfolk 1440–1580* (Oxford: Oxford University Press, 2000).

Wrigley, E.A., 'Family Reconstitution', in id. (ed.), *An Introduction to English Historical Demography* (London: Weidenfeld & Nicholson, 1966), pp. 96–159.

—— and R.S. Schofield, *The Population History of England, 1541–1871: A Reconstruction* (2nd edn, Cambridge: Cambridge University Press, 1989).

—— et al., *English Population History from Family Reconstitution, 1580–1837* (Cambridge: Cambridge University Press, 1997).

Young, A., 'Tour in Catalonia', *Annals of Agriculture*, 8 (1787), pp. 193–275.

Yun, B., 'Peasant Material Culture in Castille (1750–1900): Some Proposals', in A.J. Schuurman and L. Walsh (eds), *Material Culture: Consumption, Life-Style, Standard of Living, 1500–1900* (Milan: Bocconi, 1994), pp. 125–36.

—— *Sobre la transición al capitalismo en Castilla: Economia y sociedad en Tierra de Campos (1500–1830)* (Valladolid: Junta de Castilla y León, 1987).

Zamora, F. de, *Diario de los viajes hechos por Cataluña*, ed. R. Boixareu (Barcelona: Curial, 1973).

Zanden, J.L. van, 'A Third Road to Capitalism? Proto-Industrialization and the Moderate Nature of the Late Medieval Crisis in Flanders and Holland, 1350–1550', in P. Hoppenbrouwers and J.L. van Zanden (eds), *Peasants into Farmers? The Transformation of the Rural Economy and Society in the Low Countries (Middle Ages–19th Century) in Light of the Brenner Debate* (Turnhout: Brepols, 2001), pp. 85–101.

Index

Amat i de Cortada, Rafel de (Baró de
    Maldà) 134, 140, 150, 154, 156,
    159, 163
Anoia district 32–3, 51
Arkwright machine, *see* cotton,
    mechanisation in

Bages district 26, 32, 58, 108
baking, *see* household economy,
    self-provisioning in
Barcelona 4, 22, 53, 55, 60–1
    consumption patterns in 150–6, 160–2,
        164, 170, 174
    cotton industry 76–8, 83, 86(n.128),
        87, 90, 132, 177, 180(n.8)
    infant and child mortality 114–15
Baró de Maldà, *see* Amat i de Cortada,
    Rafel de
Bejar 59, 61, 63–4, 82
bergadana, *see* cotton, mechanisation in
birth intervals, *see* fertility
Borrull family (clothiers) 60, 62, 65–7,
    72–5, 82
bread, *see* household economy,
    self-provisioning
breastfeeding 19, 109–12, 182
    and women's work 115, 139–40, 182
Brenner, Robert 6–9, 25–6, 49, 184

Calaf 60, 134, 164
calicoes, *see also* cotton
    consumer good 4–5, 147, 160–1, 165
    manufacture 3–5, 76–7, 79, 83–4,
        87–91, 147, 151, 175
Carmona, Juan 30–1, 43–4
chocolate 4–5, 149, 155–6, 163, 171,
    174–5, 178, 183
clocks 4, 145, 149–51, 172–5, 183
cloth manufacturers, *see* clothiers
clothiers

age at marriage of 102
and clocks 151
conflict with weavers 63, 68, 72–6,
    137, 180–2
differentiation among 63–4, 66–70
inventories of 3, 66–70, 79–82, 126,
    132, 154, 174
landholdings of 126, 132
and markets 18, 59–63
and organisation of production 63–7
and shift to cotton 78–84, 87, 182
clothing 4, 61, 131, 146–8, 158–66,
    168–70, 178, 183
clothing sector 123–4, 129, 142–3
coffee 14(n.43), 155–6, 175
Conca de Barberà 59, 83, 108
Congost, Rosa 30, 50
Copons 60, 164
cotton
    consumer good 146–7, 160–1, *see also*
        calicoes
    equipment in inventories 3–4, 71,
        79–82, 86–9, 128–9
    expansion into rural areas 77–8
    importance in Igualada 22, 55–6, 179,
        181
    mechanisation in 21, 77, 80–91, 128,
        139
    origins in Catalonia 76–7
    relations of production in 87–90
    scale of production in 84–91
    shift from wool to 4, 21, 23, 55,
        76–84, 91, 182
    wages in 77, 102, 138, 176
    women's work in 132, 136–8
credit 3, 9, 17–18, 49, 63, 69, 75, 87, 97,
    122, 130, 165, 171, 176, 179, *see*
    also debt
cutlery 4–5, 149, 157–8, 171–3, 175, 178,
    183

Modern Economic and Social History Series

General Editor
Derek H. Aldcroft, University Fellow, Department of Economic and
Social History, University of Leicester, UK

Derek H. Aldcroft
Studies in the Interwar European Economy
1 85928 360 8 (1997)

Michael J. Oliver
Whatever Happened to Monetarism?
Economic Policy Making and Social Learning in the United Kingdom
Since 1979
1 85928 433 7 (1997)

R. Guerriero Wilson
Disillusionment or New Opportunities?
The Changing Nature of Work in Offices,Glasgow 1880–1914
1 84014 276 6 (1998)

Roger Lloyd-Jones and M.J. Lewis with the assistance of M. Eason
Raleigh and the British Bicycle Industry
An Economic and Business History, 1870–1960
1 85928 457 4 (2000)

Barry Stapleton and James H. Thomas
Gales
A Study in Brewing, Business and Family History
0 7546 0146 3 (2000)

Derek H. Aldcroft and Michael J. Oliver
Trade Unions and the Economy: 1870–2000
1 85928 370 5 (2000)

Ted Wilson
Battles for the Standard
Bimetallism and the Spread of the Gold Standard in the Nineteenth Century
1 85928 436 1 (2000)

Patrick Duffy
The Skilled Compositor, 1850–1914
An Aristocrat Among Working Men
0 7546 0255 9 (2000)

Robert Conlon and John Perkins
Wheels and Deals
The Automotive Industry in Twentieth-Century Australia
0 7546 0405 5 (2001)

Sam Mustafa
Merchants and Migrations
Germans and Americans in Connection, 1776–1835
0 7546 0590 6 (2001)

Bernard Cronin
Technology, Industrial Conflict and the Development of Technical
Education in 19th-Century England
0 7546 0313 X (2001)

Andrew Popp
Business Structure, Business Culture and the Industrial District
The Potteries, c. 1850–1914
0 7546 0176 5 (2001)

Scott Kelly
The Myth of Mr Butskell
The Politics of British Economic Policy, 1950–55
0 7546 0604 X (2002)

Michael Ferguson
The Rise of Management Consulting in Britain
0 7546 0561 2 (2002)

Alan Fowler
Lancashire Cotton Operatives and Work, 1900–1950
A Social History of Lancashire Cotton Operatives in the Twentieth Century
0 7546 0116 1 (2003)

John F. Wilson and Andrew Popp (eds)
Industrial Clusters and Regional Business Networks in England, 1750–1970
0 7546 0761 5 (2003)

John Hassan
The Seaside, Health and the Environment in England and Wales since 1800
1 84014 265 0 (2003)

Marshall J. Bastable
Arms and the State
Sir William Armstrong and the Remaking of British Naval Power, 1854–1914
0 7546 3404 3 (2004)

Robin Pearson
Insuring the Industrial Revolution
Fire Insurance in Great Britain, 1700–1850
0 7546 3363 2 (2004)

Andrew Dawson
Lives of the Philadelphia Engineers
Capital, Class and Revolution, 1830–1890
0 7546 3396 9 (2004)

Lawrence Black and Hugh Pemberton (eds)
An Affluent Society?
Britain's Post-War 'Golden Age' Revisited
0 7546 3528 7 (2004)

Joseph Harrison and David Corkill
Spain
A Modern European Economy
0 7546 0145 5 (2004)

Ross E. Catterall and Derek H. Aldcroft (eds)
Exchange Rates and Economic Policy in the 20th Century
1 84014 264 2 (2004)

Armin Grünbacher
Reconstruction and Cold War in Germany
The Kreditanstalt für Wiederaufbau (1948–1961)
0 7546 3806 5 (2004)

Till Geiger
Britain and the Economic Problem of the Cold War
The Political Economy and the Economic Impact of the
British Defence Effort, 1945–1955
0 7546 0287 7 (2004)

Anne Clendinning
Demons of Domesticity
Women and the English Gas Industry, 1889–1939
0 7546 0692 9 (2004)

Timothy Cuff
The Hidden Cost of Economic Development
The Biological Standard of Living in Antebellum Pennsylvania
0 7546 4119 8 (2005)

Julian Greaves
Industrial Reorganization and Government Policy in Interwar Britain
0 7546 0355 5 (2005)

Derek H. Aldcroft
Europe's Third World
The European Periphery in the Interwar Years
0 7546 0599 X (2006)

James P. Huzel
The Popularization of Malthus in Early Nineteenth-Century England
Martineau, Cobbett and the Pauper Press
0 7546 5427 3 (2006)

Richard Perren
Taste, Trade and Technology
The Development of the International Meat Industry since 1840
978 0 7546 3648 9 (2006)

Roger Lloyd-Jones and M.J. Lewis
Alfred Herbert Ltd and the British Machine Tool Industry,
1887–1983
978 0 7546 0523 2 (2006)

Anthony Howe and Simon Morgan (eds)
Rethinking Nineteenth-Century Liberalism
Richard Cobden Bicentenary Essays
978 0 7546 5572 5 (2006)

Espen Moe
Governance, Growth and Global Leadership
The Role of the State in Technological Progress, 1750–2000
978 0 7546 5743 9 (2007)

Peter Scott
Triumph of the South
A Regional Economic History of Early Twentieth Century Britain
978 1 84014 613 4 (2007)

David Turnock
Aspects of Independent Romania's Economic History with
Particular Reference to Transition for EU Accession
978 0 7546 5892 4 (2007)

David Oldroyd
Estates, Enterprise and Investment at the Dawn of the Industrial Revolution
Estate Management and Accounting in the North-East of England, c.1700–1780
978 0 7546 3455 3 (2007)

Ralf Roth and Günter Dinhobl (eds)
Across the Borders
Financing the World's Railways in the Nineteenth and Twentieth Centuries
978 0 7546 6029 3 (2008)

Vincent Barnett and Joachim Zweynert (eds)
Economics in Russia
Studies in Intellectual History
978 0 7546 6149 8 (2008)

Raymond E. Dumett (ed.)
Mining Tycoons in the Age of Empire, 1870–1945
Entrepreneurship, High Finance, Politics and Territorial Expansion
978 0 7546 6303 4 (2009)

Peter Dorey
British Conservatism and Trade Unionism, 1945–1964
978 0 7546 6659 2 (2009)

Shigeru Akita and Nicholas J. White (eds)
The International Order of Asia in the 1930s and 1950s
978 0 7546 5341 7 (2010)

Myrddin John Lewis, Roger Lloyd-Jones, Josephine Maltby
and Mark David Matthews
Personal Capitalism and Corporate Governance
British Manufacturing in the First Half of the Twentieth Century
978 0 7546 5587 9 (2010)

John Murphy
A Decent Provision
Australian Welfare Policy, 1870 to 1949
978 1 4094 0759 1 (2011)

Robert Lee (ed.)
Commerce and Culture
Nineteenth-Century Business Elites
978 0 7546 6398 0 (2011)

Martin Cohen
The Eclipse of 'Elegant Economy'
The Impact of the Second World War on Attitudes to Personal
Finance in Britain
978 1 4094 3972 1 (2012)

Gordon M. Winder
The American Reaper
Harvesting Networks and Technology, 1830–1910
978-1-4094-2461-1 (2012)